Praise for *Better Python Code*

"You'll not just be aspiring to be an expert anymore after practicing through *Better Python Code: A Guide for Aspiring Experts*, you'll be one of them! Learn from David Mertz, who's been making experts through his writing and training for the past 20 years."
—*Iqbal Abdullah, past Chair, PyCon Asia Pacific, and past board member, PyCon Japan*

"In *Better Python Code: A Guide for Aspiring Experts*, David Mertz serves up bite-sized chapters of Pythonic wisdom in this must-have addition to any serious Python programmer's collection. This book helps bridge the gap from beginner to advanced Python user, but even the most seasoned Python programmer can up their game with Mertz's insight into the ins and outs of Python."
—*Katrina Riehl, President, NumFOCUS*

"What separates ordinary coders from Python experts? It's more than just knowing best practices—it's understanding the benefits and pitfalls of the many aspects of Python, and knowing when and why to choose one approach over another. In this book David draws on his more than 20 years of involvement in the Python ecosystem and his experience as a Python author to make sure that the readers understand both *what* to do and *why* in a wide variety of scenarios."
—*Naomi Ceder, past Chair, Python Software Foundation*

"Like a Pythonic BBC, David Mertz has been informing, entertaining, and educating the Python world for over a quarter of a century, and he continues to do so here in his own pleasantly readable style."
—*Steve Holden, past Chair, Python Software Foundation*

"Being expert means someone with a lot of experience. David's latest book provides some important but common problems that folks generally learn only after spending years of doing and fixing. I think this book will provide a much quicker way to gather those important bits and help many folks across the world to become better."
—*Kushal Das, CPython Core Developer and Director, Python Software Foundation*

"This book is for everyone: from beginners, who want to avoid hard-to-find bugs, all the way to experts looking to write more efficient code. David Mertz has compiled a great set of useful idioms that will make your life as a programmer easier and your users happier."
—*Marc-André Lemburg, past Chair, EuroPython, and past Director, Python Software Foundation*

Better Python Code

Better Python Code

A Guide for Aspiring Experts

David Mertz

Hoboken, New Jersey

Cover image: StudioLondon/Shutterstock
Python and the Python Logo are trademarks of the Python Software Foundation.
Linux® is the registered trademark of Linus Torvalds in the U.S. and other countries.
macOS® is a trademark of Apple Inc.
Microsoft Windows is a trademark of the Microsoft group of companies.

For information about buying this title in bulk quantities, or for special sales opportunities (which may
include electronic versions; custom cover designs; and content particular to your business, training goals,
marketing focus, or branding interests), please contact our corporate sales department
at corpsales@pearsoned.com or (800) 382-3419.

For government sales inquiries, please contact governmentsales@pearsoned.com.

For questions about sales outside the U.S., please contact intlcs@pearson.com.

Visit us on the Web: informit.com/aw

Library of Congress Control Number: 2023944574

ISBN-13: 978-0-13-832094-2
ISBN-10: 0-13-832094-2

1 2023

Pearson's Commitment to Diversity, Equity, and Inclusion

Pearson is dedicated to creating bias-free content that reflects the diversity of all learners. We embrace the many dimensions of diversity, including but not limited to race, ethnicity, gender, socioeconomic status, ability, age, sexual orientation, and religious or political beliefs.

Education is a powerful force for equity and change in our world. It has the potential to deliver opportunities that improve lives and enable economic mobility. As we work with authors to create content for every product and service, we acknowledge our responsibility to demonstrate inclusivity and incorporate diverse scholarship so that everyone can achieve their potential through learning. As the world's leading learning company, we have a duty to help drive change and live up to our purpose to help more people create a better life for themselves and to create a better world.

Our ambition is to purposefully contribute to a world where:

- Everyone has an equitable and lifelong opportunity to succeed through learning.
- Our educational products and services are inclusive and represent the rich diversity of learners.
- Our educational content accurately reflects the histories and experiences of the learners we serve.
- Our educational content prompts deeper discussions with learners and motivates them to expand their own learning (and worldview).

While we work hard to present unbiased content, we want to hear from you about any concerns or needs with this Pearson product so that we can investigate and address them.

- Please contact us with concerns about any potential bias at https://www.pearson.com/report-bias.html.

This book is dedicated to my mother, Gayle Mertz, who always valued ideas and the relentless criticism of existing reality.

Contents

Foreword

It was a pleasure for me to be asked to write a foreword for David's new book, as I always expect David to provide useful, insightful content.

Much as I began with high expectations, I am delighted to say that they were not just met but exceeded: The book is an engaging read, offers a great deal of insight for anyone at an intermediate or advanced level to improve their Python programming skill, and includes copious sharing of precious experience practicing and teaching the language; it is easy to read and conversational in style. In spite of all this, David manages to keep the book short and concise enough to absorb quickly and fully.

Most of the book's content reflects, and effectively teaches, what amounts to a consensus among Python experts about best practices and mistakes to avoid. In a few cases in which the author's well-explained opinions on certain issues of style differ from those of other experts, David carefully and clearly points out these cases so readers can weigh the pros and cons and come to their own decisions.

Most of the book deals with Python-related issues at intermediate levels of experience and skill. These include many instances in which programmers familiar with different languages may adopt an inferior style in Python, simply because it appears to be a direct "translation" of a style that's appropriate for the languages that they know well.

An excellent example of the latter problem is writing APIs that expose *getter* and *setter* methods: In Python, direct getting and setting of the attribute (often enabled via the `property` decorator) should take their place. Reading hypothetical code like `widgets.set_count(widgets.get_count() + 1)` — where experienced Pythonistas would instead have used the direct, readable phrasing `widgets.count += 1` — would clearly show that the hypothetical coder is ignoring or unaware of Python "best practices." David's book goes a long way toward addressing this and other common misunderstandings.

Despite its overall intermediate level, the book does not hesitate to address quite a few advanced topics, including the danger of catastrophic backtracking in regular expressions, some quirks in floating-point representations of numbers, "round-tripping" problems with serialization approaches like JSON, etc. The coverage of such issues makes studying this book definitely worthwhile, not just for Python programmers of intermediate skills, but for advanced ones too.

—*Alex Martelli*

Preface

Python is a very well-designed programming language. In surprisingly many cases, the language manages to meet one of the aphorisms in Tim Peters' *The Zen of Python*: "There should be one—and preferably only one—obvious way to do it." If there is only one way to do it, it's hard to make mistakes.

Of course, that aphorism is an aspiration that is not uniformly met. Often there are many ways to perform a task in Python, many of them simply wrong, many inelegant, many leaning heavily on idioms of other programming languages rather than being *Pythonic*, and some of them not exactly *wrong* but still grossly inefficient. All the problems described in this book are ones that I've seen in real-life code, sometimes in the wild, sometimes caught during code review, and admittedly far too often in code I wrote myself before reflecting upon its flaws.

About the Book

The sections of this book each present some mistake, pitfall, or foible that developers can easily fall into, and are accompanied by descriptions of ways to avoid making them. At times those solutions simply involve a minor change in "spelling," but in most cases they require a nuance of thought and design in your code. Many of the discussions do something else as well...

I do not hope only to show you something you did not know, but in a great many cases I hope to show you something about which you did not know there *was something* to know. I believe that the most effective writing and teaching conveys to readers or students not only information, but also good *ways of thinking* about problems and reasoning about their particular solutions. The info boxes, footnotes, and silly digressions within this book all hope to allow you to think deeper about a particular domain, or a particular task, or a particular style of programming.

There is no need to read this book from cover to cover (but I believe that readers who do so will benefit). Each chapter addresses a related cluster of concepts, but stands alone. Moreover, each section within a chapter is also self-contained. Each can be read independently of the others, and most readers will learn something interesting in each one. Some of the sections are more advanced than others, but even in those that seem introductory, I think you will find nuances you did not know. And even in those that seem advanced, I hope you will find the discussions accessible and enlightening.

Notwithstanding that each section forms a sort of vignette, the chapters are generally organized in sequence of increasing sophistication, and the sections loosely build upon each other. Where it feels helpful, many discussions refer to other sections that might provide background, or foreshadow elaboration in later sections.

In general, I am aiming at a reader who is an intermediate-level Python developer, or perhaps an advanced beginner. I assume you know the basics of the Python programming language; these discussions do not teach the most basic syntax and semantics that you would find in a first course or first book on Python. Mostly I simply assume you have an inquisitive mind and a wish to write code that is beautiful, efficient, and correct.

This book is written with Python 3.12 in mind, which was released in October 2023. Code shown has been tested against 3.12 betas. The large majority of the code examples will work in Python 3.8, which is the earliest version that has not passed end-of-life as of mid-2023. In some cases, I note that code requires at least Python 3.10, which was released on October 4, 2021; or occasionally at least Python 3.11, released on October 24, 2022. The large majority of the mistakes discussed within this book were mistakes already in Python 3.8, although a few reflect improvements in later versions of Python.

Documents titled "*What's new in Python M.m.μ*"[1] have been maintained since at least the Python 1.4 days (in 1996).[2]

Code Samples

Most of the code samples shown in this book use the Python REPL (Read-Evaluate-Print-Loop). Or more specifically, they use the IPython (https://ipython.readthedocs.io) enhanced REPL, but using the `%doctest_mode` magic to make the prompt and output closely resemble the plain `python` REPL. One IPython "magic" that is used fairly commonly in examples is `%timeit`; this wraps the standard library `timeit` module, but provides an easy-to-use and adaptive way of timing an operation reliably. There are some *mistakes* discussed in this book where a result is not *per se* wrong, but it takes orders of magnitude longer to calculate than it should; this magic is used to illustrate that.

When you write your own code, of course, interaction within a REPL—including within Jupyter notebooks (https://jupyter.org) or other richly interactive environments—will only be a small part of what you write. But the mistakes in this book try to focus on samples of code that are as narrow as possible. An interactive shell is often a good way to illustrate these mistakes; I encourage you to borrow the lessons you learn, and copy them into full `*.py` files. Ideally these discussions can be adapted into rich codebases after starting as mere snippets.

At times when presenting commands run in the operating system shell (i.e., running a Python script to show results), I display the command prompt `[BetterPython]$` to provide a quick visual clue. This is not actually the prompt on my personal machine, but rather is something to which I could change if I wanted to do so. On Unix-like systems, the `$` is often (but not always) part of shell prompts.

---

1. Python does not strictly use Semantic Versioning (https://semver.org), so my implied nomenclature "major.minor.micro" is not strictly accurate.
2. See https://docs.python.org/3/whatsnew/index.html for an index of past release notes.

Note   A short introduction to a REPL

Many developers who have come from other programming languages, or who are just beginning programming in general, may not appreciate how amazingly versatile and useful an interactive shell can be. More often than not, when I wish to figure out how I might go about some programming task, I jump into a Python, IPython, or Jupyter environment to get a more solid understanding of how my imagined approach to a problem will work out.

A quick example of such a session, for me within a bash terminal, might look like this:

```
[BetterPython]$ ipython
Python 3.11.0 | packaged by conda-forge |
    (main, Oct 25 2022, 06:24:40) [GCC 10.4.0]
Type 'copyright', 'credits' or 'license' for more information
IPython 8.7.0 -- An enhanced Interactive Python. Type '?' for help.


In [1]: %doctest_mode                                    # ❶
Exception reporting mode: Plain
Doctest mode is: ON
>>> from collections import ChainMap                      # ❷
>>> ChainMap?                                             # ❸
Init signature: ChainMap(*maps)
Docstring:
A ChainMap groups multiple dicts (or other mappings) together
to create a single, updateable view.
[...]
File:            ~/miniconda3/lib/python3.11/collections/__init__.py
Type:            ABCMeta
>>> dict1 = dict(foo=1, bar=2, baz=3)
>>> dict2 = {"bar": 7, "blam": 55}
>>> chain = ChainMap(dict1, dict2)
>>> chain["blam"], chain["bar"]                          # ❹
(55, 2)
>>> !ls src/d*.adoc                                      # ❺
src/datastruct2.adoc  src/datastruct.adoc
```

❶ Use a display style similar to running just python with no script.

❷ I pressed <tab> to select a completed line after collections.

❸ I'd like information about what this object does (abridged here).

❹ Entering expressions shows their value immediately.

❺ With !, I can run a command within an external shell and see results.

There's much more to what REPLs can do than is shown, but this gives you a quick feel for their capabilities.

Different programming environments will treat copying/pasting code samples into them differently. Within IPython itself, using the `%paste` magic will ignore the leading `>>>` or `...` characters in an appropriate way. Various other shells, IDEs, and code editors will behave differently. Many of the code samples that are presented outside a REPL, and also many of the data files used, are available at https://gnosis.cx/better. Moreover, paths are mostly simplified for presentation; files often live within the `code/` or `data/` subdirectories of the book's website, but those paths are usually not shown. In other words, the code presented is used to explain concepts, not as reusable code I intend for you to copy directly. (That said, you *may* use it, of course.) In particular, much of the code shown is code that has *foibles* in it; for that code, I most certainly do not want you to use it in production.

All code blocks whose title includes "Source code of <filename>" are available for download from https://gnosis.cx/better. In some cases, the code shown in this book is an excerpt from a longer file named. All other code blocks, whether titled to aid navigation or untitled, are present only to explain concepts; of course, you are free to use them by copying, retyping, or adapting for your purpose.

Obtaining the Tools Used in This Book

The Python programming language is Free Software that may be obtained at the official site of the Python Software Foundation (PSF). A variety of other entities have also created customized Python distributions with additional or different capabilities bundled with the same core programming language. These include many operating system vendors. Most Linux distributions bundle Python. macOS (formerly stylized in slightly different ways, such as "Mac OS X" and "OS X") has included Python since 2001. It is available for Windows from the Microsoft Store.

To obtain the PSF distribution of Python, go to https://www.python.org/downloads/. Versions are available for many operating systems and hardware platforms. To follow some of the examples within this book, using the IPython terminal-based REPL (https:// ipython.org/install.html) or Jupyter notebooks (https://docs.jupyter.org/en/latest/install .html) is advisable. These enhanced interactive environments support "magics," such as `%timeit`, that are special commands not contained in the Python language itself, but which can improve interactive exploration. Throughout the book, when interactive sessions are shown, they can be easily identified by a leading `>>>` for initial lines and leading `...` for continuation lines (when present). However, Jupyter—as well as the interactive shells in many integrated development environments (IDEs) or sophisticated code editors—mark code entered and results produced by other visual indicators. The enhanced REPLs mentioned also support adding a single or double `?` at the end of a Python name to display information about the object it refers to; this is used in some examples.

I personally use Miniconda (https://docs.conda.io/en/latest/miniconda.html) as a means of installing Python, IPython, Jupyter, and many other tools and libraries. Miniconda itself contains a version of Python, but will also allow creation of *environments* with different versions of Python, or indeed without Python at all, but rather other useful tools. You will see hints in some examples about my choice of installation, but nothing in the book depends on you following my choice.

Other Useful Tools

Most of the discussions in this book are conceptual rather than merely stylistic. However, linters will often detect mistakes that at least border on conceptual, including sometimes mistakes described in this book. A particularly good linter for Python is Flake8 (https://flake8.pycqa.org/), which actually utilizes several lower-level linters as (optional) dependencies. A good linter may very well not detect important mistakes, but you cannot go wrong in at least *understanding* why a linter is complaining about your code.

The home page for the Black code formatter (https://black.readthedocs.io/) describes itself well:

> Black is the uncompromising Python code formatter. By using it, you agree to cede control over minutiae of hand-formatting. In return, Black gives you speed, determinism, and freedom from pycodestyle nagging about formatting. You will save time and mental energy for more important matters.
>
> — **Black home page**

Opinions about using Black vary among Pythonistas. I have found that even if Black occasionally formats code in a manner I wouldn't entirely choose, enforcing consistency when working with other developers aids the readability of shared code, especially on large projects.

A very impressive recent project for linting and code formatting is Ruff (https://beta.ruff.rs/docs/). Ruff covers most of the same linting rules as Flake8 and other tools, but is written in Rust and runs several orders of magnitude faster than other linters. As well, Ruff provides auto-formatting similar to Black, but cleans up many things that Black does not address. (However, Black also cleans things that Ruff does not; they are complementary.)

In modern Python development, type annotations and type-checking tools are in relatively widespread use. The most popular of these tools are probably Mypy (http://mypy-lang.org/), Pytype (https://google.github.io/pytype/), Pyright (https://github.com/Microsoft/pyright), and Pyre (https://pyre-check.org/). All of these tools have virtues, especially for large-scale projects, but this book generally avoids discussion of the Python type-checking ecosystem. The kinds of mistakes that type checking can detect are mostly disjointed from the semantic and stylistic issues that we discuss herein.

Acknowledgments

A number of participants in the Python-Help Discourse board (https://discuss.python.org/c/users/7) have suggested nice ideas for these mistakes. For many of their suggestions, I had already included their idea, or some variation of it, but in other cases, their thoughts prompted an addition to or modification of the mistakes I address. I greatly thank Chris Angelico, Charles Machalow, John Melendowski, Steven D'Aprano, Ryan Duve, Alexander Bessman, Cooper Lees, Peter Bartlett, Glenn A. Richard, Ruben Vorderman, Matt Welke, Steven Rumbalski, and Marco Sulla for their suggestions.

Other friends who have made suggestions include Brad Huntting, Adam Peacock, and Mary Ann Sushinsky.

This book is far better thanks to the suggestions I received; all errors remain my own.

About the Author

David Mertz, Ph.D., has been a member of the Python community for a long time: about 25 years—long enough to remember what was new about Python 1.5 versus 1.4. He has followed the development of the language closely, given keynote talks about many of the changes over versions, and his writing has had a modicum of influence on the directions Python and popular libraries for it have taken. David has taught Python to scientists, developers coming from other languages, and programming neophytes.

You can find voluminous details about his publications at https://gnosis.cx/publish/resumes/david-mertz-publications.pdf. You can learn more about where he has worked at https://gnosis.cx/publish/resumes/david-mertz-resume.pdf.

Introduction

Python is a powerful, and also a reasonably opinionated, programming language. While there are often many ways you *could* accomplish a task in Python, there is very often exactly one way you *should* accomplish that task. Some programs are considered "Pythonic," and others are not.

Note   Being Pythonic

The slightly joking term *Pythonic* is widely used in the Python community. In a general way it means "reflecting good programming practices for the Python language." But there is also something just slightly *ineffable* about the term in a way similar to how other programmers use *fragile*, *elegant*, or *robust* in describing particular code. You'll see the terms *Pythonic* and *unpythonic* quite a bit in this book.

In a related bit of Pythonic humor—the language was, after all, named after the Monty Python comedy troupe—we often use the term *Pythonista* for developers who have mastered Pythonic programming.

To a fairly large extent, being Pythonic is a goal to improve the *readability* of your programs so that other users and contributors can easily understand your intention, the behavior of the code, and indeed identify its bugs. There are, as well, many times when being unpythonic leads to unexpected behavior, and hence harms *functionality* in edge cases you may not have considered or tried out during initial usage.

In this book, I am not shy in being opinionated about good Python practices. Throughout the discussions, I try to explain the motivations for these opinions, and reflect on my long experience using, teaching, and writing about Python. It is a truly delightful programming language, about which I have sincere enthusiasm.

Much of what we hope for in Python code is explained by *The Zen of Python*.

```
>>> import this
The Zen of Python, by Tim Peters

Beautiful is better than ugly.
Explicit is better than implicit.
Simple is better than complex.
```

```
Complex is better than complicated.
Flat is better than nested.
Sparse is better than dense.
Readability counts.
Special cases aren't special enough to break the rules.
Although practicality beats purity.
Errors should never pass silently.
Unless explicitly silenced.
In the face of ambiguity, refuse the temptation to guess.
There should be one---and preferably only one---obvious way to do it.
Although that way may not be obvious at first unless you're Dutch.
Now is better than never.
Although never is often better than *right* now.
If the implementation is hard to explain, it's a bad idea.
If the implementation is easy to explain, it may be a good idea.
Namespaces are one honking great idea---let's do more of those!
```

There are many topics within the world of Python programming that are very important, but are not addressed in this short book. The appendix, *Topics for Other Books*, gives some pointers to resources, and brief summaries of the ideas I think you would do well to pursue when learning them.

1

Looping Over the Wrong Things

As in most procedural programming languages, Python has two kinds of loops: `for` and `while`. The semantics of these loops is very similar to that in most analogous languages. However, Python puts a special emphasis on looping *over* iterables—including *lazy* iterables along with concrete collections—which many languages do not do. Many of the mistakes in this chapter are "best practices" in other programming languages but are either stylistically flawed or unnecessarily fragile when translated too directly into Python.

Technically, Python also allows for recursion, which is another way of "looping," but recursion depth is limited in Python, and tail-call optimization (see https://en.wikipedia.org/wiki/Tail_call) is absent. Recursion can be enormously useful for problems that are naturally *subdivided* as a means of reaching their solution, but it is rarely a good approach in Python for constructing a mere *sequence* of similar actions.

None of the mistakes in this chapter deal specifically with recursion, but programmers coming from Lisp-family languages, ML-family languages, or perhaps Haskell, Rust, Lua, Scala, or Erlang should note that while recursion may be a good habit in the language you used to program, it *can be* a bad habit for Python.

1.1 (Rarely) Generate a List for Iteration

A common pattern in many Python programs is to generate a sequence of items to process, append them to a list, and then loop through that list, processing each item as we get to it. In fact, structuring programs this way is often perfectly sensible and wholly intuitive. Except when it is not.

When the sequence of items might be very long (or potentially infinite) or when each item might be a memory-hungry object, creating and populating a list often consumes more memory than is needed. As well, when the processing operation might be concurrent with the generating operation, we might spend a long time generating the list, followed by a similarly long time processing the list. If actual parallelism is possible, we might instead be able to complete the overall program in half as much time. But when parallelism is possible, it isn't always easy. (For more on concurrency, see this book's Appendix.)

Let's suppose that we have a function called `get_word()` that will return a word each time it is called, generally different words on different calls. For example, this function might be responding to data sent over a wire in some manner or calculated dynamically based on something else about the state of the program. For this toy function, if `get_word()` returns None, its data source is depleted; moreover, a "word" for the purpose of this example is a sequence of ASCII lowercase letters only.

It is straightforward, and commonplace, to write code similar to the following.

Creating a list from generated items

```
# source = <some identifier for how we generate data>
words = []
while True:
    word = get_word(src=source)
    if word is None:
        break
    words.append(word)

print(f"{len(words):,}") # -> 267,752
```

Readers of other discussions in this book might recognize the number of words generated and guess the implementation of `get_word()` from that. But let's assume that the number of words and what they are can vary across each program run, and can vary across multiple orders of magnitude.

In a bit of crude numerology, we assign a magic number to each word simply by valuing `'a'` as 1, `'b'` as 2, and so on, through `'z'` as 26, and adding those values. This particular transformation isn't important, but the idea of "calculate a value from each datum" is very commonplace. We use the following function for this calculation.

Numerological word magic number

```
def word_number(word):
    magic = 0
    for letter in word:
        magic += 1 + ord(letter) - ord('a')
    return magic
```

We might visualize the distribution of these numerological values as shown in Figure 1.1.

```
# words = <regenerated list from another source>
import matplotlib.pyplot as plt                          # ❶
plt.plot([word_number(word) for word in words])
plt.title(f"Magic values of {len(words):,} generated words")
plt.show()
```

❶ `pip install matplotlib` or `conda install matplotlib`

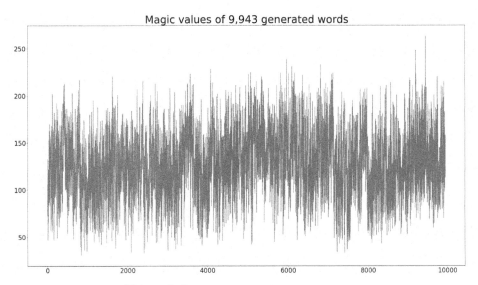

Figure 1.1   Magic values of generated words.

Assuming that all we care about is this final generated chart, there is no reason we needed to instantiate the full collection of words, only their magic numbers. Admittedly, the toy example is too simple to show the full advantage of the refactoring, but a sensible approach is to lazily construct a generator of only the data we actually care about and to only utilize the intermediate data as it is needed. For example, this code produces the chart shown in Figure 1.2.

Lazily calculating only what is needed within a generator

```
def word_numbers(src):
    while (word := get_word(src=src)) is not None:
        yield word_number(word)


# source2 = <some different identifier for data source>
magic_nums = list(word_numbers(source2))
plt.plot(magic_nums)
plt.title(f"Magic values of {len(magic_nums):,} generated words")
plt.show()
```

The example shown in Figure 1.2 still needed to instantiate the list of numbers, but not the list of actual words. If the "words" were some much larger, memory-consuming object, this change would become more significant. For many scenarios, exclusively incrementally processing each value from a generator individually, with no intermediate collection at all, will suffice, and save considerable memory.

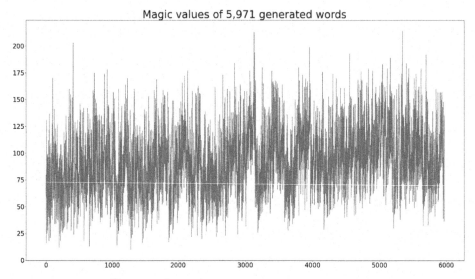

Figure 1.2   More magic values of generated words.

1.2   Use `enumerate()` **Instead of Looping Over an Index**

Developers coming from C-derived languages sometimes reach automatically for loops over the index elements of a list or other data structure. This is usually an unpythonic way to write a loop. Code written in this manner is not significantly slower than using `enumerate()`, but it is less readable, is more verbose, and generally simply feels like a "code smell."

For example, in C++, an idiom like this is common:

```
// `items` could be array, vector, or other collection types
for (int i = 0; i < items.size(); i++) {
    process(i, items[i]);
}
```

A closely analogous option is available in Python, and in Python's somewhat distant past, such an approach was the standard available mechanism:

```
for i in range(len(items)):
    process(i, items[i])
```

Indeed, if you are not required to utilize the index position within a loop, utilizing the index at all is generally a code smell in Python. A much more idiomatic option is simply:

```
for item in items:
    process(None, item)
```

On those fairly common occasions when you need both the index and the underlying item, using enumerate() is much more expressive and idiomatic:

```
for i, item in enumerate(items):
    process(i, item)
```

In the relatively uncommon situations when I want the index but not the item itself, I often use enumerate() anyway, and I use the Python convention of _ (single underscore) representing "a value I don't care about":

```
for i, _ in enumerate(items):
    process(i, None)
```

An approach that I use from time to time, when I actually want to maintain several increments, is to initialize the several counters prior to a loop, even if one of them could derive from enumerate():

```
total, n_foo, n_bar = 0, 0, 0
for item in items:
    if is_foo(item):
        process_foo(item)
        n_foo += 1
    elif is_bar(item):
        process_bar(item)
        n_bar += 1
    else:
        pass
    total += 1
```

In the example, total could equally well be reset while enumerating the loop itself, but you might wish to emphasize the parallel with n_foo and n_bar, and that is probably better expressed as shown here.

1.3 Don't Iterate Over `dict.keys()` When You Want `dict.items()`

There is a sense in which you can *almost* think of Python lists as mappings from index positions to values. Within a dictionary, integers are perfectly well able to act as keys; hence, `obj[7]` might equally well be an index into a `dict` (or other mapping) or an index into a `list` (or other sequence).

In much the same way as you sometimes see unpythonic code that loops over the index positions of a list but then looks up that index within the body, you also sometimes see unpythonic code that loops over `dict.keys()`. Actually, let's back up just a bit: there are two stylistic mistakes that were just named. Imagine code like this:

```
for key in my_dict.keys():
    process(key, my_dict[key])
```

This is nonidiomatic in the first instance because looping over `my_dict.keys()` is equivalent to looping over `my_dict` itself. Behind the scenes, slightly different types of objects are produced: `dict_keys` for `my_dict.keys()` and `dict_keyiterator` from the dictionary itself. However, little real code depends on this difference since they behave the same for most purposes:

```
>>> my_dict = {c:ord(c) for c in "Bread and butter"}
>>> type(my_dict.keys())
<class 'dict_keys'>
>>> type(iter(my_dict))
<class 'dict_keyiterator'>
```

Specifically, the following identity will always apply, for every dictionary (unless, with great perversity, you could break this identity in a subclass of `dict` or in some custom mapping):

```
>>> all(a is b for a, b in zip(iter(my_dict), iter(my_dict.keys())))
True
```

In other words, if you wish to loop over keys, you should just write:

```
for key in my_dict:
    process(key, my_dict[key])
```

However, it is relatively uncommon to wish to loop *only* over the keys of a dictionary. Even if you only rarely, in one branch of the code, actually use the value, it costs nearly nothing to include it as a loop variable. Remember, Python objects are accessed by reference; you just assign a reference to an existing object by binding a loop variable; you don't copy or create an object.

In other words, don't bother with:

```
for key in my_dict:
    if rare_condition(key):
        val = my_dict[key]
        process(key, val)
```

Simply write the clean, Pythonic code:

```
for key, val = my_dict.items():
    if rare_condition(key):
        process(key, val)
```

This problem is one that linters are likely to warn about—as was probably the prior one about using `enumerate()`—but *understanding* the mechanisms of loops goes further than just reading a warning.

1.4 Mutating an Object During Iteration

You should not mutate objects that you are iterating over. At times you can "get away with" it without bad effects, but the habit remains a bad one.

The first thing that we should note is that some Python objects are immutable. If you iterate over a `str`, `bytes`, `tuple`, or `frozenset` object, for example, the question simply does not arise of mutating the underlying collection.

Still, a lot of Python objects are both iterable and mutable—most notably `list`, `dict`, `set`, and `bytearray`, although of course, custom or third-party objects might be also. Attempting to mutate during iteration over an object can go wrong in several different ways.

Baseline iteration over immutable object
```
>>> s = "Mary had a little lamb!"
>>> for c in s:
...     if c <= "s":
...         print(c, end="")
... print()
Mar had a lile lamb!
```

This toy code is mostly pointless in itself, but we do a selective operation on only those elements of an iterable that meet some predicate. One thing we could certainly do rather than print off individual characters is re-aggregate those passing the filter into some new collection. That approach is generally a perfectly good solution to all of the mutation issues, so keep it in your pocket as an option.

Suppose we want to try something similar using mutable collections rather than an immutable string.

Quick failure in mutation of iterables

```
>>> my_set
{'r', 'M', 'm', 'a', 'e', 'h', 'l', 't', 'd', 'b', '!', ' ', 'i'}
>>> my_set = set("Mary had a little lamb!")
>>> for c in my_set:
...     if c > "s":
...         my_set.discard(c)
...
Traceback (most recent call last):
[...]
RuntimeError: Set changed size during iteration

>>> my_dict = {c:ord(c) for c in "Mary had a little lamb!"}
>>> for c in my_dict:
...     if c > "s":
...         del my_dict[c]
...
Traceback (most recent call last):
[...]
RuntimeError: dictionary changed size during iteration
```

The temptation to mutate these iterables is reduced by hitting a `RuntimeError` quickly. However, we are less fortunate for ordered collections. Something goes wrong, but the error can be much more subtle and harder to notice.

Hidden failure in mutation of iterables

```
>>> my_list = list("Mary had a little lamb!")
>>> for i, c in enumerate(my_list):
...     if c > "s":
...         del my_list[i]
...
>>> my_list
['M', 'a', 'r', ' ', 'h', 'a', 'd', ' ', 'a', ' ', 'l', 'i',
't', 'l', 'e', ' ', 'l', 'a', 'm', 'b', '!']
>>> "".join(my_list)
'Mar had a litle lamb!'
```

```
>>> my_ba = bytearray("Mary had a little lamb!", "utf8")
>>> for i, c in enumerate(my_ba):
...     if c > ord("s"):
...         del my_ba[i]
...
>>> my_ba
bytearray(b'Mar had a litle lamb!')
```

In this code, things appear superficially to work correctly. No execeptions are raised. We genuinely do get a `list` or `bytearray` with some characters removed. However, looking slightly more closely we see that one of the `t` characters that should be filtered out remains in the mutated object. This happened because once an element was deleted, the index position no longer aligned with the actual underlying sequence. A corresponding problem would arise with insertion of new elements.

The correct way to approach this requirement is simply to create a brand-new object based on the predicate applied and selectively append to it. An append is a cheap operation on a Python `list` or `bytearray` (however, insertion into the *middle* of a new sequence can easily hit quadratic complexity—a danger warned about in other parts of this book).

Creating a new object as a filter of a sequence

```
>>> my_list = list("Mary had a little lamb!")
>>> new_list = []
>>> for c in my_list:
...     if c <= "s":
...         new_list.append(c)
...
>>> new_list
['M', 'a', 'r', ' ', 'h', 'a', 'd', ' ', 'a', ' ', 'l', 'i',
'l', 'e', ' ', 'l', 'a', 'm', 'b', '!']
>>> "".join(new_list)
'Mar had a lile lamb!'
```

Even more compactly:

```
>>> new_list = [c for c in my_list if c <= "s"]
>>> "".join(new_list)
'Mar had a lile lamb!'
```

Recall that you can also make a (shallow) copy of a sequence simply by taking the null slice of it. In slightly different scenarios, `my_list[:]` or `my_ba[:]` can often be useful as easy syntax for creating a new sequence containing the same items.

1.5   for **Loops Are More Idiomatic Than** while **Loops**

When possible, a Pythonic loop looks like: for item in iterable. This is the basic idiom, and when you find yourself doing something else, think about whether that other thing is actually better.

In writing a loop in a program, you are often faced with the choice between for and while. Or to be precise, you *could* always use either one for any given loop. It may not be obvious, but you could get by in a language that only had for if it has infinite iterators.

Equivalent of while predicate(a, b) using only for

```
>>> from itertools import repeat
>>> a, b = 17, 23  # Initial example values have no special meaning
>>> for _ in repeat(None):                          # ❶
...     print("Current values:", a, b)
...     if predicate(a, b):                         # ❷
...         break
...     a = get_data(a)                             # ❸
...     b = get_data(b)                             # ❸
...
Current values: 857 338
Current values: 613 500
Current values: 611 47
Current values: 387 871
Current values: 689 812
Current values: 406 892
Current values: 817 522
```

❶ An infinite iterator always yielding None

❷ Deliberately vague about what predicate() is checking

❸ Deliberately vague about what get_data() is doing

The preceding code is a standard example of a while True loop, but written without while. That is, we get data to work on in a stateful way. Then we evaluate that data with an expectation that it *might* reach a state where we wish to exit the loop (but it might also be an eternally running server).[1]

Expressing for in terms of while is even simpler as a translation.

Equivalent of for item in iterable using only while

```
>>> # iterable = <collection, generator, something else>
>>> iterator = iter(iterable)
```

---

1. Readers are welcome to try to guess what get_data() and predicate() are doing. Come prepared with a deep understanding of the Mersenne Twister pseudo-random number generator (PRNG).

```
>>> try:
...     while True:
...         item = next(iterator)
...         print("Current item:", item)
... except StopIteration:
...     pass
...
Current item: 2
Current item: 3
Current item: 5
Current item: 7
Current item: 11
```

Obviously, you can do the same conditional branching, `break`, `continue`, or all the other actions you might put inside a `for` loop in the preceding `while` construct.

Notwithstanding their formal equivalence (possibly with a small number of extra lines to force it), it is far more common for a `for` loop to feel Pythonic than it is for a `while` loop. This general advice has *many* exceptions, but you will find that *almost always* when you loop in Python, it is either over a collection or over an iterable (such as a generator function, generator comprehension, or custom iterable class). In many of the times when this is not the case, it is a call to refactor the part of your code that provides data to operate *into* an iterable.

It is *not* a mistake to use `while`, but whenever you find yourself writing it, you should still ask yourself: "Can I do this as a `for` loop?" Ask yourself the same question for code you are in a position to refactor. The answer may well be that the `while` loop is the most expressive and clearest version, but the question should still have occurred to you. Thinking in terms of (potentially infinite) sequences usually promotes clear and elegant design in Python.

1.6 The Walrus Operator for "Loop-and-a-Half" Blocks

A pattern that Python programmers—and programmers in many other programming languages—have often used has always been just slightly ugly. This is the "loop-and-a-half" pattern. In fact, a number of languages have been designed with, or later grown, a construct like `do … while` or `repeat … until` specifically to avoid exactly this minor wart. For example, the following code uses the same mysterious `get_data()` and `predicate()` functions from the previous sections.

Old-style loop-and-a-half in Python

```
>>> val = get_data()
>>> while not predicate(val):
```

```
...         print("Current value acceptable:", val)
...         val = get_data()
...
Current value acceptable: 869
Current value acceptable: 805
Current value acceptable: 632
Current value acceptable: 430
```

The repetition of the assignment to `val` both before the loop and within the loop body just feels slightly wrong from a stylistic and code-clarify perspective (although, it's not an actual *mistake*).

A probably even less aesthetically pleasing variant on this pattern is to use `break` within the body to avoid the repetition.

Internal-break-style loop-and-a-half in Python

```
>>> while True:
...         val = get_data()
...         if predicate(val):
...             break
...         print("Current value acceptable:", val)
...
Current value acceptable: 105
Current value acceptable: 166
Current value acceptable: 747
```

Since Python 3.8, we've had the option of using the so-called "walrus operator" to simplify this structure. The operator is fancifully named for its resemblance to an emoticon of a walrus with eyes and tusks. The walrus operator (`:=`) allows you to assign a value within an expression rather than only as a statement.

New-style loop-and-a-half in Python

```
>>> while not predicate(val := get_data()):
...         print("Current value acceptable:", val)
...
Current value acceptable: 859
Current value acceptable: 296
Current value acceptable: 235
Current value acceptable: 805
Current value acceptable: 383
```

In both cases where the predicate is inside the `while` statement, the loop might be entered as few as zero times. With a `while True`, the loop is always entered at least once, but it might terminate early (the "and-a-half") if some condition occurs.

Using the walrus operator within an `if` statement is very similar in both providing a value and perhaps not running the suite based on that value.

An `if` suite without and with inline initialization

```
>>> val = get_data()
>>> if val:
...     print("Current value acceptable:", val)
...
Current value acceptable: 247

>>> if val := get_data():
...     print("Current value acceptable:", val)
...
Current value acceptable: 848
```

1.7 `zip()` Simplifies Using Multiple Iterables

As with many of the discussions in this chapter, let's look at a mistake that is mostly stylistic and one of code clarity. An unpythonic way of looping over multiple iterables, such as multiple lists, might look like the following code. In the example, the several data files contain information on 1,255 NOAA-monitored weather stations.

Parallel access to multiple lists of the same length

```
>>> from pprint import pprint
>>> from pathlib import Path
>>> from collections import namedtuple

>>> Station = namedtuple("Station",
...     "name latitude longitude elevation")
...
>>> names = Path("station-names.txt").read_text().splitlines()
>>> lats = Path("station-latitudes.txt").read_text().splitlines()
>>> lons = Path("station-longitudes.txt").read_text().splitlines()
>>> els = Path("station-elevations.txt").read_text().splitlines()
>>> assert len(names) == len(lats) == len(lons) == len(els) == 1255

>>> stations = []
>>> for i in range(1255):
...     station = Station(names[i], lats[i], lons[i], els[i])
...     stations.append(station)
```

```
...
>>> pprint(stations[:4])
[Station(name='JAN MAYEN NOR NAVY', latitude='70.9333333',
    longitude='-8.6666667', elevation='9.0'),
 Station(name='SORSTOKKEN', latitude='59.791925',
    longitude='5.34085', elevation='48.76'),
 Station(name='VERLEGENHUKEN', latitude='80.05',
    longitude='16.25', elevation='8.0'),
 Station(name='HORNSUND', latitude='77.0',
    longitude='15.5', elevation='12.0')]
```

The assertion in the example checks that all these files indeed have the same amount of data. More robust error handling is possible, of course. The use of `pathlib` in the example assures that files are closed after they are read in. Using `pathlib` gives you a similar guarantee about proper cleanup to using context managers, which are discussed in Chapter 3.

The prior code is not terrible, but it can be made more Pythonic. As one improvement, we can notice that open file handles are themselves iterable. As the main point, we do not need intermediate lists to perform this action, nor do we need to separately access corresponding index positions within each. This calls back to several mistakes discussed in this chapter of focusing on *where* a datum occurs in a collection rather than directly on the data itself.

Cleaner code to build a list of station data `namedtuples` might look like this.

Using `zip()` to read multiple open files

```
>>> stations = []
>>> with (                                          # ❶
...     open("station-names.txt") as names,
...     open("station-latitudes.txt") as lats,
...     open("station-longitudes.txt") as lons,
...     open("station-elevations.txt") as els,
... ):
...     for data in zip(names, lats, lons, els):
...         data = (field.rstrip() for field in data)
...         stations.append(Station(*data))
...
>>> assert len(stations) == 1255
>>> pprint(stations[:4])
[Station(name='JAN MAYEN NOR NAVY', latitude='70.9333333',
    longitude='-8.6666667', elevation='9.0'),
 Station(name='SORSTOKKEN', latitude='59.791925',
    longitude='5.34085', elevation='48.76'),
 Station(name='VERLEGENHUKEN', latitude='80.05',
    longitude='16.25', elevation='8.0'),
```

```
Station(name='HORNSUND', latitude='77.0',
    longitude='15.5', elevation='12.0')]
```

❶ Parenthesized context managers were introduced in Python 3.10.

The aesthetics of having to strip the extra newlines from the file iterators isn't ideal, but overall this code is just as safe (in terms of guaranteeing closed files), only holds one datum from each file in memory at a given time, and is more concise and expressive. The extra names remain within the namespace, but they are merely closed files that take minimal memory:

```
>>> names
<_io.TextIOWrapper name='station-names.txt' mode='r' encoding='UTF-8'>
>>> next(names)
Traceback (most recent call last):
[...]
ValueError: I/O operation on closed file.
```

# 1.8 zip(strict=True) **and**
     itertools.zip_longest()

In the preceding section, we looked at improvements in readability that use of zip() can often accomplish. But that section also glossed over a possible problem in the underlying task. The iterables that we zip() together might be different lengths, and when they are, zip() will silently ignore the unconsumed items from the longer iterator.

Recall that we had several data files with information on the name, latitude, longitude, and elevation of NOAA-monitored weather stations. One can notice pretty quickly that this is a fragile arrangement of data, since the process that created the files may fail to assure accurate synchronization of their data. However, data often becomes available to us in forms that have upstream flaws that we cannot control.

The code we wrote to illustrate the good use of zip() was a good approach to remedying some flaws in the format of the original data by putting all attributes of each station within the same object (a namedtuple in the example, although other objects like dataclasses, dictionaries, or custom objects might also be good choices).

The use of zip() in its simplest form, from the "solution" to the prior section, can actually *mask* errors rather than the much better option of failing noisily. Recall the sound advice from *The Zen of Python*: "Errors should never pass silently."

Previously we had used this code, but let's substitute the data file *station-lattrunc.txt* for *station-latitude.txt*. That is, the former is a truncated version of the latter, which I have constructed for this example.

Using `zip()` can mask mismatches in iterables

```
>>> stations = []
>>> with (
...      open("station-names.txt") as names,
...      open("station-lattrunc.txt") as lats,
...      open("station-longitudes.txt") as lons,
...      open("station-elevations.txt") as els,
... ):
...      for datum in zip(names, lats, lons, els):
...          datum = (d.rstrip() for d in datum)
...          stations.append(Station(*datum))
...
>>> assert len(stations) == 1255
Traceback (most recent call last):
[...]
AssertionError
>>> len(stations)
1250
```

The assertion shown catches that the length of the generated list of objects isn't exactly 1,255; but we would like code that is flexible enough to handle corresponding data with a different number of items than that precise number.

There are two reasonable approaches we can take when we want to enforce a degree of data consistency but do not necessarily know an exact data size to expect: requiring that all the data files *in fact* are of matching length, or padding fields where data is not available. Either is reasonable, depending on your purpose.

Using `zip(strict=True)` to enforce iterator length consistency

```
>>> stations = []
>>> with (
...      open("station-names.txt") as names,
...      open("station-lattrunc.txt") as lats,
...      open("station-longitudes.txt") as lons,
...      open("station-elevations.txt") as els,
... ):
...      for datum in zip(names, lats, lons, els, strict=True):
...          datum = (d.rstrip() for d in datum)        # ❶
...          stations.append(Station(*datum))
...
Traceback (most recent call last):
[...]
ValueError: zip() argument 2 is shorter than argument 1
```

❶ The optional `strict` argument was added in Python 3.10.

This approach is very helpful in working independently of the length of the several streams of data, merely enforcing that they are the same. And it is very much a "fail fast" approach, which is almost universally desirable.

However, there are likewise definitely situations where imputing sentinel values for missing data is more appropriate. A *sentinel* is a special value that can mark a "special" situation for a data point. A very common sentinel, in many contexts, is None. Sometimes you might use a value like -1 as a sentinel to indicate that "normal" values are positive. At other times, you might include a defined name like my_sentinel = object() to guarantee that this value is distinct from everything else in your program. Filling in imputed values is easy with zip_longest().

Using `itertools.zip_longest()` to impute missing data

```
>>> from itertools import zip_longest
>>> stations = []
>>> with (
...     open("station-names.txt") as names,
...     open("station-lattrunc.txt") as lats,
...     open("station-longitudes.txt") as lons,
...     open("station-elevations.txt") as els,
... ):
...     for datum in zip_longest(
...             names, lats, lons, els, fillvalue="-1"):
...         datum = (d.rstrip() for d in datum)
...         stations.append(Station(*datum))
...
>>> pprint(stations[-6:])
[Station(name='SCUOL', latitude='46.8',
    longitude='10.2833333', elevation='1295.0'),
 Station(name='NALUNS', latitude='-1',
    longitude='10.2666666', elevation='2400.0'),
 Station(name='BUOCHS AIRPORT STANS', latitude='-1',
    longitude='8.4', elevation='450.0'),
 Station(name='SITTERDORF', latitude='-1',
    longitude='9.2666666', elevation='506.0'),
 Station(name='SCALOTTAS', latitude='-1',
    longitude='9.5166666', elevation='2323.0'),
 Station(name='VADUZ', latitude='-1',
    longitude='9.5166666', elevation='463.0')]
```

In the case of zip_longest(), shorter iterables are simply filled in with some sentinel. None is the default, but it is configurable using the argument fillvalue.

Neither of the approaches in this section is flawless, of course. In particular, having items from iterables *correspond* correctly is a much stricter requirement than having them *align* correctly. If one series drops item 10 and another drops item 20, they could still fortuitously be the same length overall. These functions are powerful, but they cannot answer all the important questions about data consistency.

1.9 Wrapping Up

One of the loveliest elements of modern Python is its emphasis on looping over iterables, including those that are not concrete collections. In some mistakes in Chapter 4, *Advanced Python Usage*, we look at explicit "iterator algebra." This chapter reflects patterns and habits you will use nearly every time you write Python code; we have emphasized Python's focus on looping *over* the data you are actually concerned with rather than over indirections towards it.

Beyond those mistakes that guide you to emphasize the right things to loop over, we also looked at the danger of mutating concrete collections during iteration and at how while loops, when they are the more elegant approach, can benefit from use of the newish walrus operator.

Confusing Equality with Identity

Most objects in Python are mutable. Moreover, *all objects* in Python are accessed by reference. For objects that are immutable, such as strings, numbers, and `frozensets`, comparing for equality or inequality rarely raises a concern about whether those objects are also identical. However, for mutable objects such as mutable collections, it becomes very important to distinguish identity from mere equality.

In many programming languages, a distinction is made between *pass by value*, *pass by address*, and *pass by reference* (occasionally *pass by name* occurs as well). Python behaves most similarly to reference passing, but in Python lingo we often emphasize Python's semantics by calling the behavior *pass by object reference*. Being thoroughly object oriented, Python always encapsulates its objects, regardless of the scope they exist within. It's not the value that is passed into functions, nor is it a memory address, nor is it a variable name, it's simply an *object*.

What becomes important to consider is whether an object passed into a function or method is *immutable*. If it is, then it behaves very much like a passed value in other languages (since it cannot be changed at all and therefore is not in the calling scope). The particular name an object has in different scopes can vary, but the object remains the same under each name. If that object is mutable, it might be mutated within a child scope, changing it within the calling scope (or elsewhere within the runtime behavior of a program).

2.1 Late Binding of Closures

The scoping behavior of Python can cause surprises for programmers coming from other dynamic programming languages. An expectation of many developers is that if a function—including a `lambda` function—is created within a loop (including within the loop element of a list, set, dict, or generator comprehension), then the created function will utilize the value of a variable that exists at the time the function is created.

> **Note   Interning commonly used immutable objects**
>
> As an optimization strategy, CPython (and other implementations) sometimes reuses the memory allocation for certain objects by treating them as pseudo-eternal. Most notably, *small integers* and *short strings* will often reuse the identical objects to refer to equal objects that go by different names.
>
> The specific details of when this happens are implementation and version dependent, and you should never rely on such behavior within your programs. They merely might go faster as a result of these optimizations. For example, CPython and PyPy take very different approaches to "interning" but no well-written programs will notice this implementation difference.
>
> **Integer interning**
> ```
> >>> a = 5
> >>> b = 2 + 3
> >>> a == b, a is b
> (True, True)
> >>> c = 1_000_000
> >>> d = 999_999 + 1
> >>> c == d, c is d
> (True, False)
> ```
>
> **String interning**
> ```
> >>> e = "foobar"
> >>> f = "foo" + "bar"
> >>> e == f, e is f
> (True, True)
> >>> g = "flimflam"
> >>> h = "".join(["flim", "flam"])
> >>> g == h, g is h
> (True, False)
> ```

However, Python *binds by name* in this circumstance, rather than binding by value. The value eventually utilized is the *final* value a variable takes on at the time the closure function is eventually called.

Surprising behavior of functions created as closures

```
>>> def make_adders(addends):
...     funcs = []
...     for addend in addends:
...         funcs.append(lambda x: x + addend)     # ❶
...     return funcs
...
```

```
>>> adders = make_adders([10, 100, 1000])          # ❷
>>> for adder in adders:
...     print(adder(5))
...
1005
1005
1005
```

❶ The `lambda` does nothing special here; using a `def adder` inner function definition produces the exact same behavior.

❷ Notice that `adders` is a list of functions, each of which is called in the loop.

Note So what is a closure, anyway?

The term *closure* is a bit of computer science lingo that, while important, might not be familiar to people who are new to programming or have not studied theoretical aspects. Don't worry, it's not as bad as it seems.

In programming languages, a (lexical; i.e., nested scope) closure means that variables defined outside the current scope of a function definition are "closed over." That is to say, the function itself in some manner captures those variables and they can continue to be used later when the function is called.

As we will see, however, whereas many programming languages "capture" variables as their values, Python captures them as their names.

In contrast, if we were to write a very closely analogous program in (fairly) modern JavaScript, the behavior is probably what we would expect. Older JavaScript *does* contain the keyword `function` that would be even more closely parallel with the Python version; but preference for "arrow functions" has become predominant over the last few years.

Less surprising behavior of JavaScript closures

```
// Welcome to Node.js v18.10.0.
> const make_adders = (addends) => {
...     const funcs = [];
...     for (const addend of addends) {
...         funcs.push((x) => x + addend);
...     };
...     return funcs;
... };
undefined
> const adders = make_adders([10, 100, 1000]);
undefined
> for (const adder of adders) {
```

```
...         console.log(adder(5));
... };
15
105
1005
undefined
```

In the JavaScript comparison, the const keyword is forcing "expected" scoping, but we can accomplish the same thing in Python by using keyword binding to force more obvious scoping. To get the output that most newcomers—and probably most experienced Python developers as well—expect, force early binding by assigning default arguments.

Less surprising behavior of Python closures

```
>>> def make_adders(addends):
...     funcs = []
...     for addend in addends:
...         funcs.append(lambda x, *, _addend=addend: x + _addend)
...     return funcs
...
>>> adders = make_adders([10, 100, 1000])      # ❶
>>> for adder in adders:
...     print(adder(5))
...
15
105
1005
```

❶ adders is a list of (lambda) function objects.

We have required that only one positional argument is passed, and used a "private" name for the keyword argument. Technically, of course, we could still override the behavior of the closure function, though:

```
>>> add10 = adders[0]
>>> add10(5, 6)
Traceback (most recent call last):
  Cell In[272], line 1
    add10(5, 6)
TypeError: make_adders.<locals>.<lambda>() takes 1 positional
  argument but 2 were given

>>> add10(5, _addend=6)
11
```

2.2 Overchecking for Boolean Values

Nearly all objects in Python are "truthy" or "falsy." That is to say that in a *Boolean context*, almost all objects are perfectly usable "bare" without wrapping them in `bool()`, and especially not with a completely pointless comparison of `obj is True` or `obj is False`.

While often the `is True` and `is False` are simply unecessary, they can sometimes cause actual bugs. The value you obtain from a function call—specifically from a function that you did not write yourself, such as a function from a library—may not be `True` or `False` since the API only guarantees or attempts to return a truthy or falsy value. Quite often, assuming a value is an actual Boolean will *often* work, then fail unexpectedly where the function utilizes a different type of object, such as to communicate a sentinel.

> **Note   Special cases of truthiness**
>
> As a quick guide, numbers that are equal to zero are falsy. So are collections that are empty. So are string-like objects of length zero. Naturally, so are the singletons `False` and `None`. When you see those values in a "Boolean context" they are equivalent to an actual `False`. Most other objects are truthy.
>
> Well-known objects that are neither truthy nor falsy are NumPy arrays and Pandas Series and DataFrames.
>
> ```
> >>> import numpy as np
> >>> import pandas as pd
> >>> arr = np.array([1, 2])
> >>> bool(arr)
> ValueError: The truth value of an array with more than one
>   element is ambiguous. Use a.any() or a.all()
>
> >>> series = pd.Series([1, 2], index=["A", "B"])
> >>> series
> A    1
> B    2
> dtype: int64
> >>> bool(series)
> ValueError: The truth value of a Series is ambiguous.
>   Use a.empty, a.bool(), a.item(), a.any() or a.all().
> ```
>
> You can define the truthiness of your own classes by including a `.__bool__()` dunder method. While you *can* do something else, as we see with NumPy and Pandas, you almost always want to return `True` or `False` from that method, according to whatever criteria make sense for instances of your custom class.

Whereas `is True` and `is False` have a narrow edge case where they can make sense, using `obj == True` or `obj == False` will always cause a feeling of unease among Pythonistas since `True` and `False` are unique identities already. In Python, numbers that aren't zero and collections that aren't empty are truthy, and zeros and empty collections are falsy. This is as much as we want to know for most constructs.

Idiomatic Python checks for truthiness

```
>>> tuples = [ (1, 2, 3), (), (4, 5), (9,) ]
>>> [max(tup) for tup in tuples if tup]         # ❶
[3, 5, 9]
>>> for tup in tuples:
...     if tup:                                 # ❶
...         print(len(tup))
...     else:
...         print("EMPTY")
...
3
EMPTY
2
1
```

❶ Rely on implicit truthiness

Some variations you might see will try to check more than explicitly needed.

Unidiomatic Python checks for truthiness

```
>>> [min(tup) for tup in tuples if len(tup)]    # ❶
[1, 4, 9]
>>> [min(tup) for tup in tuples if bool(tup)]   # ❷
[1, 4, 9]
>>> for tup in tuples:
...     if (len(tup) > 0) is True:              # ❸
...         print(min(tup))
...
1
4
9
```

❶ Unnecessary `len()` check

❷ Unnecessary `bool()` check

❸ Triply unnecessary `len()`, inequality comparison, and `is True`

For the most part, the mistake of coercing actual `True` or `False` values from merely "truthy" or "falsy" is simply stylistic and does not harm program operation. But such use has a strong code smell that should be avoided.

Often the habit of spelling out `is True` is borrowed from SQL, where database columns might both be of Boolean type and be nullable.[1] However, sometimes you encounter a similar usage in existing Python code. In SQL, these checks actually do make sense, as shown in the following code.

Use of = TRUE in SQL

```
SQLite version 3.37.2 2022-01-06 13:25:41
sqlite> CREATE TABLE test (name TEXT, flag BOOL NULL);
sqlite> INSERT INTO test VALUES ("Bob", TRUE), ("Ann", FALSE),
    ("Li", NULL);
sqlite> SELECT name FROM test WHERE flag IS NULL;
Li
sqlite> SELECT name FROM test WHERE flag = TRUE;
Bob
sqlite> SELECT name FROM test WHERE flag = FALSE;
Ann
sqlite> SELECT name FROM test WHERE NOT flag;      # ❶
Ann
```

❶ In many SQL dialects, we can get away with Python-like bare values, but best practice in that language remains to be explicit.

Sometimes in Python code, you will see a sentinel used within a function that normally returns an actual `True` or `False`. Often this sentinel is `None`, but sometimes other values are used. The problem here, of course, is that a sentinel almost certainly has a truthiness that can be deceptive in code using such a function.

If you are writing code from scratch, or refactoring it, you are better off using an explicit enumeration, utilizing the well-designed `enum` standard library module. But in the real world, you will probably encounter and need to use code that does not do this.

"Almost Boolean" function with a sentinel

```
>>> import re
>>> def has_vowel(s):
...      "Vowels are a, e, i, o, u ... and sometimes y"
```

---

1. Effectively, the nullable Boolean type gives you a trinary, or "three-valued," logic (https://en.wikipedia.org/wiki/Three-valued_logic).

```
...        class Maybe:
...            def __repr__(self):
...                return "MAYBE"
...
...        if re.search(r"[aeiou]", s):
...            return True
...        elif "y" in s:
...            return Maybe()
...        else:
...            return False
...
>>> has_vowel("Oh no!")                          # ❶
True
>>> has_vowel("My my!")                           # ❶
MAYBE
>>> if has_vowel(my_phrase) is True:              # ❷
...     print("The phrase definitely has a vowel")
...
```

❶ Arguably OK for printing an answer

❷ The three-valued logic makes us resort to unpythonic style.

If you are free to redesign this function, you might define Vowel =
enum.Enum("Vowel", ["Yes", "No", "Maybe"]) then return Vowel.Yes, Vowel.No,
or Vowel.Maybe within the function, as appropriate. Comparisons will require an explicit
identity (or equality) check, but that clarifies the intention better for this case anyway.

2.3 Comparing x == None

This problem is a simple one, perhaps as a breather from many others with broad
background information. In Python, None is a *singleton* constant. True and False are also
unique, but in a hyper-technical sense are the *two* possible instances of the bool class. That
is to say, there can only ever be one None during a particular execution of the Python
interpreter.

If you ever see code using if obj == None you immediately know that whoever
wrote it was a newcomer to Python, and this should be cleaned up in code review. Most
linters and style checking tools will complain about this.

The correct spelling is always simply if obj is None. You will make your colleagues
happy when you write this, or when you fix it in legacy code.

> **Note Singletons and the Borg**
>
> The famous 1994 "Gang of Four" book (*Design Patterns: Elements of Reusable Object-Oriented Software*, by Erich Gamma, Richard Helm, Ralph Johnson, and John Vlissides) popularized the software concept of a "singleton." In their case, they meant a class (in C++ or Smalltalk) that can only have a single instance.
>
> Narrowly speaking, Python's None fulfills this definition:
>
> ```
> >>> type(None)
> <class 'NoneType'>
> >>> None.__class__() is None
> True
> >>> (1).__class__() is 1                    # ❶
> <>:1: SyntaxWarning: "is" with a literal. Did you mean "=="?
> False
> ```
>
> ❶ Warnings in Python 3.10, 3.11, and 3.12 have gotten noticeably more precise. This friendly reminder is a good example.
>
> For your own classes, the "singleton pattern" is a poor choice in Python. It is *possible* to implement, yes, but to accomplish all the same goals, Alex Martelli's "Borg idiom" is uniformly more Pythonic:
>
> ```python
> class Borg:
>     _the_collective = {}
>     def __init__(self):
>         self.__dict__ = self._the_collective
>
>     def __eq__(self, other):
>         return isinstance(other, self.__class__)
> ```
>
> Many Borg can exist, but every attribute and method is shared between each of them. None, however, remains properly a singleton.

2.4 Misunderstanding Mutable Default Arguments

The behavior of mutable default arguments is surprising to many developers. In fact, many programmers—including many experienced Python developers—would describe it as simply a wart or antipattern of the language.[2]

---

2. In a provocative blog post title, Florimond Manca declared in 2018 that "Python Mutable Defaults Are The Source of All Evil." A great many other writers have given the same warning with somewhat less florid language.

I take a somewhat more sympathetic view of Python behavior around mutable values used as named arguments than do many of my colleagues; however, I will probably admit that my affection arises in overly large part from knowing the "trick" for a long time, and having written about it in more-or-less positive terms in 2001. Moreover, in Python 2.1 where I first wrote about playing with this behavior, many alternatives that now exist had not yet entered the language.

Let's look at a simple function to illustrate the issue. We have several word list files on disk:

```
>>> for fname in Path("data").glob("?-words.txt"):
...     print(f"{fname}: {Path(fname).read_text().strip()}")
...
data/a-words.txt: acclimations airways antinarrative astrocyte
data/b-words.txt: buggiest biros bushvelds begazed braunite
data/z-words.txt: zonate zoophyte zumbooruk zoozoos
```

We would like to process the separate words within lists.

Read words from a file, arrange them in a list
```
>>> def wordfile_to_list(fname, initial_words=[]):
...     with open(fname) as words:
...         initial_words.extend(words.read().split())
...     return initial_words
...
>>> wordfile_to_list("data/z-words.txt", ["zlotys", "zappier"])
['zlotys', 'zappier', 'zonate', 'zoophyte', 'zumbooruk', 'zoozoos']
```

So far, so good. We might want to start with some initial list elements but add more from a file. Straightforward enough. Let's try it again.

Read words from file to list, take two
```
>>> wordfile_to_list("data/a-words.txt")
['acclimations', 'airways', 'antinarrative', 'astrocyte']
>>> wordfile_to_list("data/b-words.txt")
['acclimations', 'airways', 'antinarrative', 'astrocyte',
 'buggiest', 'biros', 'bushvelds', 'begazed', 'braunite']
>>> wordfile_to_list("data/b-words.txt", ['brine'])
['brine', 'buggiest', 'biros', 'bushvelds', 'begazed', 'braunite']
```

At the first pass of just reading *a-words.txt*, all seems well. At the second pass of also reading in *b-words.txt*, we notice with surprise that our results are becoming cummulative rather than calls being independent. However, it gets even weirder on the third pass in which we read in *b-words.txt* anew, but it stops being cummulative again.

Understanding what is occurring is not genuinely difficult once you think about the execution model of Python. Keyword arguments are evaluated at definition time. *All lines of Python*, within a given scope, are evaluated at definition time, so this *should be* unsurprising. The list `initial_words` is defined once at definition time, and the same object gets extended during each call (unless a different object is substituted for a call). But OK, I get it. It's weird behavior.

If we want statefulness in a function call (or in something equivalent) we have several good approaches to doing that which don't use the "immutable default value" *hack*.

2.4.1 First Approach, Use a Class

I like functional programming styles, but classes are great ways to encapsulate stateful behavior.

Class-based stateful word reader

```
>>> class Wordlist:
...     def __init__(self, initial=[]):
...         self._words = initial
...
...     def add_words(self, fname):
...         self._words.extend(Path(fname).read_text().split())
...
...     def reset(self, initial=None):
...         self._words = initial if initial is not None else []
...
...     def __repr__(self):
...         return str(self._words)
...
>>> words = Wordlist(["microtubules", "magisterial"])
>>> words
['microtubules', 'magisterial']
>>> words.add_words("data/b-words.txt")
>>> words
['microtubules', 'magisterial', 'buggiest', 'biros',
 'bushvelds', 'begazed', 'braunite']
>>> words.reset(["visioning", "virulency"])
>>> words
['visioning', 'virulency']
>>> words.add_words("data/a-words.txt")
>>> words
['visioning', 'virulency', 'acclimations', 'airways',
 'antinarrative', 'astrocyte']
```

You can easily tweak this API to your precise needs, but it clearly gets both statefulness and easy comprehensibility.

2.4.2 Second Approach, Use a None Sentinel

The most common "solution" you will read elsewhere is simply to use None rather than a mutable default, and put the initialization within a function body. This keeps code in functions, which are often simpler than classes, and sticks with built-in collection types.

Sentinel None as function named parameter

```
>>> def wordfile_to_list(fname, initial_words=None):
...     words = [] if initial_words is None else initial_words
...     with open(fname) as wordfile:
...         words.extend(wordfile.read().split())
...     return words
...
>>> words = wordfile_to_list("data/a-words.txt")
>>> words
['acclimations', 'airways', 'antinarrative', 'astrocyte']
>>> words = wordfile_to_list("data/b-words.txt")
>>> words
['buggiest', 'biros', 'bushvelds', 'begazed', 'braunite']
>>> words = wordfile_to_list("data/z-words.txt", words)
>>> words
['buggiest', 'biros', 'bushvelds', 'begazed', 'braunite',
  'zonate', 'zoophyte', 'zumbooruk', 'zoozoos']
```

We can control statefulness in this design simply by deciding whether or not to pass in a current state to mutate or by skipping that argument for a fresh list result.

2.4.3 Third Approach, Take Advantage of Stateful Generators

The final solution I will suggest is the one I've seen least often discussed in public fora. At the same time, it's probably the one I like the best, and one that was not available in 2001 when I first started seeing hands wrung over the issue of mutable default parameters.

Generator-based statefulness

```
>>> def word_injector(initial_words=None):
...     words = [] if initial_words is None else initial_words
...     while True:
...         fname = (yield words)
...         if fname is not None:
```

```
...                with open(fname) as wordfile:
...                    words.extend(wordfile.read().split())
...
>>> words = word_injector(["microtubules", "magisterial"])
>>> next(words)                                   # ❶
['microtubules', 'magisterial']
>>> words.send("data/a-words.txt")                # ❷
['microtubules', 'magisterial', 'acclimations', 'airways',
 'antinarrative', 'astrocyte']
>>> words.send("data/z-words.txt")                # ❷
['microtubules', 'magisterial', 'acclimations', 'airways',
 'antinarrative', 'astrocyte', 'zonate', 'zoophyte', 'zumbooruk',
 'zoozoos']
>>> words2 = word_injector()
>>> next(words2)                                  # ❶
[]
>>> words2.send("data/b-words.txt")               # ❷
['buggiest', 'biros', 'bushvelds', 'begazed', 'braunite']
>>> next(words2)                                  # ❶
['buggiest', 'biros', 'bushvelds', 'begazed', 'braunite']
```

❶ A plain next() call will always simply retrieve the current state of the word list.

❷ Read about the .send() method on generators at https://docs.python.org/3 /reference/expressions.html#generator.send.

This approach resembles functional programming paradigms. If we want multiple stateful "instances" of a word list, we do not instantiate a class, but rather simply create new generator objects from a generator function. All statefulness is purely internal to the position of the generator within the while True loop.

If we really wanted to, we could use a sentinel like _RESET to inject (.send()) in place of a filename; but that is not really necessary. It is easier simply to create a new generator that is started with values from an existing generator using either next(old_words) or old_words.send(newfile). Or, for that matter, you can simply start a new generator with a list from any arbitrary code that might have created a word list by whatever means.

2.5 Copies versus References to Mutable Objects

We saw in the preceding section that it is easy to forget that *all Python expressions* within a given scope are evaluated at definition time. Users are sometimes bitten by mutable default arguments, but other constructs also provide an attractive nuisance.

For example, it is commonplace to wish to initialize a list of lists.[3] An *obvious* way to do so is as follows.

Creating a "blank" Python list of lists (the wrong way)

```
>>> from pprint import pprint
>>> from enum import Enum
>>> Color = Enum("C", ["BLANK", "RED", "GREEN", "BLUE"])
>>> grid = [[Color.BLANK] * width] * height
>>> pprint(grid)
[[<C.BLANK: 1>, <C.BLANK: 1>, <C.BLANK: 1>, <C.BLANK: 1>],
 [<C.BLANK: 1>, <C.BLANK: 1>, <C.BLANK: 1>, <C.BLANK: 1>],
 [<C.BLANK: 1>, <C.BLANK: 1>, <C.BLANK: 1>, <C.BLANK: 1>],
 [<C.BLANK: 1>, <C.BLANK: 1>, <C.BLANK: 1>, <C.BLANK: 1>],
 [<C.BLANK: 1>, <C.BLANK: 1>, <C.BLANK: 1>, <C.BLANK: 1>]]
```

It seems like we have a nice grid, as we wished for. However, let's try populating it:

```
>>> grid[1][0] = Color.RED
>>> grid[3][2] = Color.BLUE
>>> grid[3][1] = Color.GREEN
>>> grid[4][1:4] = [Color.RED] * 3
>>> pprint(grid)
[[<C.RED: 2>, <C.RED: 2>, <C.RED: 2>, <C.RED: 2>],
 [<C.RED: 2>, <C.RED: 2>, <C.RED: 2>, <C.RED: 2>],
 [<C.RED: 2>, <C.RED: 2>, <C.RED: 2>, <C.RED: 2>],
 [<C.RED: 2>, <C.RED: 2>, <C.RED: 2>, <C.RED: 2>],
 [<C.RED: 2>, <C.RED: 2>, <C.RED: 2>, <C.RED: 2>]]
>>> pprint([id(sublist) for sublist in grid])
[139768215997440,
 139768215997440,
 139768215997440,
 139768215997440,
 139768215997440]
```

Rather than having created a grid, we've create a list of five references to the identical object (a list in this case, but the same danger lurks for any mutable object type).

There are a number of ways you might fix this once you remember the problem. Probably the easiest solution is to use comprehensions rather than the list multiplication shortcut.

---

3. If you work with tabular data, however, do consider whether NumPy or Pandas, or another DataFrame library, is a better choice for your purpose.

Creating a blank Python list of lists (a good way)

```
>>> grid = [[Color.BLANK for _w in range(width)] for _h in
    range(height)]
>>> pprint(grid)
[[<C.BLANK: 1>, <C.BLANK: 1>, <C.BLANK: 1>, <C.BLANK: 1>],
 [<C.BLANK: 1>, <C.BLANK: 1>, <C.BLANK: 1>, <C.BLANK: 1>],
 [<C.BLANK: 1>, <C.BLANK: 1>, <C.BLANK: 1>, <C.BLANK: 1>],
 [<C.BLANK: 1>, <C.BLANK: 1>, <C.BLANK: 1>, <C.BLANK: 1>],
 [<C.BLANK: 1>, <C.BLANK: 1>, <C.BLANK: 1>, <C.BLANK: 1>]]
>>> grid[1][0] = Color.RED
>>> grid[3][2] = Color.BLUE
>>> grid[3][1] = Color.GREEN
>>> grid[4][1:4] = [Color.RED] * 3
>>> pprint(grid)
[[<C.BLANK: 1>, <C.BLANK: 1>, <C.BLANK: 1>, <C.BLANK: 1>],
 [<C.RED: 2>, <C.BLANK: 1>, <C.BLANK: 1>, <C.BLANK: 1>],
 [<C.BLANK: 1>, <C.BLANK: 1>, <C.BLANK: 1>, <C.BLANK: 1>],
 [<C.BLANK: 1>, <C.GREEN: 3>, <C.BLUE: 4>, <C.BLANK: 1>],
 [<C.BLANK: 1>, <C.RED: 2>, <C.RED: 2>, <C.RED: 2>]]
>>> pprint([id(sublist) for sublist in grid])
[139768305000064,
 139768302388864,
 139768304216832,
 139768302374976,
 139768216006464]
```

We have a list of length 5, each item being a distinct list (as indicated by their different IDs) that can be modified independently.

2.6 Confusing is with == (in the Presence of Interning)

Earlier in this chapter, we looked at == and is in some depth. In some sense, this section is an extension of those discussions. However, the issue here is *accidental identity*; or at least *non-guaranteed identity*.

A sidenote to the introduction of this chapter discussed the fact that *small integers* and *short strings* will often reuse the identical objects to refer to equal objects that go by different names. I strongly suspect that the "Faster CPython" project (https://github.com /faster-cpython/) will extend the range of objects that are interned, especially starting with Python 3.12. Already, PyPy (https://www.pypy.org/) is much more aggressive about object interning; albeit that element is only a very small aspect of the huge speedups it obtains via its tracing JIT (https://en.wikipedia.org/wiki/Tracing_just-in-time_compilation).

A prior discussion looked at why you should never use x == None in your code; but ultimately, that was a stylistic issue and one of Pythonicity. Ultimately, none of your programs would break if you used that style violation. Interned values are different. You might notice something like this:

```
>>> a = 5 * 5
>>> b = 21 + 4
>>> a is b, a == b
(True, True)
```

Thinking too cleverly along these lines, you might conclude that identity comparison is probably faster than equality comparison. To a small extent you would be correct (at least for Python 3.11, on my CPU and operating system):

```
>>> def intern_id(a, b):
...     for _ in range(20_000_000):
...         a is b
...
>>> def intern_eq(a, b):
...     for _ in range(20_000_000):
...         a == b
...
>>> %timeit intern_id(a, b)
361 ms ± 2.8 ms per loop (mean ± std. dev. of 7 runs, 1 loop each)
>>> %timeit intern_eq(a, b)
448 ms ± 9.96 ms per loop (mean ± std. dev. of 7 runs, 1 loop each)
```

The problem, of course, is that only some numbers (and some strings) that are equal are also identical, and actual programs almost always need to make comparisons on values that vary at runtime. Other than special singletons, or when you genuinely care whether two custom objects (for example, objects at different positions in a collection) are identical, stick with equality checks:

```
>>> fb1 = "foobar"
>>> fb2 = "foo" + "bar"
>>> fb3 = "   foobar   ".strip()
>>> fb1 is fb2, fb1 == fb2
(True, True)
>>> fb1 is fb3, fb1 == fb3
(False, True)

>>> c = 250 + 9
>>> d = 7 * 37
```

```
>>> c is d, c == d
(False, True)
```

2.7 Wrapping Up

The puzzles of equality and identity have stymied many accomplished programmers. In Common Lisp, developers distinguish among `eq`, `equal`, `eql`, and `equalp`. In Scheme, they settle for just =, `eqv?`, and `equal?`. In JavaScript, equality is notoriously, and humorously, non-transitive. A well-known diagram (shown in Figure 2.1 as the "theological trinity") about JavaScript gives us a perspective into the comparative sanity of Python, which maintains transitivity (absent deliberately pathological custom classes, which can make all horrors possible).

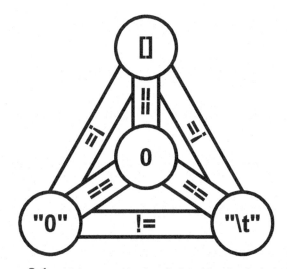

Figure 2.1   A joke comparing JavaScript with a theological trinity.

In Python we do not have quite so many variations on a theme. Instead, we have a test for *identical* objects with `is` and a test for *equivalent* objects with ==. The semantics are relatively straightforward, but many mistakes still occur as developers try to decide what they mean between these concepts.

A footnote to this chapter might add that while Python's standard library has the very useful function `copy.deepcopy()` to recursively copy nested collections, there does not exist in the standard library any function for `deepequality()` that would, hypothetically, recursively compare such nested collections. A great many recipes you can find online have implemented such a thing, but they are each slightly different and none ascend to a ubiquity meriting inclusion in these discussions. This provides an opportunity for you to make your very own novel mistake.

A Grab Bag of Python Gotchas

This chapter looks at concerns one encounters—and mistakes one might often make—strictly within the Python language itself. Like the prior two chapters on respectively looping and equality versus identity, these discussions are about the core of the Python language. Later chapters look at less common language constructs, less used or more specialized standard library modules, and some very common third-party modules.

While the discussions in this chapter are somewhat heterogeneous, they also address a few of the most failings real-world Python code encounters, in my experience. A fair number of the issues in this chapter reflect the use of habits developed for other programming languages that are less well suited to Python code.

3.1 Naming Things

As the famous saying goes:

> There are two hard things in computer science: cache invalidation, naming things, and off-by-one errors.

In this section, we will look at where naming can go wrong. The kinds of mistakes addressed in this section are somewhat heterogeneous, but all pertain in one way or another to ways that choosing names badly can either cause your programs to break outright, or at the least make them fragile, ugly, and unpythonic.

3.1.1 Naming a File Identically to a Standard Library Module

The mechanism Python uses for determining where to import modules from is fairly convoluted. There are a lot of options, to provide a lot of flexibility. Setting the environment variable PYTHONPATH can affect this. Use of virtual environments can affect this. Runtime manipulation of sys.path—including within imported modules themselves—can affect this. Use of _pth files can affect this. The -E, -I, -s, and -S command-line options can affect this.

Unfortunately, it's *just complicated*. This is not the book to explore the details of Python's import system, but a good summary write-up is available at https://docs.python.org/3/library/sys_path_init.html.

The upshot of this complication is that developers are very well served by avoiding filenames that conflict with the names of standard library modules—or indeed with the names of any other third-party packages or modules they intend to use. Unfortunately, there are a lot of names in the latter category especially, and conflicts can arise innocently.

If you are uncertain about a conflict, or fear one may occur as you add later dependencies, use of *relative imports* can often avoid these mistakes.

Let's take a look at a short shell session:

```
[BetterPython]$ python code/hello.py
Hello World!
[BetterPython]$ cd code
[code]$ python hello.py
Program goes BOOM!
```

There are many "magical" ways I could obtain this odd behavior, but the one I used is really not *all that* magical.

Source code of code/hello.py

```
# The special path manipulation
import sys, os
if 'code' not in os.path.abspath('.'):
    sys.path = [p for p in sys.path if "BetterPython" not in p]

# The "regular" program
import re
pat = re.compile("hello", re.I)
s = "Hello World!"
if re.match(pat, s):
    print(s)
```

Notice that the message "Program goes BOOM!" is completely absent from this script. That's because it lives in *re.py*; not the version of that file that comes with the Python standard library, but the version that happens to be at */home/dmertz/git/BetterPython/code/re.py* on my computer.

Source code of code/re.py

```
import sys
print("Program goes BOOM!")
sys.exit()
```

Of course, if you use NumPy or Pandas, the same kind of conflict might occur with naming a local module `numpy.py` or `pandas.py`. So simply looking at the standard library module list does not assure absence of conflict. But there *are* a lot of ways to come up with distinctive names for the files in your own project.

Let's suppose, however, that you really want to use a particular name. For example, `calendar` is a standard library module, but one that is very old and that you've probably never even thought about using. However, it's a pretty good, generic name, one that could very easily be a good choice for a submodule name within your own brand-new project.

Note   The oldest Python module(s)

When I mention that `calendar` is *old*, I really mean it. It was in Python 0.9 with largely the same capabilities, in 1991:

```
[BetterPython]$ grep '0\.9' \
    /home/dmertz/miniconda3/envs/py0.9/README
This is version 0.9 (the first beta release), patchlevel 1.
[BetterPython]$
/home/dmertz/miniconda3/envs/py0.9/bin/python
>>> import calendar
>>> calendar.prmonth(2023, 2)
Mon Tue Wed Thu Fri Sat Sun
              1   2   3   4   5
  6   7   8   9  10  11  12
 13  14  15  16  17  18  19
 20  21  22  23  24  25  26
 27  28
```

Python has a pretty strong commitment to backward compatibility.

Rather trivially, we might write our own `calendar.py` module as follows.

Source code of `code/calendar.py`

```
from datetime import datetime
this_year = datetime.now().year
this_month = datetime.now().month
```

We can utilize this code within a script.

Source code of `code/thismonth.py`

```
from .calendar import this_year, this_month          # ❶
from calendar import TextCalendar
TextCalendar().prmonth(this_year, this_month)         # ❷
```

❶ One or more dots before a module name indicate a *relative import* (see https://docs.python.org/3/reference/import.html).

❷ Yes! The API changed modestly in the 32 years between Python 0.9 and Python 3.12.

This script uses both the global and the local `calendar.py` module (the standard library provides `TextCalendar`; the local module provides `this_year` and `this_month`). Let's run it:

```
[BetterPython]$ python -m code.thismonth
    February 2023
Mo Tu We Th Fr Sa Su
       1  2  3  4  5
 6  7  8  9 10 11 12
13 14 15 16 17 18 19
20 21 22 23 24 25 26
27 28
```

You can, of course, use relative imports for less trivial modules and subpackages, including across multiple levels of a directory hierarchy. See https://docs.python.org/3/reference/import.html#package-relative-imports for details.

Avoid using the same names as other libraries, including the standard library, wherever it feels reasonable to do so. As a fallback, relative imports are a reasonable solution to the problem.

3.1.2 Avoid Using `import *`

It is *usually* a bad idea to use `from modname import *` in your Python modules and scripts. This pattern is dangerous even when purely restricted to the standard library, but becomes worse when used with the dizzying array of third-party modules that define their own names. This bad idea is one you will encounter in a lot of existing code, and in thousands of answers on Stack Overflow.

The reason why the pattern is dangerous is quite plainly because many modules use the same names for objects, especially for functions (but sometimes for classes, constants, or other things). The number of different meanings given to `encode()`, `open()`, `connect()`, or `add()` are numerous. If you use the `import *` pattern, the behavior of your program can change dramatically based only on the order of your import statements. This is made much worse when many imports may be indirect or dynamic.

Let's take a look at three Python programs.

Source code of `math1.py`

```
from math import *
from cmath import *
from numpy import *
```

```
inf = float('inf')
for fn, num in zip([sqrt, ceil, isfinite], [-1, 4.5, inf*1j]):
    try:
        print(f"{fn.__name__}({num}) -> {fn(num)}")
    except Exception as err:
        print(err)
```

These three only vary in the order of their import lines.

Source code of math2.py

```
from cmath import *
from numpy import *
from math import *

inf = float('inf')
for fn, num in zip([sqrt, ceil, isfinite], [-1, 4.5, inf*1j]):
    try:
        print(f"{fn.__name__}({num}) -> {fn(num)}")
    except Exception as err:
        print(err)
```

Finally, one more import order.

Source code of math3.py

```
from math import *
from numpy import *
from cmath import *

inf = float('inf')
for fn, num in zip([sqrt, ceil, isfinite], [-1, 4.5, inf*1j]):
    try:
        print(f"{fn.__name__}({num}) -> {fn(num)}")
    except Exception as err:
        print(err)
```

Is it apparent at a glance what each of these scripts will do?

Try to reason about the results before reading the outputs that follow. What makes this still more complicated is that some of the functions used are in all the modules they were imported from while, others are in only some of the modules. So the actual meanings of the names sqrt, ceil, and isfinite is only obvious if you know all three of these modules intimately (and know the specific versions of the modules you are working with).

Outputs from running the sample scripts

```
[BetterPython]$ python code/math1.py
RuntimeWarning: invalid value encountered in sqrt
  print(f"{fn.__name__}({num}) -> {fn(num)}")
sqrt(-1) -> nan
ceil(4.5) -> 5.0
isfinite((nan+infj)) -> False

[BetterPython]$ python code/math2.py
math domain error
ceil(4.5) -> 5
must be real number, not complex

[BetterPython]$ python code/math3.py
sqrt(-1) -> 1j
ceil(4.5) -> 5.0
isfinite((nan+infj)) -> False
```

Clearly, we have used three different versions of `sqrt()` since we arrived at three different answers. It is less clear what is occurring for `ceil()` and `isfinite()`.

`ceil()` has produced two different answers, varying in datatype. But that might be two implementations, and it might be three implementations. As it turns out, `cmath` lacks an implementation of `ceil()`, so one of the implementations in `math` and `numpy` is active for the differing scripts; those different implementations merely happen to produce the same result in this example.

`isfinite()` has also produced two different answers, although one answer isn't really a result but rather an exception. In any case, it turns out that there are three different implementations of `isfinite()` involved here, with the `numpy` version accepting a variety of optional arguments and being happy to operate elementwise on arrays, as well as on scalars.

It is, of course, *possible* to overwrite a name imported from one module with a later import from another module, even if the names are specified. But explicitly including the names makes reasoning about what is happening much more obvious.

Named imports of common names from multiple modules

```
from numpy import sqrt
from cmath import sqrt
from math import sqrt
# ...more code...
```

In the preceding example, it jumps out that we are repeatedly overwriting the name `sqrt`, and whatever definitions `cmath` or `numpy` might provide are inaccessible because only the definition in math will be used. If that name had not been present in one of the earlier modules, we would see an immediate ImportError. Of course, we could change our imports to use the namespaced cmath.sqrt instead; or we could use from cmath import sqrt as csqrt to provide an alternate name. Whatever choice we make becomes apparent from the code itself.

Note   Rules have exceptions

Many experienced Pythonistas will disagree with me about the following. However, I believe that there are a few standard library modules where the import * pattern remain OK to use.

The module itertools contains many useful functions for performing "lazy iterator algebra" that, by design, play nicely with one another and have distinctive names relatively unlikely to occur elsewhere. If you start a program using filterfalse() and takewhile(), you are likely to later discover a related need for repeat() and chain(). In a sense, I believe that all the names in itertools would be reasonable to have put into __builtins__. I have a similar attitude towards the third-party more_itertools (which has a lot more names, and is discussed elsewhere), which likewise "plays nice" with itself and with itertools.

On the other hand, it isn't all that difficult to explicitly begin your script with:

```
from itertools import (
    filterfalse, takewhile, repeat, chain, groupby, tee)
```

If you want to use a few others, just add them to the list. I would make the same comment about collections.abc, in which names like AsyncIterable and MutableMapping are extremely unlikely to be accidentally reused by some unrelated module (even a third-party module). There is nothing there where import * is likely to cause harm.

There are some other modules where I also do not worry about name conflicts very much, but the specific functionalities you want are very limited. If you want collections.namedtuple, there is little reason you will necessarily want the handful of other collections inside it. dataclasses.dataclass, fractions.Fraction, and decimal.Decimal are nearly the *only* names inside those modules. In the last case, however, decimal.getcontext, decimal.setcontext, and decimal.localcontext are actually likely to be useful; so probably decimal is another of the few modules where I personally would not object to import *.

3.1.3 **Bare or Overly Generic** except **Statements**

Mostly for legacy reasons, Python allows the except statement to occur in bare form, without naming specific exceptions to be caught. This is categorically a mistake to use. Catching a broad exception where a subclass is more appropriate is also often a mistake; however, there are gray areas about exactly how broad an exception it is best to catch, with judgment needed for each individual decision.

Broadly speaking, when you only identify that "something went wrong" in a block of code, the remediation you apply can easily fail to match the actual underlying problem that occurred. By narrowing exceptions caught to those you genuinely know how to correct, you express your intentions accurately. This is true even when the best action in some exception case is halt-and-catch-fire; at least you are doing it with deliberation.

Python has a rich exception hierarchy, and most third-party libraries extend it with additional exceptions specific to their purpose. As well, numerous modules in the standard library also extend the built-in exceptions, but do not expose them unless they are imported (since you'll only ever see them if you use that module).

It's easy to see this hierarchy generated by a brief Python program and shown in Figure 3.1.

Source code of code/exception-hierarchy.py

```
def asciiDocTree(cls, level=1):
    print (f"{'*' * level} {cls.__module__}.{cls.__name__}")
    for i in cls.__subclasses__():
        asciiDocTree(i, level+1)


asciiDocTree(BaseException)
```

I am writing this book in the AsciiDoc format (https://asciidoc.org/), so as a convenience for myself, I've used its style of nested bullets. You can easily modify this code to present a tree with cosmetic differences. You will notice that in a few cases, built-in exceptions themselves reference exceptions in other modules. In the listing, descendants of builtins.Exception are italicized, which includes most of the hierarchy.

Suppose that we want to write a program that reads numbers from two files, and creates a collection that represents the numerator from the first file divided by the denominator from the second file. There are a variety of ways that this program might go wrong. Many—indeed most—programs you will write have many potential failure modes.

A naive first attempt might use a *bare except* (which most linters or style checkers will already complain about).

```
builtins.BaseException
  builtins.BaseExceptionGroup
    builtins.ExceptionGroup
  builtins.Exception
    builtins.ArithmeticError              builtins.ReferemceError
      builtins.FloatingPointError         builtins.RuntimeError
      builtins.OverflowError                builtins.NotImplementedError
      builtins.ZeroDivisionError            builtins.RecursionError
    builtins.AssertopmError               _frozen_importlib._DeadlockError
    builtins.AttributerError             builtins.StopAsyncIteration
    builtins.BufferError                 builtins.StopIteration
    builtins.EOFError                    builtins.SyntaxError
    builtins.ImportError                   builtins.IndentationError
      builtins.ModuleNotFoundError            builtins.TabError
      zipimport.ZipImportError           builtins.SystemError
    builtins.LookupError                 encodings.CodeRegistryError
      builtins.IndexError                builtins.TypeError
      builtins.KeyError                  builtins.ValueError
      encodings.CodeRegistryError          builtins.UnicodeError
    builtins.MemoryError                     builtins.UnicodeDecodeError
    builtins.NameError                       builtins.UnicodeEncodeError
      builtins.UnboundLocalError             builtins.UnicodeTranslateError
    builtins.OSError                     io.Unsupportedoperation
      builtins.BlockingIOError           builtins.Warning
      builtins.ChildProcessError           builtins.BytesWarning
      builtins.ConnecationError            builtins.DeprecationWarning
        builtins.BrokenPipeError           builtins.EncodingWarning
        builtins.ConnectionAbortedError    builtins.FutureWarning
        builtins.ConnectionRefusedError    builtins.ImportWarning
        builtins.ConnectionResetError      builtins.PendingDeprecationWarning
      builtins.FileExistsError             builtins.ResourceWarning
      builtins.FileNotFoundError           builtins.RuntimeWarning
      builtins.InterruptedError            builtins.SyntaxWarning
      builtins.ISADirectoryError           builtins.UnicodeWarning
      builtins.NotADirectoryError          builtins.UserWarning
      builtins.PermissionError           builtins.ExceptionGroup
      builtins.ProcessLookupError        warnings._OptionError
      builtins.TimeoutError
      io.unsupportedoperation
      signal.itimer_error
  builtins.GeneratorExit
  builtins.KeyboardInterrupt
  builtins.SystemExit
```

Figure 3.1   Hierarchy of built-in exceptions.

Source code of code/divide1.py

```
#!/usr/bin/env python
import sys
numerators = sys.argv[1]
denominators = sys.argv[2]

try:
    ratios = []
    num_fh = open(numerators)                          # ❶
    den_fh = open(denominators)
    for string_a, string_b in zip(num_fh, den_fh, strict=True):
        a = float(string_a.strip())
        b = float(string_b.strip())
        ratios.append(a/b)
    print(ratios)
except:
    print("Unable to perform divisions")
finally:
    num_fh.close()
    den_fh.close()
```

❶ Another section discusses why a context manager around open() might be better. However, the finally will perform cleanup of the open files and illustrates this concern better.

Let's run the existing program:

```
[BetterPython]$ code/divide1.py numerators1.txt denominators1.txt
Unable to perform divisions
```

Something went wrong in the suite of the try block. We have little information about what kind of problem occurred, though. Let's try to get a bit better visibility by modifying the except on line 15-16 to use the following.

Source code of code/divide2.py (partial)

```
except Exception as err:
    print(f"Unable to perform divisions:\n    {err}")
    print(f"Partial results: {ratios}")
```

Floating point numbers displayed by this script are shown with no more than six digits following the decimal point to make the presentation cleaner. You will see longer representations if you run this code on your system. To duplicate the permission error listed, you will probably need to run `chmod -r denominators3.txt` or the equivalent for your operating system.

When we run this, we get better insight into what went wrong that is impossible with a bare `except`. Let's try running using several different sets of data files:

```
[BetterPython]$ code/divide2.py numerators1.txt denominators1.txt
Unable to perform divisions:
    float division by zero
Partial results: [0.737704, 1.15, 2.0]

[BetterPython]$ code/divide2.py numerators1.txt denominators2.txt
Unable to perform divisions:
    zip() argument 2 is shorter than argument 1
Partial results: [0.737704, 1.15, 2.0, 0.326086, 0.0]

[BetterPython]$ code/divide2.py numerators1.txt denominators3.txt
Unable to perform divisions:
    [Errno 13] Permission denied: 'denominators3.txt'
Partial results: []
Traceback (most recent call last):
[...]
NameError: name 'den_fh' is not defined

[BetterPython]$ code/divide2.py numerators1.txt denominators4.txt
Unable to perform divisions:
    [Errno 2] No such file or directory: 'denominators4.txt'
Partial results: []
Traceback (most recent call last):
[...]
NameError: name 'den_fh' is not defined

[BetterPython]$ code/divide2.py numerators1.txt denominators5.txt
[0.737704, 1.15, 2.0, 0.326086, 0.0, 0.962962]
```

Several different distinct errors occurred. The program can be made less fragile by treating each of these errant conditions more specifically. Here is an example.

Source code of code/divide3.py

```
#!/usr/bin/env python
import sys

numerators = sys.argv[1]
denominators = sys.argv[2]
```

```python
try:
    ratios = []
    num_fh = open(numerators)
    den_fh = open(denominators)
    line = 0
    for string_a, string_b in zip(num_fh, den_fh, strict=True):
        line += 1
        a = float(string_a.strip())
        b = float(string_b.strip())
        ratios.append(a / b)
    print([f"{r:.3f}" for r in ratios])
except ZeroDivisionError:
    print(f"Partial results: {[f'{r:.3f}' for r in ratios]}")
    print(f"Attempt to divide by zero at input line {line}")
except ValueError as err:
    print(f"Partial results: {[f'{r:.3f}' for r in ratios]}")
    desc = err.args[0]
    if "zip()" in desc:
        print(desc)
    elif "could not convert" in desc:
        print(f"String is not numeric at input line {line}")
except PermissionError:
    print(f"Partial results: {[f'{r:.3f}' for r in ratios]}")
    print("Insufficient permission to file(s). Run as sudo?")
except FileNotFoundError as err:
    print(f"Partial results: {[f'{r:.3f}' for r in ratios]}")
    print(f"File {err.filename} does not exist")
except OSError as err:
    # Superclass after PermissionError and FileNotFoundError
    print(f"Partial results: {[f'{r:.3f}' for r in ratios]}")
    print(err)
finally:
    try:
        num_fh.close()
        den_fh.close()
    except NameError:
        # Opened in same order as closed, if failure with open()
        # on second, the first file will still get closed here.
        pass
```

Clearly there is a lot more going on in this expanded version. In a non-demonstration program, you would probably perform some actual remediation in the various except suites rather than simply print some varying messages based on the type of error encountered.

One notable feature of the preceding code is that we catch `PermissionError` and `FileNotFoundError`, but then also catch their parent class `OSError` *later* in the sequence of `except` clauses. We have a specific behavior we want if those exact things went wrong, but still recognize that there are other ways that `open()` might fail that we haven't specifically thought about.

In some suites, there might be a final `except Exception` that does generic logging of "everything that we haven't thought of that could go wrong." Such a suite might either decide to continue the rest of the program, or use a bare `raise` to re-raise the same exception, depending on what served the program's purpose better.

Let's run the new version:

```
[BetterPython]$ code/divide3.py numerators1.txt denominators1.txt
Partial results: ['0.738', '1.150', '2.000']
Attempt to divide by zero at input line 4

[BetterPython]$ code/divide3.py numerators1.txt denominators2.txt
Partial results: ['0.738', '1.150', '2.000', '0.326', '0.000']
zip() argument 2 is shorter than argument 1

[BetterPython]$ code/divide3.py numerators1.txt denominators3.txt
Partial results: []
Insufficient permission to file(s). Run as sudo?

[BetterPython]$ code/divide3.py numerators1.txt denominators4.txt
Partial results: []
File denominators4.txt does not exist

[BetterPython]$ code/divide3.py numerators1.txt denominators5.txt
['0.738', '1.150', '2.000', '0.326', '0.000', '0.963']
```

I have not bothered to display the contents of the several data files because those don't really matter. They are all text files with one number listed per line. However, do notice that the code considers the case of a line containing a string that cannot be converted to a `float`.

Unfortunately, the `zip(strict=True)` and the `float("abc")` cases both raise `ValueError` rather than more specific subclasses. We have to tease them apart inside the `except` suite by looking at the actual messages contained inside the exception object. This remains slightly fragile because Python does not guarantee it will not change the wording of error messages between versions, and we are simply looking for substrings that currently occur inside those messages. Actually, even more than not guaranteeing, a conscious effort is being made to improve the quality of error messages since 3.10; but "improve" obviously means "change."

3.2 Quadratic Behavior of Naive String Concatenation

> **Note   Understanding runtime complexity**
>
> The title of this pitfall discussion includes a little bit of computer science jargon. The word *quadratic* in mathematics refers to a polynomial with degree two. It actually means exactly the same thing in computer science, but the connection is perhaps not obvious immediately.
>
> In computer science, we often talk about the "big-O" behavior of various algorithms (see https://en.wikipedia.org/wiki/Big_O_notation). This concern arises in a number of discussions in this book.
>
> In quick synopsis, big-O complexity expresses the relationship between the size of the data being operated on and the time a computer will take to perform the operation. The best we can hope for is O(1), which means that the code will take the same amount of time no matter what size the data is. More commonly, O(N) is achievable, which means that the compute time increases in lockstep with the data size. A bit worse, but frequently seen, is O(N×log N); this says that the compute time is the size of the data multiplied by the logarithm of that size.
>
> We start to become worried when we see quadratic, that is, $O(N^2)$, behavior. Worse behaviors are possible, though. Some computation might take time equal to the cube, or the 4th power, of the data size. The worst behavior we commonly encounter is called exponential, that is, $O(2^N)$. These algorithms become intractable very quickly as data size grows; some so-called "hard problems" cannot be improved over exponential complexity.

Python string concatenation uses an intuitive plus operator, although this same operator has a very different meaning for other types. For example, + (which under the hood calls the "dunder"[1] methods .__add__() or .__radd__() on the class of the objects involved) means addition of numbers and aggregation of lists as well.

Code such as this is intuitive, readable, and perfectly Pythonic:

```
firstname = "David"
lastname = "Mertz"
degree = "Ph.D."

fullname = firstname + " " + lastname            # ❶
```

---

1. The term *dunder* is commonly used by Python programmers to refer to names that have both two leading and two trailing underscores. These are discussed in a number of places throughout the book.

```
if degree:
    fullname += ", "  + degree
```

❶ This might be better as an f-string.

However, this good code can quickly go bad if we do too many concatenation operations:

```
>>> from pprint import pprint
>>> def lorem_ipsum(n=10):
...     phrase = ""
...     for _ in range(n):
...         phrase = phrase + get_word() + " "       # ❶
...     return phrase
...
>>> pprint(lorem_ipsum(), width=68)
('engobe rereads hussif bethwacks aubade followup rabic '
 'privateerings nonsegregation sniffed ')
```

❶ String concatenation

So far, this code remains reasonably Pythonic, and *as used* I have no complaint about it. As with other examples ancillary to the main point of a section, or requiring larger datasets, the source code and data file can be found at https://gnosis.cx/better. All that matters for the current discussion is that `get_word()` returns some string each time it is called.[2]

But what happens if we try to generate larger phrases with this code?

```
>>> %timeit lorem_ipsum(10)
5.85 µs ± 54 ns per loop (mean ± std. dev. of 7 runs, 100,000 loops
each)
>>> %timeit lorem_ipsum(1000)
957 µs ± 8.09 µs per loop (mean ± std. dev. of 7 runs, 1,000 loops
each)
>>> %timeit lorem_ipsum(100_000)
5.64 s ± 33.8 ms per loop (mean ± std. dev. of 7 runs, 1 loop each)
```

Going from 10 words to 1,000 words is still mostly dominated by the time it takes to randomly select from the 267,752 available words. So rather than taking 100 times as long, we increase to about 200 times as long. However, increasing the size of the concatenated

---

2. Picking random words from the SOWPODS English word list (https://en.wikipedia.org/wiki/Collins _Scrabble_Words) may not have the specific letter-spacing distributions that typesetters like for "Lorem ipsum" samples, but we don't really care for the purposes within this book.

string by another 100 times (approximately; words vary in length) takes about 5,500 times as long.

What is happening here is that immutable strings are being allocated and deallocated with many of the concatenations. It's not quite on every concatenation since CPython uses some overallocation internally, but it is common. This leads to approximately quadratic (i.e., $O(N^2)$ on number of words) growth in the complexity.

It happens that for the toy code I show, there is a solution that involves almost no change to the `lorem_ipsum()` function. However, this approach does not generalize if you are doing much more than building one single long string. Python is optimized to treat *in-place* string concatenation more like it does appending to a list, which has amortized $O(N)$ behavior (the section "Deleting or Adding Elements to the Middle of a List" in Chapter 7, *Misusing Data Structures*, discusses amortized cost further).

In-place string concatenation

```
>>> def lorem_ipsum(n=10):
...       phrase = ""
...       for _ in range(n):
...           phrase += get_word() + " "          # ❶
...       return phrase
...
>>> %timeit lorem_ipsum()
5.37 µs ± 194 ns per loop (mean ± std. dev. of 7 runs, 100,000 loops
each)
>>> %timeit lorem_ipsum(1000)
549 µs ± 6.04 µs per loop (mean ± std. dev. of 7 runs, 1,000 loops
each)
>>> %timeit lorem_ipsum(100_000)
53.1 ms ± 765 µs per loop (mean ± std. dev. of 7 runs, 10 loops
each)
```

❶ The += operator is called "in-place."

This is perfect scaling! However, for functions or loops that cannot be expressed quite as simply as this, it is worth keeping in mind two additional options. These will often be practical in situations where in-place concatenation does not allow straightforward expression of your requirement.

Concatenation of constructed list

```
>>> def lorem_ipsum(n=10):
...       words = []
...       for _ in range(n):
```

```
...            words.append(get_word())
...        return " ".join(words)
...
>>> %timeit lorem_ipsum()
4.55 µs ± 54.4 ns per loop (mean ± std. dev. of 7 runs, 100,000 loops
each)
>>> %timeit lorem_ipsum(1000)
426 µs ± 3.43 µs per loop (mean ± std. dev. of 7 runs, 1,000 loops
each)
>>> %timeit lorem_ipsum(100_000)
47.5 ms ± 917 µs per loop (mean ± std. dev. of 7 runs, 10 loops each)
```

Using a final `str.join()` is a few percent faster, which is not particularly important
(and doesn't necessarily generalize). But the important thing is that it maintains linear
scaling as the size of the list/string grows.

Another approach is to use an `io.StringIO` stream.

Streams for file-like appending of strings

```
>>> from io import StringIO
>>> def lorem_ipsum(n=10):
...        buff = StringIO()
...        for _ in range(n):
...            buff.write(get_word() + " ")
...        return buff.getvalue()
...
>>> %timeit lorem_ipsum()
5.69 µs ± 176 ns per loop (mean ± std. dev. of 7 runs, 100,000 loops
each)
>>> %timeit lorem_ipsum(1000)
548 µs ± 9.33 µs per loop (mean ± std. dev. of 7 runs, 1,000 loops
each)
>>> %timeit lorem_ipsum(100_000)
57.2 ms ± 430 µs per loop (mean ± std. dev. of 7 runs, 10 loops each)
```

Again, `io.StringIO` has the same linear scaling we are looking for, and is within a few
percent of the same speed as the other approaches. Using streams might be just slightly
slower in the simple case, but having a file-like object lets you do operations like `.seek()`,
`.tell()`, and `.readlines()` that are often independently useful. Moreover, if you need
to "scale up" to using an actual filesystem (for persistence, for example), many file-like
objects can be a drop-in replacement within the code.

I summarize the performance of several approaches to appending strings in Table 3.1.

Table 3.1 Approaches to appending strings, time in μs, per data size.

Approaches (μs)	10 strings	1,000 strings	100,000 strings
Appending strings	5.85	957	5,640,000
In-place concat	5.37	549	53,100
Final list.join()	4.55	426	47,500
StringIO writes	5.69	548	57,200

3.3 Use a Context Manager to Open a File

Context managers are an important mechanism for managing resources that require cleanup. The most common example of this is opening files.

In the very ancient days of Python, context managers did not exist, and it was the responsibility of programmers to explicitly close files when they were done working with them. Many developers—out of haste, because a script is a "one-off", or under the assumption it "won't matter"—still sometimes approach file handling this way. I am myself guilty of this bad habit, and have probably done it more recently than I would like to admit.

In such a quick-and-dirty approach, I have written many scripts similar to the following.

Source code of code/wordcount

```python
#!/usr/bin/env python
import os

n_words = 0
for root, dir_, files in os.walk("src"):
    for name in files:
        if name.endswith(".adoc"):
            filepath = os.path.join(root, name)
            fh = open(filepath)
            n_words += len(fh.read().split())

print(f"Total words in book draft: {n_words:,}")
```

With this script, which I wrote just a few minutes ago, I can check my progress in writing this book. The many smaller files in nested directories that make up the book are written in a textual format called AsciiDoc (which is similar to reStructuredText or Markdown; the only important focus here is that it's basically just text files):

```
[BetterPython]$ code/wordcount
Total words in book draft: 65,376
```

As a word-count algorithm it's fairly crude. More relevantly for this discussion, I have relied solely on implicit garbage collection by Python. This will *probably* work fine for this limited purpose. The reference count on the open file object will drop to zero when fh is repeatedly rebound, and the .__del__() method of the TextIOWrapper object (which fh is an instance of) will be called during this cleanup, closing the file.

This reasoning can quickly become less clear in more complex programs, however, especially ones that utilize concurrency. At least two dangers, explained in the following subsections, exist when files might not be closed because neither does flow control actually arrive at a call to fh.close() nor does scoping or program termination succeed in forcing garbage collection. Flow control can fail because if/elif/else branches are not fully analyzed, or similarly for match/case (in Python 3.10+), but most often because uncaught exceptions are raised that prevent a program reaching the explicit fh.close() and dangling file handles stay around.

3.3.1 First Danger

The first danger is encountering the file handle limit your operating system imposes.

Operating system file handle limit

```
>>> files = [open(f"tmp-{n:04d}.txt", mode="w") for n in range
(10_000)]
Traceback (most recent call last):
[...]
OSError: [Errno 24] Too many open files: 'tmp-1011.txt'

>>> from glob import glob
>>> sorted(glob("tmp-*.txt"))[-4:]
['tmp-1007.txt', 'tmp-1008.txt', 'tmp-1009.txt', 'tmp-1010.txt']
```

Considerably fewer than 10,000 files were created. We could, in concept, adjust the specific number using resource.setrlimit(), but at some point we will hit limits of the operating system itself; moreover, increasing it will cause lag in other operations the computer is performing. Trying to open 10,000 temporary files at once is simply not a good idea. Rather, we should take an approach that uses only a few files at a time, and reopens them when needed rather than in advance.

Safe use of many temporary files

```
# If filenames are completely reproducible from index, then
# pregenerating them in a list is not needed.  Suppose the names
# are created by a more complex procedure than simple numbering
filenames = [f"tmp-{n:04d}.txt" for n in range(10_000)]

while (index := more_work_needed()) is not None:
```

```
    if not 0 <= index <= 9999:
        raise IndexError(f"Cannot access temporary file {index}")
    with open(filenames[index], mode="a") as tmpfile:    # ❶
        data = get_information_to_store()                # ❷
        tmpfile.write(data)
```

❶ Under the presumption that the same index is repeated, append mode is likely better.

❷ As in other sections, a sample implementation of this function is at https://gnosis.cx /better; any function that returns varying strings is equally illustrative.

3.3.2   Second Danger

The second danger is that failure to close an open file may leave some queued changes unwritten to disk. In fact, even the permissions or existence of an unclosed file could be messed up. Again, using a context manager assures safety around this.

Unsafe open file in code/crash.py

```
import os
fh = open("crash.txt", mode="w")
fh.write("Hello, world!\n")
fh.flush()
fh.write("Goodbye!\n")
os._exit(1)
fh.close()
```

Obviously this program is a toy example. Notice, however, that it *has* a .close() method call included (which is not reached):

```
[PythonMistakes]$ python code/crash.py      # ❶
[BetterPython]$ cat crash.txt               # ❷
Hello, world!
```

❶ Run the program.

❷ Show the full output generated within *crash.txt*.

3.3.3   Correcting the Fragility

Simply by enclosing every open() within a context manager, the dangers are mitigated.

Safe open file in code/safe-crash.py

```
import os
with open("crash.txt", mode="w") as fh:
```

```
    fh.write("Hello, world!\n")
    fh.write("Goodbye!\n")
os._exit(1)
```

Admittedly, a genuine system-level crash such as simulated by os._exit() will interfere with flushing unclosed files. That is, if the crash occurred between the "Hello" and "Goodbye" writes, we still wouldn't get all the data to disk. But keeping writes inside the with block at least minimizes the exposure to that danger:

```
[PythonMistakes]$ python code/safe-crash.py
[BetterPython]$ cat crash.txt
Hello, world!
Goodbye!
```

Done correctly, all the fh.write() lines produce output to *crash.txt*. You can read more about writing your own context managers at https://docs.python.org/3/reference/datamodel.html#context-managers. The excellent description in the Python documentation describes the "guts" of how context managers work internally.

3.4 Optional Argument key to .sort() and sorted()

Using the optional key argument to sorted() and list.sort() can make your code cleaner, faster, and more robust. Failing to use a key function where relevant is a common mistake.

The requirements for sorting collections or iterables in Python are suprisingly minimal. Each object must be able to perform a *less than* comparison with the objects adjacent to it in a sequence.

Given that all we need is less-than inequality, providing sortability of custom objects is extremely easy to make available. Here is an example.

Creating custom objects that can be sorted

```
>>> class Thing:
...     def __init__(self, value):
...         self.value = value
...     def __lt__(self, other):
...         return self.value < other.value
...     def __repr__(self):
...         return f"Thing({self.value})"
...
>>> sorted([Thing(2), Thing(-17), Thing(55), Thing(7)])
```

```
[Thing(-17), Thing(2), Thing(7), Thing(55)]
>>> things = [Thing(2), Thing(-17), Thing(55), Thing(7)]
>>> things.sort()
>>> things
[Thing(-17), Thing(2), Thing(7), Thing(55)]
```

Note   The pointy edges of sorting

Not all objects can be compared for less-than inequality, which can occasionally have the surprising effect that the sortability of a sequence depends on the original order of elements.

   While this can possibly occur, far more often sorting heterogeneous iterables simply fails with some variety of TypeError. Still, we *can* see situations like this:

```
>>> sorted([5, Strange(), 1, Strange(), 2+3j])
[1, 5, StrangeObject, StrangeObject, (2+3j)]
>>> sorted([5, Strange(), 2+3j, Strange(), 1])
[1, 5, StrangeObject, StrangeObject, (2+3j)]
>>> sorted([5, Strange(), 1, 2+3j, Strange()])
Traceback (most recent call last):
[...]
TypeError: '<' not supported between instances of
'complex' and 'int'
```

   To really understand when this will succeed and when it will fail, for a given sequence of objects that are partially incompatible, you need to understand the details of the Timsort algorithm (https://en.wikipedia.org/wiki/Timsort). Doing so is a worthwhile goal, but is not required to understand anything in this book.

A more useful "thing" would presumably have additional attributes and methods, but this suffices to show the scaffolding needed (the .__repr__() is optional, but it makes for a more attractive display).

If a developer is not aware of the optional keyword argument key, which can be passed to sorted() or to list.sort(), the code they write is likely to perform inefficiently or just plain wrongly. In particular, such flawed code can sometimes wind up sorting on a basis other than the sort order that is useful for the objects involved.

For example, suppose we wanted to sort "Things" not based on their numeric order, but rather based on their numeric order within a ring of a given modulus (called $\mathbb{Z}_n$). A first inclination might be to subclass Thing to have this behavior.

> **Note Iterables are sortable (if the corresponding concrete collection is)**
>
> Python really does emphasize iterables over concrete collections wherever they are feasible to use. The result of sorting is still a concrete collection, but the iterable need not have started out as such. For example:
>
> ```
> >>> from random import randint
> >>> def make_things():
> ...         for _ in range(5):
> ...             yield Thing(randint(1, 1000))        # ❶
> ...
> >>> sorted(make_things())
> [Thing(544), Thing(651), Thing(666), Thing(799),
> Thing(920)]
> ```
>
> ❶ The presence of yield makes this a *generator function*.

Unnecessary use of subclass merely for sort order

```
>>> class ModThing(Thing):
...         def __init__(self, value: int, mod: int=7):
...             self.value = value
...             self._mod = mod
...         def __lt__(self, other):
...             return self.value % self._mod < other.value % other._mod
...
...
>>> sorted([ModThing(2), ModThing(-17), ModThing(55), ModThing(7)])
[Thing(7), Thing(2), Thing(-17), Thing(55)]
```

There might well be additional reasons to attach the modulus to the class itself, but supposing we only cared about sorting, we could achieve the same effect more easily using the following.

Using the key function in decorate-sort-undecorate sorting

```
>>> sorted([Thing(2), Thing(-17), Thing(55), Thing(7)],
...         key=lambda thing: thing.value % 7)
[Thing(7), Thing(2), Thing(-17), Thing(55)]
```

Anything that can represent a consistent transformation of the underlying objects being sorted is suitable as a key function. The decorate-sort-undecorate pattern is vastly more efficient as a big-O complexity than using a comparison function between every pair of items. See a discussion at https://en.wikipedia.org/wiki/Schwartzian_transform. The less efficient comparison function idiom is still used in many other programming languages, and was long ago used in Python, prior to version 2.4.

Lambda functions are absolutely appropriate to use in this context, even if in most other places a named function would serve clarity better. But very often it is useful to use `operator.itemgetter` or `operator.attrgetter` as faster and more expressive functions than custom lambda functions. One place we see this need very commonly is in manipulating deserialized JSON data, which tends to be highly nested.

Using `operator.itemgetter` to sort based on a dict key

```
>>> from operator import itemgetter
>>> students = [
...     dict(name="Xian", grade="B", age=10),
...     dict(name="Jane", grade="B", age=12),
...     dict(name="John", grade="A", age=15)
... ]
>>> sorted(students, key=itemgetter('age'), reverse=True)
[{'name': 'John', 'grade': 'A', 'age': 15},
 {'name': 'Jane', 'grade': 'B', 'age': 12},
 {'name': 'Xian', 'grade': 'B', 'age': 10}]
>>> sorted(students, key=itemgetter('name'))
[{'name': 'Jane', 'grade': 'B', 'age': 12},
 {'name': 'John', 'grade': 'A', 'age': 15},
 {'name': 'Xian', 'grade': 'B', 'age': 10}]
```

For data held in classes `operator.attrgetter` is very similar, but simply accesses the attribute that is passed as an argument for each instance being sorted.

3.5 Use `dict.get()` for Uncertain Keys

An occasionally forgotten convenience of the `dict` object is its `.get()` method. It's really handy, and code that takes other approaches is usually slightly cumbersome and less friendly.

Remember the students used in the prior section about sorting? Let's return to them. But let's add a few more of them:

```
students = [
    dict(name="Xian", grade="A-", age=10),
    dict(name="Jane", grade="B", age=12),
    dict(name="John", grade="C", age=15),
    dict(name="Pema", age=14),
    dict(name="Thandiwe", grade="B+")
```

We'd like to create a little report from our student list. A somewhat awkward approach to the missing data might be the following.

Look-before-you-leap approach (LBYL)

```
>>> print("| Name      | Grade | Age")
... print("+----------+-------+-----")
... for student in students:
...     name = student['name'] if 'name' in student else "MISSING"
...     grade = student['grade'] if 'grade' in student else "PASS"
...     age = student['age'] if 'age' in student else "?"
...     print(f"| {name:9s} | {grade:<4s}  | {age}")
...
| Name      | Grade | Age
+----------+-------+-----
| Xian      | A-    | 10
| Jane      | B     | 12
| John      | C     | 15
| Pema      | PASS  | 14
| Thandiwe  | B+    | ?
```

Despite what I warn in Chapter 4, *Advanced Python Usage*, there are times when forgiveness–not–permission makes code worse.

Easier-to-ask-forgiveness-than-permission approach (EAFP)

```
>>> print("| Name      | Grade | Age")
... print("+----------+-------+-----")
... for student in students:
...     try:
...         name = student['name']
...     except KeyError:
...         name = "MISSING"
...     try:
...         grade = student['grade']
...     except KeyError:
...         grade = "PASS"
...     try:
...         age = student['age']
...     except KeyError:
...         age = "?"
...     print(f"| {name:9s} | {grade:<4s}  | {age}")
...
```

```
| Name       | Grade | Age
+-----------+-------+-----
| Xian       | A-    | 10
| Jane       | B     | 12
| John       | C     | 15
| Pema       | PASS  | 14
| Thandiwe   | B+    | ?
```

In this example, and in many where we work with dictionaries, neither of these approaches is ideal. Both LBYL and EAFP require too much code and impede readability for this task. The cleanest solution is simply "pick a default."

Just-use-default approach

```
>>> print("| Name       | Grade | Age")
... print("+-----------+-------+-----")
... for student in students:
...     print(f"| {student.get('name', 'MISSING'):9s} "
...           f"| {student.get('grade', 'PASS'):<4s}   "
...           f"| {student.get('age', '?')}")
...
| Name       | Grade | Age
+-----------+-------+-----
| Xian       | A-    | 10
| Jane       | B     | 12
| John       | C     | 15
| Pema       | PASS  | 14
| Thandiwe   | B+    | ?
```

Breaking the `print()` argument across lines means we only save one line (although a few more characters are saved). More importantly, we simply express the intention to default to certain values and avoid introducing extra variables within the loop.

3.6 Wrapping Up

In this chapter, we examined some very everyday features that can easily be used in ways causing problems. These ordinary pitfalls range from code that gets the right results but does so with far worse runtime expense than is needed, to ways that poor choices of names can create ambiguities or conflicts, to failing to recognize the need for familiar and idiomatic Pythonic approaches (which incidentally save you from problems in edge cases).

In this book we learn that many things are possible, and that many of them are nonetheless best avoided. Chapter 5, *Just Because You Can, It Doesn't Mean You Should...*, looks at what we might call "impulsive" uses of rather advanced features. The pitfalls in this chapter, however, express tasks you perform almost every time you sit down to write a Python program, or modify or expand an existing one. Even these simple things can be done wrongly.

While such is not the only source of mistakes, often those in this chapter reflect habits brought by developers from other programming languages they may have used earlier. Adapting your Python habits to utilize Pythonic code shows kindness to yourself and to your colleagues.

4

Advanced Python Usage

This chapter continues to focus on features of pure Python—that is to say, primarily on built-in functions and a few standard library functions within the "almost built-in" subset. However, as the title suggests, the mistakes herein concern features that new or occasional Python programmers do not (yet) use every day.

In Chapter 3, *A Grab Bag of Python Gotchas*, we addressed the importance of good naming in regard to several patterns, antipatterns, and some outright broken code. Some of the mistakes we look at in this chapter very much reiterate that same theme, but present mistakes advanced developers—arguably *too* advanced for their own good—are likely to make.

Other features that are often misused—and sometimes simply unused when they should be—include checking the types of objects, using *iterator algebra*, decorators, and a small bit of magic with f-strings. Some of the topics in this chapter might not yet be familiar to you, but reading about them will help you become aware of new possibilities.

4.1 Comparing `type(x) == type(y)`

It is common to wish for Python functions to be polymorphic. A great many of the built-in functions operate on numerous kinds of objects. For example, `len()`, `repr()`, `float()`, and `sum()` can each accept a variety of objects (not the same variety for each, though).

When you wish to write your own functions, very often you can do so by *duck typing*. In such instances, any kind of typing is bypassed. Often a `try/except` block, under the EAFP approach, is used ("easier to ask forgiveness than seek permission"). Nonetheless, there are definitely times when you specifically want to do something different depending on the type of values passed to a function (or to local variables created in its body).

Let's create a function that performs a binary operation in a vectorized manner across a concrete sequence. Later chapters deal with inherently vectorized libraries like NumPy and Pandas. For this example, in which we are directly comparing types, we only pay attention to pure Python.

> **Note   Quacking like a duck**
>
> Wikipedia provides a good definition of "duck typing"
> (https://en.wikipedia.org/wiki/Duck_typing):
>
> > Duck typing in computer programming is an application of the duck
> > test—"If it walks like a duck and it quacks like a duck, then it must
> > be a duck"—to determine whether an object can be used for a
> > particular purpose. With nominative typing, an object is of a given
> > type if it is declared to be. [...] In duck typing, an object is of a given
> > type if it has all methods and properties required by that type. Duck
> > typing can be viewed as a usage-based structural equivalence
> > between a given object and the requirements of a type.
>
> Pythonic programming very often utilizes the idea of duck typing.

Function `vector_op()` (flawed implementation)

```python
from operator import add                         # ❶

def vector_op(seq1, seq2, op=add):
    if type(seq1) != type(seq2):
        raise ValueError(
            "Both sequences must have same collection type")

    if type(seq1) == list:                        # ❷
        return [op(x, y) for x, y in zip(seq1, seq2, strict=True)]

    if type(seq1) == tuple:                       # ❸
        return tuple(op(x, y)
                for x, y in zip(seq1, seq2, strict=True))

    if type(seq1) == str:                         # ❹
        nums1 = seq1.split()
        nums2 = seq2.split()
        new = (op(float(x), float(y))
                for x, y in zip(nums1, nums2, strict=True))
        return " ".join(str(n) for n in new)

    raise ValueError("Unsupported type for collections")
```

❶ Addition as a named function

❷ Comparing type to only list, and not to any subclass

❸ Comparing type to only `tuple`, and not to any subclass

❹ Comparing type to only `str`, and not to any subclass

We can use this function with various arguments:

```
>>> from operator import mul
>>> vector_op("3 4 7", "2 -1 3", mul)
'6.0 -4.0 21.0'
>>> vector_op((3, 4, 7), (2, -1, 3), mul)
(6, -4, 21)
>>> vector_op([3, 4, 7], [2, -1, 3], mul)
[6, -4, 21]
>>> vector_op((3, 4, 7), (2, -1, 3), lambda x, y: (2*x) ** y)
(36, 0.125, 2744)
>>> vector_op([3, 4, 7], (2, -1, 3), mul)
Traceback (most recent call last):
[...]
ValueError: Both sequences must have same collection type
>>> vector_op([3, 4, 7], [2, -1], mul)
Traceback (most recent call last):
[...]
ValueError: zip() argument 2 is shorter than argument 1
```

This function is plausibly useful. It also will fail to work on many arguments that are useful in an obvious way. Unless we genuinely need to avoid supporting subclasses (which is unusual, but not *inconceivable*), a more general implementation based around `isinstance()` is much more sensible. For example:

```
>>> from collections import namedtuple
>>> Vector3D = namedtuple("Vector3D", "x y z")
>>> vec1 = Vector3D(3, 4, 4)
>>> vector_op(vec1, (2, -1, 3))
Traceback (most recent call last):
[...]
ValueError: Both sequences must have same collection type

>>> vec2 = Vector3D(x=2, y=-1, z=3)
>>> vector_op(vec1, vec2)
Traceback (most recent call last):
[...]
ValueError: Unsupported type for collections

>>> isinstance(vec1, tuple)
True
```

We can easily support specializations of the types supported by the `vector_op()` function. It would feel much more useful if the failing calls in the preceding code simply worked; similarly, why not allow any subtypes of `list` or `str` to work seamlessly when doing so is no extra work?

While we are at it, why not simply support the abstract protocols to which `list`, `tuple`, and `str` belong? If some object is simply structurally typed in a manner "close enough" to what we need for the work of each branch, we can use capabilities rather than precise type.

Function `vector_op()` (good and generic implementation)

```python
from collections.abc import MutableSequence, Sequence, ByteString
from operator import add

def vector_op(seq1, seq2, op=add):
    if isinstance(seq1, (ByteString, str)) \         # ❶
            and isinstance(seq2, (ByteString, str)):
        nums1 = seq1.split()
        nums2 = seq2.split()
        new = (op(float(x), float(y))
                for x, y in zip(nums1, nums2, strict=True))

        if isinstance(seq1, ByteString):
            as_str = " ".join(str(n) for n in new)
            return type(seq1)(as_str.encode("ascii"))    # ❷
        else:
            sep = type(seq1)(" ")                         # ❷
            return sep.join(type(seq1)(n) for n in new)

    # Since issubclass(MutableSequence, Sequence), we could
    # specialize implementation of mutable versus immutable.
    # However, since we construct the concrete collection from a
    # generator comprehension, this is handled for us here.
    if isinstance(seq1, Sequence) and isinstance(seq2, Sequence):
        new = (op(x, y) for x, y in zip(seq1, seq2, strict=True))
        try:
            return type(seq1)(new)                        # ❷
        except TypeError:
            # Unfortunately, namedtuple must be instantiated
            # with separate arguments, not one generator
            return type(seq1)(*new)

    raise ValueError("Unsupported type for collections")
```

❶ Since `issubclass(str, Sequence)`, we need to check for string-like objects first.

❷ We defer to the type of the first sequence, where the two sequences are "compatible" but distinct.

The new implementation is much more flexible while also being slightly shorter (if you remove the extra comments). We can try it out:

```
>>> vector_op(vec1, vec2)
Vector(x=5, y=3, z=7)
>>> vector_op(vec1, (2, -1, 3))
Vector(x=5, y=3, z=7)
>>> vector_op(vec1, [2, -1, 3])              # ❶
Vector(x=5, y=3, z=7)
>>> vector_op("3 4 7", "2 -1 3", mul)
'6.0 -4.0 21.0'
>>> vector_op(b"3 4 7", b"2 -1 3", mul)
b'6.0 -4.0 21.0'
>>> vector_op(b"3 4 7", "2 -1 3")            # ❶
b'5.0 3.0 10.0'

>>> vector_op([3, 4, 4], (2, -1, 3))         # ❶
[5, 3, 7]
>>> vector_op((3, 4, 4), [2, -1, 3])         # ❶
(5, 3, 7)
```

❶ If you wish for less flexibility in mixing non-subtypes, the code could be tweaked easily enough.

There remains a little bit of magic in the second implementation in that we inspect `type(seq1)` to decide on a precise class to use when constructing the result. A somewhat less magical version might simply return a list whenever a mixture of `Sequence` types are passed as arguments. However, a little bit of magic is not always unpythonic; at times this power can be used wisely and powerfully.

4.2 Naming Things (Revisited)

Good use of names is a basic feature of Pythonic programming. Chapter 3, *A Grab Bag of Python Gotchas*, discussed some concerns with good names. Here we expand upon them. These more advanced cases should equally be attended to.

4.2.1 Overriding Names in Built-ins

Python has a quite large standard library module called __builtins__, and a relatively small collection of actual keywords. Between Python versions, just a few things have slowly migrated from the former to the latter, but for the most part Python programmers do not regularly think about the distinction that much.

Whenever the Python interpreter starts (at least CPython, the reference and by far most common implementation), everything in __builtins__ is loaded automatically. So on the surface, it's all just "a bunch of names."

Let's take a look at what the actual keywords in Python 3.12 are.

Python 3.12 keywords

```
>>> import keyword
>>> keyword.kwlist
['False', 'None', 'True', 'and', 'as', 'assert', 'async', 'await',
 'break', 'class', 'continue', 'def', 'del', 'elif', 'else', 'except',
 'finally', 'for', 'from', 'global', 'if', 'import', 'in', 'is',
 'lambda', 'nonlocal', 'not', 'or', 'pass', 'raise', 'return', 'try',
 'while', 'with', 'yield']
>>> len(keyword.kwlist)
35
```

In contrast, the built-in, but not technically reserved, names are a fair bit larger. The dunders like __name__ and __package__ are a bit special in being set differently depending on what code is being run. But the regular names are simply functionality you will always have available by default. It's a long list, but useful to skim over (you might learn names you were not familar with, or be reminded of ones you have partially forgotten).

Python 3.12 built-ins, excluding dunders

```
>>> [b for b in dir(__builtins__)
...     if not b.startswith("_") and b not in keyword.kwlist]
['ArithmeticError', 'AssertionError', 'AttributeError',
 'BaseException', 'BaseExceptionGroup', 'BlockingIOError',
 'BrokenPipeError', 'BufferError', 'BytesWarning', 'ChildProcessError',
 'ConnectionAbortedError', 'ConnectionError', 'ConnectionRefusedError',
 'ConnectionResetError', 'DeprecationWarning', 'EOFError', 'Ellipsis',
 'EncodingWarning', 'EnvironmentError', 'Exception', 'ExceptionGroup',
 'FileExistsError', 'FileNotFoundError', 'FloatingPointError',
 'FutureWarning', 'GeneratorExit', 'IOError', 'ImportError',
 'ImportWarning', 'IndentationError', 'IndexError', 'InterruptedError',
 'IsADirectoryError', 'KeyError', 'KeyboardInterrupt', 'LookupError',
 'MemoryError', 'ModuleNotFoundError', 'NameError',
 'NotADirectoryError', 'NotImplemented', 'NotImplementedError',
 'OSError', 'OverflowError', 'PendingDeprecationWarning',
 'PermissionError', 'ProcessLookupError', 'RecursionError',
 'ReferenceError', 'ResourceWarning', 'RuntimeError', 'RuntimeWarning',
 'StopAsyncIteration', 'StopIteration', 'SyntaxError', 'SyntaxWarning',
 'SystemError', 'SystemExit', 'TabError', 'TimeoutError', 'TypeError',
 'UnboundLocalError', 'UnicodeDecodeError', 'UnicodeEncodeError',
```

```
'UnicodeError', 'UnicodeTranslateError', 'UnicodeWarning',
'UserWarning', 'ValueError', 'Warning', 'ZeroDivisionError', 'abs',
'aiter', 'all', 'anext', 'any', 'ascii', 'bin', 'bool', 'breakpoint',
'bytearray', 'bytes', 'callable', 'chr', 'classmethod', 'compile',
'complex', 'copyright', 'credits', 'delattr', 'dict', 'dir', 'divmod',
'enumerate', 'eval', 'exec', 'exit', 'filter', 'float', 'format',
'frozenset', 'getattr', 'globals', 'hasattr', 'hash', 'help', 'hex',
'id', 'input', 'int', 'isinstance', 'issubclass', 'iter', 'len',
'license', 'list', 'locals', 'map', 'max', 'memoryview', 'min',
'next', 'object', 'oct', 'open', 'ord', 'pow', 'print', 'property',
'quit', 'range', 'repr', 'reversed', 'round', 'set', 'setattr',
'slice', 'sorted', 'staticmethod', 'str', 'sum', 'super', 'tuple',
'type', 'vars', 'zip']
>>> len([b for b in dir(__builtins__)
...          if not b.startswith("_") and b not in keyword.kwlist])
146
```

There are a few oddballs like `True` and `None` that are both keywords and also in `__builtins__`. The difference between these different "always available" names is simply in whether they are assignable.

Assigning to keywords versus built-ins

```
>>> FutureWarning = "FutureWarning"
>>> lambda = "λ"
  File "<stdin>", line 1
    lambda = "λ"
           ^
SyntaxError: invalid syntax
```

Few Python developers can necessarily rattle off a complete list of either keywords or built-ins, but most of us have used almost all of these names from time to time.

The override in the preceding example is unlikely to be something you would do inadvertently, and it will only cause problems relatively uncommonly. A `FutureWarning` is used by a library that intends to deprecate some API "in the future." However, unless you put that override inside the library itself (either as author, or by monkey patching), the library itself will retain the genuine version.

However, there are a handful of names in `__builtins__` that are relatively easy to overwrite simply by not giving the question a lot of thought. For many of these, I have committed this "mistake" myself, sometimes in code that predated the addition to the `__builtins__` module that later added the name.

Inadvertently overwriting built-in names

```
# Using a natural-seeming name within a function
def total_receipts(receipts):
```

```
    sum = 0
    for receipt in receipts:
        sum += receipt.amount
    return sum

# A database index column:
sql = "SELECT id, firstname, lastname, age FROM persons"
for row in cur.execute(sql):
    id, first, last, age = row
    if id = prior_person_id:
        raise ValueError("Cannot re-process this record")
    # ... other code
```

For uses like this, the "mistake" is probably not that important. If the built-in function sum() is not used later on in the total_receipts() user function, the fact that we have (locally) overwritten a standard name stops mattering once we leave the function scope.

> **Note   Python scoping rules**
>
> Python uses a rule called LEGB (Local, Enclosing, Global, and Built-in) for scoping variables. That is, when the runtime sees a name, it looks in each of those scopes, in the order listed. Enclosing means an outer function or a class in which a method is defined. Local means within the body of the function or method where the code lives.
>
> The important thing about scopes is that when you leave them, the names they define are released, and do not affect the use of the same names in the enclosing scope (nor in some other local scope you enter later).

In the case of overwriting id, the use feels natural, but is *slightly* more error-prone. A loop like the one I constructed *might* occur within the body of a larger function or method, and that same function *might* want to use the actual __builtins__.id() function. That said, the function *does* remain available in the __builtins__ namespace (which could, in principle, itself be overwritten, which is *definitely* a bad idea to do).

There are only a handful of names where a developer might naturally want to use that name as a custom variable. However, a few of these *do* genuinely feel natural to use. Here is an example.

Harmful overwriting of built-in name

```
>>> input = input("Your name? ")                            # ❶
Your name? David Mertz
>>> input
'David Mertz'
```

```
>>> input = input("Your name? ")              # ❷
Traceback (most recent call last):
  File "<stdin>", line 1, in <module>
TypeError: 'str' object is not callable
```

❶ Built-in function input() at this point

❷ Now the name input has been bound to a string.

I wish I could write honestly that this example is a purely hypothetical mistake which I have never myself committed in real code. I *can* state honestly that I have never had the unreflective inclination to call a local variable StopAsyncIteration because that just seemed like an intuitive name for a custom value within my program. There are fewer than 20 names for which the inclination to make this mistake arises naturally.

In general, the standard solution to this concern is to append a trailing underscore to a custom name in a program. For example:

```
>>> input_ = input("Your name? ")
Your name? Bob Loblaw
>>> input_
'Bob Loblaw'
>>> input_ = input("Your name? ")
Your name? Kitty Sanchez
>>> input_
'Kitty Sanchez'
```

4.2.2 Directly Accessing a Protected Attribute

It is (usually) a mistake to access "protected" names outside the class or module that defines them for its own use. Python itself provides no programmatic limitation about this, and it can be very tempting to utilize these members directly simply because it is so easy. You should avoid doing this. A great deal of Python code, however, fails to utilize this advice, and often later breaks as a result.

Python has a convention that names that live inside namespaces—whether inside modules, classes, or other objects that define namespaces—can use one or two leading underscores to declare those names "protected" or "private" (in analogy with languages like C++ and Java). In a very approximate way, one leading underscore is more like *protected* and two leading underscores is more like *private*; but this is a weak analogy at best.

Python also has a convention of using "dunder" names, which have both leading and trailing double underscores. You should *never* use those names other than for their documented purpose of overriding some operator or supporting some built-in and standard library function.

It's just barely permissible for genuine *frameworks* to invent their own dunders for private use; but even there, I'd advise framework creators to avoid that pattern. For example, you should absolutely override .__lshift__() or .__call__() if that is relevant for your class, but try to avoid inventing .__modify__() in your own code, if for no other reason than some future version of Python might discover a need for that name.

Creators of modules and classes commonly follow a convention of using attribute names that begin with underscores as a way of telling users "don't use this attribute directly." Those developers cannot *enforce* that request upon users downstream, but the intention is made clear.

As an example, let's write a `LinearCongruentialGenerator` (LCG) class (see https://en.wikipedia.org/wiki/Linear_congruential_generator) with reasonable behavior and code. In Chapter 8, *Security*, in the section *Kinds of Randomness*, I discuss in much more detail Python's actual pseudo-random number generator (PRNG), the Mersenne Twister. Suffice it to say that LCGs are less good PRNGs than what Python provides you; but LCGs were and are used in actual production software PRNGs, so they aren't absurdly bad (depending on configuration of parameters).

Class implementation of a linear congruential generator

```python
class LinearCongruentialGenerator:
    def __init__(self, seed: int = 123):            # ❸
        self.__seed: int = seed                      # ❶
        self._multiplier: int = 1_103_515_245       # ❷
        self._modulus: int = 2**32                   # ❷
        self._increment: int = 1                     # ❷

        # Simple constraints we should follow
        assert 0 < self._modulus
        assert 0 < self._multiplier < self._modulus
        assert 0 <= self._increment < self._modulus
        assert 0 <= seed < self._modulus

        # One initial application of recurrence relation
        self._state = (
            (self._multiplier * self.__seed + self._increment)
            % self._modulus)

    @property
    def seed(self):
        return self.__seed

    def next(self):
        # Increment the state
        self._state = (
            (self._multiplier * self._state + self._increment)
            % self._modulus)
        return self._state / self._modulus
```

❶ "Private" attribute

❷ "Protected" attribute

❸ Type annotations are not runtime enforced but document intention.

This class will produce a pretty good sequence of pseudo-random numbers, each between 0 (closed) and 1 (open), and a different such sequence for nearly every different integer seed below 2**32. Let's take a quick look at using this class:

```
>>> lcg = LinearCongruentialGenerator(456)
>>> [lcg.next() for _ in range(8)]
[0.9508262551389635, 0.8921057728584856, 0.5018460648134351,
0.16488368925638497, 0.7462635268457234, 0.6617225247900933,
0.06575838476419449, 0.07386434846557677]
>>> lcg2 = LinearCongruentialGenerator(9876)
>>> [lcg2.next() for _ in range(8)]
[0.9167962749488652, 0.9652843165677041, 0.09186752885580063,
0.6128534006420523, 0.5585974934510887, 0.8420640060212463,
0.9102171016857028, 0.9698882394004613]
```

For our purposes, we are happy for users to be able to examine the seed used by a given generator, but definitely do not want them to modify the (purported) seed:

```
>>> lcg.seed
456
>>> lcg.seed = 789
Traceback (most recent call last):
[...]
AttributeError: property 'seed' of 'LinearCongruentialGenerator'
  object has no setter
```

This pattern of using a read-only property to access a "private" attribute is a good one to follow. As creator, I want instances of my class always to honestly report the seed that was used to initialize them.

Those attributes that only begin with a single underscore ("protected") are not quite as sensitive. You *might* be able to change them and allow the functionality to remain "reasonable" (but you might not be so able):

```
>>> lcg3 = LinearCongruentialGenerator(456)
>>> [lcg3.next() for _ in range(3)]                # ❶
[0.9508262551389635, 0.8921057728584856, 0.5018460648134351]

>>> lcg3._multiplier = 22695477                    # ❷
```

```
>>> [lcg3.next() for _ in range(3)]
[0.8215138253290206, 0.1279368051327765, 0.818344411207363]

>>> lcg3._multiplier = 0                              # ❸
>>> [lcg3.next() for _ in range(2)]
[2.3283064365386963e-10, 2.3283064365386963e-10]
```

❶ Initial numbers based on seed are reproducible

❷ Reasonable multiplier, but breaks reproducibility from seed

❸ Bad choice of multiplier badly breaks the generator

In the example, the *very bad* multiplier of zero causes the generator to produce the same fixed number forever. However, other bad choices can merely weaken the distribution. The specific details of good multiplier, modulus, and increment get into relatively heavy number theory, with primality, relative primality, the divisibility of the multiplier by 4 specifically, and other factors coming into play. In other words, the ordinary users of the class probably do not know the relevant considerations and should not touch these attributes.

Note   The first rule of underscores is "don't talk about name mangling"

Python initial double underscores have a dirty little secret. They are *not* truly private and users can get at them if they know about name mangling. Let's take a look:

```
>>> lcg.__seed
Traceback (most recent call last):
[...]
AttributeError: 'LinearCongruentialGenerator' object has no
  attribute '__seed'

>>> lcg._LinearCongruentialGenerator__seed
456
>>> lcg._LinearCongruentialGenerator__seed = 123
>>> lcg.seed
123
```

If you ever find yourself breaking through the privacy of names this way, you are making a mistake or are an actual core developer of a Python framework. However, it can certainly be both things.

The other danger with using private or protected attributes is that the author of a module or library is explicitly *not* promising they will continue to exist in the next version of that software. They may very reasonably decide to redesign or refactor their code, and only maintain backward compatibility with documented interfaces, such as `lcg.seed` and `lcg.next()` in the example class.

Perhaps as author of my LCG, I decide that I definitely want to use a power-of-two modulus. This is hard-coded into the implementation shown, but a subclass, for example, might change that but preserve the official APIs. Given this decision, I might change my implementation to:

```python
class LinearCongruentialGenerator:
    def __init__(self, seed: int=123):
        self.__seed: int = seed
        self._multiplier: int = 1_103_515_245
        self._modpow: int = 32
        self._increment: int = 1

    # ...other code...

    def next(self):
        # Increment the state
        self._state = (
            (self._multiplier * self._state + self._increment)
            % 2**self._modpow)
        return self._state / self._modulus
```

This new implementation has *all* the same documented behaviors. Given the same seed, the new implementation will produce exactly the same sequence of numbers from the PRNG. However, the protected attribute `._modulus` has simply stopped existing in this version. A downstream user who improperly relied on that attribute, even simply to check its value, would find their code broken by the change. If their code actually modified the protected attribute, the failure could be less obvious since Python instances can attach attributes that are unused for any purpose; changing `._modulus` would now have no effect on the sequence produced, again probably surprising the misbehaving downstream user.

As a final thought, I will mention that modules are much like classes in regard to leading underscores. Often modules will have such private or protected names inside them. The mechanism of `import` makes these slightly less accessible, but not completely invisible. Nonetheless, if a module author has requested that you not use certain names, you should believe them, and only use the documented and exported names.

4.3 Keep Less-Used Features in Mind

There are a number of brilliant features in Python that you very often do not need to think about. However, when the need does arise, it is a mistake not to be aware of and utilize these capabilities.

> **Note   Rules have occasional exceptions**
>
> There are a few odd corners where the advice in this section is properly violated, even within the Python standard library. The most notable of these is:
>
> ```
> >>> from collections import namedtuple
> >>> Person = namedtuple("Person", "first last handedness")
> >>> david = Person("David", "Mertz", "Left")
> >>> david
> Person(first='David', last='Mertz', handedness='Left')
> >>> david._fields
> ('first', 'last', 'handedness')
> >>> david._asdict()
> {'first': 'David', 'last': 'Mertz', 'handedness': 'Left'}
> ```
>
> The special problem `namedtuple` had to solve is that *anything* could be an attribute of a constructed special object, such as `Person`. For some `namedtuple` classes, a field called `.fields` might be perfectly reasonable (perhaps less so one called `.asdict`).
>
> For this situation—and a very few others—the actual documented and promised API for `namedtuple` includes having several attributes and methods whose names begin with a single underscore.

Knowledge is power. Or at least often it is: The next chapter looks at cases where a better mantra might be "ignorance is bliss."

4.3.1   F-String Debugging

There are a few gotchas throughout this book where the mistake in question is simply ignorance of a useful feature. Everything that we can do using *debugging f-strings* is perfectly well possible by other means; using this technique just makes code look nicer and lets you debug your code just a little bit more easily.

A small, but surprisingly cool, feature introduced in Python 3.8 was a format for f-strings using the pattern `f"{var=}"`. All this formatting style does is create a formatted string with a variable *name* accompanying its value that is formatted per the usual f-string (format string) rules. A slightly more verbose spelling is merely `f"var={var}"`.

In an earlier discussion, in Chapter 3, *A Grab Bag of Python Gotchas*, we looked at why "bare" or overly generic exceptions are a mistake, and how to fix that. The following code arguably uses an overly generic exception, but it can be useful in the process of getting exception handling as fine-tuned as we would like it to be.

Source code of `code/divide1b.py`

```
#!/usr/bin/env python
import sys
```

```
numerators = sys.argv[1]
denominators = sys.argv[2]

try:
    ratios = []
    num_fh = open(numerators)
    den_fh = open(denominators)
    for string_a, string_b in zip(num_fh, den_fh, strict=True):
        a = float(string_a.strip())
        b = float(string_b.strip())
        ratios.append(a/b)
    print([f"{r:.3f}" for r in ratios])
except Exception as err:
    print("Unable to perform divisions")
```

As we saw with that earlier discussion utilizing almost this same small program, a great many different things can go wrong in this script. In a few paragraphs we'll see specific causes of the errors shown generically in:

```
[BetterPython]$ code/divide1b.py numerators1.txt denominators1.txt
Unable to perform divisions
[BetterPython]$ code/divide1b.py numerators1.txt denominators2.txt
Unable to perform divisions
[BetterPython]$ code/divide1b.py numerators1.txt denominators3.txt
Unable to perform divisions
[BetterPython]$ code/divide1b.py numerators1.txt denominators4.txt
Unable to perform divisions
[BetterPython]$ code/divide1b.py numerators1.txt denominators5.txt
['0.738', '1.150', '2.000', '0.326', '0.000', '0.963']
```

The example here, as in most discussions, is toy code. However, one might easily find similar logic inside a function within a library or application being developed. In fact, this function might be in use for a long while without any of these constructed error cases being encountered. We would like to sort out *what* is going wrong in each example.

Using an actual debugger is absolutely a worthwhile approach.[1] Moreover, sending the more detailed information printed in the following code to a logging system is often desirable. For the example, let's just make the printed errors more informative.

---

1. I personally have a special fondness for PuDB (https://documen.tician.de/pudb/), which like IPython pdb (https://github.com/gotcha/ipdb) is built on the standard library module pdb (https://docs.python.org/3/library/pdb.html). Most developers, however, probably prefer the more graphical debuggers incorporated with GUI editors or IDEs like VS Code or PyCharm.

Source code of `code/divide1c.py`

```python
#!/usr/bin/env python
import sys
numerators = sys.argv[1]
denominators = sys.argv[2]
num_fh = den_fh = string_a = string_b = None

try:
    ratios = []
    num_fh = open(numerators)
    den_fh = open(denominators)
    for string_a, string_b in zip(num_fh, den_fh, strict=True):
        a = float(string_a.strip())
        b = float(string_b.strip())
        ratios.append(a/b)
    print([f"{r:.3f}" for r in ratios])
except Exception as err:
    print("Unable to perform divisions")
    print(f"{err=}\n{numerators=}\n{denominators=}\n"
          f"{num_fh=}\n{den_fh=}\n{string_a=}\n{string_b=}")
```

Trying out two of the broken cases, it becomes much easier to understand what goes wrong. From there, we can decide how best to go about preventing or catching the specific problems:

```
[BetterPython]$ code/divide1c.py numerators1.txt denominators1.txt
Unable to perform divisions
err=ZeroDivisionError('float division by zero')
numerators='data/numerators1.txt'
denominators='data/denominators1.txt'
num_fh=<_io.TextIOWrapper name='data/numerators1.txt' mode='r'
    encoding='UTF-8'>
den_fh=<_io.TextIOWrapper name='data/denominators1.txt' mode='r'
    encoding='UTF-8'>
string_a='3\n'
string_b='0\n'

[BetterPython]$ code/divide1c.py numerators1.txt denominators3.txt
Unable to perform divisions
err=PermissionError(13, 'Permission denied')
numerators='data/numerators1.txt'
denominators='data/denominators3.txt'
num_fh=<_io.TextIOWrapper name='data/numerators1.txt' mode='r'
```

```
    encoding='UTF-8'>
den_fh=None
string_a=None
string_b=None
```

You are free to use the regular formatting options for f-strings in combination with the special = marker. For example:

```
>>> from math import pi
>>> f"{pi=:<0.6f}"
'pi=3.141593'
```

4.3.2 The Elegant Magic of Decorators

As with the one prior and following two discussions, the problem discussed here is a sin of omission rather than a sin of commission. There is nothing you can do with decorators that you cannot do without them; yet they nonetheless very often improve the quality and readability of code.

Note The literalness of "nothing more"

In commenting that decorators are *stricto sensu* never required, I mean that even more literally than I do of other convenient features one *could* do without. For any decorator you use, you could rewrite it with a small and mechanical translation into code that was decorator free.

Use of decorator
```
@some_decorator
def my_function(this, that):
    # do some stuff
    return a_value
```

With *exactly* the same semantics, and yet drawing attention to the meaning less well, we could write the following.

Rewriting without a decorator
```
def my_function(this, that):
    # do some stuff
    return a_value

my_function = some_decorator(my_function)
```

This equivalence fully explains precisely what a decorator actually does. It is nothing more, and nothing less, than rebinding a name that was used in defining a function (or a class) to some new object based on taking the original function (or class) as an argument and returning the transformed version.

The value of decorators is often to give Python a kind of *aspect-oriented programming* (https://en.wikipedia.org/wiki/Cross-cutting_concern) in which a common behavior can be "injected" into many functions or classes without needing to put a shared aspect of their functionality separately into the bodies of those functions.

In a sense, you can think of a function as performing a specific task, but a decorator (aspect) as recasting the means by which many functions go about peforming their respective tasks. Within a very object-oriented way of thinking, base classes or mixins can be used to give different objects a common behavior. More often than not, using a decorator to give functions such a common behavior is more concise, more readable, and much less fragile than OOP designs.

As well, a number of decorators are built into Python itself or available within standard library modules (particularly `functools`). Only a couple of these relate to crosscutting concerns, but rather each performs some special configuration of functions, classes, or methods within classes that is most elegantly expressed as a prefix to the definition that follows.

This discussion is divided into subsections, first looking at how to write useful decorators yourself—particularly *aspect-oriented* ones—then looking at some of the most common and useful "standard" decorators. Both elements are worth knowing about, and your code will be worse for not availing yourself of these opportunities where relevant.

Writing Decorators

In general, a decorator is simply a function that takes one other function as an argument and returns *something*. Within Python semantics, that something *could be* any Python object. However, in almost all cases, useful decorators for functions and methods almost always return a callable. Moreover, this callable almost always has the same, or almost the same, calling signature as the decorated function or method. Useful decorators for classes return new classes, but ones that serve a closely related purpose to the class directly in the code—merely "tweaked" or "enhanced" in some respect.

Very simple good and bad examples follow; read a bit later to understand a better way to write even the "good" decorator.

(Pretty) good and bad decorators

```
>>> def bad_decorator(fn):                              # ❶
...       return 42
...
>>> @bad_decorator
... def fused_multiply_add(a, b, c):
...       return (a * b) + c
...
>>> fused_multiply_add(4, 7, 3)
Traceback (most recent call last):
[...]
TypeError: 'int' object is not callable
```

```
>>> import sys
>>> def ok_decorator(fn):
...     def inner(*args, **kws):
...         print(f"Calling {fn.__name__}{args}", file=sys.stderr)
...         return fn(*args, **kws)
...     return inner
...
>>> @ok_decorator
... def fused_multiply_add(a, b, c):
...     return (a * b) + c
...
>>> fused_multiply_add(4, 7, 3)
Calling fused_multiply_add(4, 7, 3)                    # ❷
31
>>> fused_multiply_add.__name__                        # ❸
'inner'
```

❶ A kind phrase used to describe this decorator is "abuse of notation."

❷ This injected, crosscutting behavior is "pretty good."

❸ Losing details of introspection is less good, but curable.

Let's write two reasonably good decorators that express crosscutting concerns. In the process, we will use a very nice decorator factory that is included in Python's standard library.

A vectorization decorator

```
>>> from functools import wraps
>>> from collections.abc import Sequence
>>> def vectorize(fn):
...     @wraps(fn)                                     # ❶
...     def inner(*args):
...         if len(args) > 1:                          # ❷
...             return fn(*args)
...         elif isinstance(args[0], Sequence):
...             return [fn(*a) for a in args[0]]
...         else:                                      # ❸
...             raise ValueError(
...                 "Requires original arguments or "
...                 "sequence of tuples")
...     return inner
...
>>> @vectorize
... def fused_multiply_add(a, b, c):
...     "Multiply and accumulate"
...     return (a * b) + c
...
```

```
>>> fused_multiply_add(4, 7, 3)
31
>>> fused_multiply_add([(4, 7, 3), (7, 2, 4), (12, 1, 5)])
[31, 18, 17]

>>> fused_multiply_add.__name__
'fused_multiply_add'
>>> fused_multiply_add?                          # ❹
Signature: fused_multiply_add(a, b, c)
Docstring: Multiply and accumulate
File:      ~/git/PythonFoibles/...
Type:      function
```

❶ A handy *decorator factory* that helps preserve function signatures

❷ We *do* assume that the original function takes two or more `args`

❸ Will break on vectorizing a function that already takes one sequence

❹ All the function attributes are preserved by using `@wraps(fn)`.

Note   Decorators and decorator factories

There is an often glossed-over distinction between *decorators* and *decorator factories*. In much of what you will read, even within the official Python documentation itself, this is not kept clear.

An actual decorator takes a function (or method or class) and returns a modified version. However, many very common and useful "decorators" are actually parameterized "decorator factories." That is, these factories take completely different arguments, and themselves *return a decorator*. In fact, many useful "decorators" are cleverly configured to act in both of these roles (probably adding to the confusion of nomenclature but making the functions themselves more useful).

For example, the excellent standard library `lru_cache` provides this dual functionality:

```
>>> def mandelbrot(z0:complex, orbits:int=255) -> int:   # ❶
...     z = z0
...     for n in range(orbits):
...         if abs(z) > 2.0:
...             return n
...         z = z * z + z0
>>> %timeit mandelbrot(0.0965-0.638j)                     # ❷
1.7 µs ± 6.82 ns per loop (mean ± std. dev. of 7 runs,
1,000,000 loops each)
```

```
>>> from functools import lru_cache
>>> @lru_cache
... def mandelbrot(z0, orbits=255):
...     z = z0
...     for n in range(orbits):
...         if abs(z) > 2.0:
...             return n
...         z = z * z + z0
...
>>> %timeit mandelbrot(0.0965-0.638j)              # ❸
91.8 ns ± 0.507 ns per loop (mean ± std. dev. of 7 runs,
10,000,000 loops each)

>>> @lru_cache(maxsize=50, typed=True)             # ❹
... def mandelbrot(z0, orbits=255):
...     z = z0
...     for n in range(orbits):
...         if abs(z) > 2.0:
...             return n
...         z = z * z + z0
```

❶ Type annotations only for documentation; no effect on behavior

❷ Undecorated mandelbrot() is fastish for one point and 255 iterations.

❸ Since %timeit makes many calls, almost all are cached and faster.

❹ Decorator factory changes details of @lru_cache behavior

The big win of this decorator is that we are completely free to reuse it on *any* function that takes multiple arguments without having to rewrite the conditional logic about whether to vectorize inside each of them. Every function we decorate can focus solely on the numeric (or other) operation it needs to perform and leave the "vectorized" aspect to the decorator.

Of course, NumPy "ufuncs" (https://numpy.org/doc/stable/reference/ufuncs.html) do this same thing for sequences that are specifically NumPy arrays, with a more optimized implementation for that case. But this version works for *any* Python sequence that might be operated on in a vectorized manner.

In a similar spirit, suppose that we want to keep track of how often a function is called.

Counting calls to a function

```
>>> def count_calls(fn):
...     @wraps(fn)
...     def inner(*args):
...         inner.num_calls += 1
...         return fn(*args)
```

```
...        inner.num_calls = 0
...        return inner
...
>>> @count_calls
... def fused_multiply_add(a, b, c):
...        return (a * b) + c
...
>>> [fused_multiply_add(*args)
...        for args in [(4, 7, 3), (7, 2, 4), (12, 1, 5)]]
[31, 18, 17]
>>> fused_multiply_add.num_calls
3
>>> fused_multiply_add(7, 6, 5)
47
>>> fused_multiply_add.num_calls
4
```

Python functions are perfectly free to have additional attributes attached to them, and that serves us well for keeping state associated with the runtime use of the function.

Standard Decorators

The Python standard library includes a number of very useful decorators. The previous section touched on using @property, which is a name in __builtins__. The decorators @staticmethod and @classmethod are similar as ways of modifying the behavior of methods within a class.

Early in this discussion, we had a chance to see how @functools.lru_cache can speed up pure functions (ones that should always return the same answer given the same arguments). An interesting standard library decorator is @dataclasses.dataclass, which can "enhance" the behavior of a class used primarily to store "records." Dataclasses are discussed in Chapter 6, *Picking the Right Data Structure*.

Similar to @functools.lru_cache is @functools.cache, which was added in Python 3.9. It is simply an unbounded variation of "least-recently-used" (LRU) caching. There are trade-offs between the two: Unbounded caching can be faster, but can also increase memory usage indefinitely.

A very interesting decorator for a class is functools.total_ordering. If we wish for instances of a custom class to be sortable and support inequality and equality comparisons, we need to implement .__lt__(), .__le__(), .__gt__(), or .__ge__() and .__eq__(). That's a lot of work that can be made easier using a decorator.

Comparable persons

```
>>> import random
>>> from functools import total_ordering, cached_property
>>> @total_ordering
... class Person:
```

```
...        def __init__(self, firstname, lastname):
...            self.firstname = firstname
...            self.lastname = lastname
...
...        def __eq__(self, other):                       # ❶
...            return (self.firstname == other.firstname and
...                    self.lastname == other.lastname)
...
...        def __gt__(self, other):                       # ❶
...            return ((self.lastname, self.firstname) >
...                    (other.lastname, other.firstname))
...
...        @cached_property                               # ❷
...        def lucky_number(self):
...            print(f"Generating for {self.firstname} {self.lastname}")
...            return random.randint(1, 100)
...
>>> person1 = Person("David", "Mertz")
>>> person2 = Person("Guido", "van Rossum")
>>> person3 = Person("Grace", "Hopper")
>>> person1 <= person3                                     # ❸
False

>>> person1.lucky_number
Generating for David Mertz
88
>>> person1.lucky_number                                   # ❹
88
>>> person2.lucky_number
Generating for Guido van Rossum
17
>>> person2.lucky_number                                   # ❹
17
```

❶ Any two of the comparison dunders may be implemented for the rest to be built for us.

❷ This property is only calculated once and then cached.

❸ A comparison, .__le__(), we did not directly implement

❹ Second access has no side effect, nor does it call randint() again

There are a good number of additional useful decorators scattered around Python's standard library, and many libraries and frameworks supply their own. Much of the time, use of decorators provides a clean, minimal, and expressive way of creating code without explicitly writing it. As with most things, decorators have their abuses; when well used, they make code even more Pythonic.

4.3.3   Use `itertools` (Sufficiently)

This pitfall joins others in this section in simply describing how developers may take approaches that are *less good* than those enabled by versions using the `itertools` module. This "less good" is rarely a matter of producing the wrong results, but is often a matter of producing the right result more slowly, sometimes worse in big-O complexity behavior (i.e., quickly exceeding available time and computer resources).

The basic Python language is very powerful. One of the concepts Python has moved toward emphasizing is *lazy computation*. Specifically, iterables in Python may be large or infinite. Concrete collections are also (usually) iterable, but many iterables that are not concrete collections have a nice property of producing exactly one object at a time, and requiring almost no memory beyond that needed for that one object.

Note   Iterables and iterators

Users new to the concept can often overlook the somewhat subtle distinction between *iterables* and *iterators*. The fact that many iterables are their own iterator does not help in sorting out that confusion. These types of things are programmatically defined by `collections.abc.Iterable` and `collections.abc.Iterator`, respectively.

In brief, an iterable is an object that, when passed to the built-in function `iter()`, returns an iterator. An iterator is simply an object that, when passed to the built-in function `next()`, either returns a value or raises `StopIteration`. These two simple properties make iterables and iterators *play nice* with loops, comprehensions, and other "iterable contexts."

Generator functions return iterators when called. But iterables and iterators may also be defined by custom classes. As usual, it is the presence of dunder methods that allows objects to work with operators and built-in functions. A typical such class might look like the following.

An iterable class that is its own iterator

```
>>> class Ones:
...     def __next__(self):
...         return 1
...     def __iter__(self):
...         return self
...
>>> list(zip(Ones(), "ABC"))
[(1, 'A'), (1, 'B'), (1, 'C')]
```

Since an instance of the `Ones` class returns itself when passed to `iter()` (which occurs implicitly in any iterable context, such as in an argument to `zip()`), `Ones()` is both an iterable and an iterator. We could spell this equivalently as `itertools.repeat(1)`, which likewise yields infinitely many values (in the example, the number 1 infinitely many times).

When producing each object yielded by an iterable is resource intensive—whether requiring significant computation, significant I/O, or utilizing significant memory—doing so once at a time makes for better programs. For example, programs that don't crash with out-of-memory errors or take months to finish creating a collection are better than those that do. For big data, being able to process *one datum* now, and produce one partial result, is almost always better than needing to produce only final aggregate collections. For time-sensitive data, doing so is often a hard requirement (think of self-adjusting industrial equipment or stock tickers, which are effectively infinite data streams).

As with other features in this section, nothing you can do using the functions in the standard library `itertools` module cannot be done without them. In fact, in the documentation of the module (https://docs.python.org/3/library/itertools.html), every provided function is accompanied by a sample (approximate) implementation in Python (often the underlying CPython version is coded in C, and might behave subtly differently in a few edge cases). The purpose of the functions in `itertools` is to provide a kind of embedded language for working with infinite or very large iterators. However, even though you *could* write each of the relatively few functions in `itertools` yourself, most have pitfalls where a subtly wrong implementation will wind up using large amounts of memory rather than remaining fully lazy.

The documentation for `itertools` itself contains almost as many recipes as there are functions within the module. Each of these is only a handful of lines (often fewer than five), but combines the building blocks of the module in the *right way* rather than getting some subtlety wrong that might break edge cases or result in bad big-O behavior.

Reading FASTA

Let's look at a small program that uses iterators, then we'll use `itertools` functions to combine them. The FASTA format (https://www.ncbi.nlm.nih.gov/BLAST/fasta.shtml) is a textual format used in bioinformatics to describe nucleotide or amino acid sequences. Very often, a single file with an extension like *.fa*, *.fna*, *.fra*, or *.fasta* will contain hundreds of thousands of sequences, each containing tens of thousands of single-letter codes. For example, such a file might represent an analysis of the genetic diversity in a milliliter of soil or seawater, with each record describing a distinct bacterium species (diversity of microscopic organisms is amazing).

Generator function to read a FASTA file incrementally

```
from collections import namedtuple
FASTA = namedtuple("FASTA", "Description Sequence")

def read_fasta(filename):
    with open(filename) as fh:
        line = next(fh)
        if not line.startswith(">"):
            raise ValueError(
                f"{filename} does not appear to be in FASTA format")
```

```
        description = line[1:].rstrip()
        nucleic_acids = []
        for line in fh:
            if line.startswith(">"):
                yield FASTA(description, "".join(nucleic_acids))
                description = line[1:].rstrip()
                nucleic_acids = []
            else:
                nucleic_acids.append(line.rstrip())    # ❶
        yield FASTA(description, "".join(nucleic_acids))
```

❶ FASTA files typically, but not uniformly, have 80-width lines within sequence blocks; but the newline is not meaningful.

Here is an example of reading a file that contains just two sequences, the putative mRNA sequences for the Pfizer and Moderna COVID-19 vaccines, respectively:[2]

```
>>> for vaccine in read_fasta("COVID-19-vax-mRNA.fasta"):
...     print(f">{vaccine.Description}")
...     print(vaccine.Sequence[:60] + "...")
...
>Spike-encoding_contig_assembled_from_BioNTech/Pfizer_BNT-162b2
GAGAATAAACTAGTATTCTTCTGGTCCCCACAGACTCAGAGAGAACCCGCCACCATGTTC...
>Spike-encoding_contig_assembled_from_Moderna_mRNA-1273
GGGAAATAAGAGAGAAAAGAAGAGTAAGAAGAAATATAAGACCCCGGCGCCGCCACCATG...
```

Let's move on to *doing something* with this FASTA data that we can iterate over.

Run-Length Encoding

In data that is expected to have many consecutive occurrences of the same symbol, run-length encoding (RLE) can often offer significant compression of the representation. RLE is often used as one component within sophisticated compression algorithms.

In particular, we can write extremely compact implementations of run-length encoding and run-length decoding by using `itertools`. These implementations also have the virtue of being able to operate lazily. That is, both of the following functions can be consumed one value at a time, and accept iterables as arguments, and hence operate efficiently on large, or even infinite, streams of data.

---

2. The data used can be obtained at https://gnosis.cx/better/data/COVID-19-vax-mRNA.fasta. It is taken from "Assemblies of putative SARS CoV2 spike encoding mRNA sequences for vaccines BNT-162b2 and mRNA-1273," by Dae-Eun Jeong, Matthew McCoy, Karen Artiles, Orkan Ilbay, Andrew Fire, Kari Nadeau, Helen Park, Brooke Betts, Scott Boyd, Ramona Hoh, and Massa Shoura (https://github.com/NAalytics).

Run-length functions

```
from collections.abc import Iterable, Iterator
from itertools import groupby, chain, repeat

def rle_encode(it: Iterable) -> Iterator:
    for k, g in groupby(it):
        yield (k, len(list(g)))

def rle_decode(it: Iterable) -> Iterator:
    yield from chain.from_iterable(repeat(x, n) for x, n in it)
```

The functions are annotated only to emphasize that they operate lazily. They utilize the itertools functions groupby(), chain.from_iterable(), and repeat() to keep the code compact and lazy. The argument *to* chain.from_iterable() is itself a generator comprehension, as well. Exactly *why* these work so elegantly is left, to some degree, for readers who should read the official documentation of each function (and of the other handy functions in the module). It's worth seeing these operate to understand what's going on:

```
>>> from itertools import islice
>>> for vaccine in read_fasta("COVID-19-vax-mRNA.fasta"):
...     encoded = rle_encode(vaccine.Sequence)          # ❶
...     first5_regions = islice(encoded, 5)             # ❶
...     print(vaccine.Description)
...     print(list(first5_regions))                     # ❷
...
Spike-encoding_contig_assembled_from_BioNTech/Pfizer_BNT-162b2
[('G', 1), ('A', 1), ('G', 1), ('A', 2), ('T', 1)]
Spike-encoding_contig_assembled_from_Moderna_mRNA-1273
[('G', 3), ('A', 3), ('T', 1), ('A', 2), ('G', 1)]
```

❶ The objects seq and first5_regions are lazy iterators, not concrete.

❷ Only by creating a list from iterator do we allocate memory.

We can verify that our paired functions are symmetrical:

```
>>> for vaccine in read_fasta("data/COVID-19-vax-mRNA.fasta"):
...     encoded = rle_encode(vaccine.Sequence)
...     decoded = rle_decode(encoded)
...     print(vaccine.Description)
...     print(decoded)
...     print("".join(islice(decoded, 60)) + "...")
...
```

```
Spike-encoding_contig_assembled_from_BioNTech/Pfizer_BNT-162b2
<generator object rle_decode at 0x7f5441632810>
GAGAATAAACTAGTATTCTTCTGGTCCCCACAGACTCAGAGAGAACCCGCCACCATGTTC...
Spike-encoding_contig_assembled_from_Moderna_mRNA-1273
<generator object rle_decode at 0x7f54416f7440>
GGGAAATAAGAGAGAAAAGAAGAGTAAGAAGAAATATAAGACCCCGGCGCCGCCACCATG...
```

Notice that the functions `rle_encode()` and `rle_decode()` are not limited to encoding or decoding characters; such is merely handy for the examples. In fact, any kind of iterable of any kind of value that might be repeated successively will work equally well in being encoded or decoded by these functions. They will also work on infinitely long iterators of values to encode or decode, as long as you only ask for a finite number of the values at once.

More "Iterator Algebra"

It is, of course, somewhat silly and unnecessary to worry so much about laziness in concretizing iterators for a file that has exactly two relatively short nucleotide sequences. As mentioned, though, similar files can be far larger collections of far longer sequences. Many other data sources can also be large, or slow to produce subsequent data (such as ones obtained from slow remote online sources); the techniques discussed in this section apply equally to those.

Some of the additional functions in `itertools` include `dropwhile()`, `takewhile()`, `pairwise()`, `accumulate()`, `tee()`, `permutations()`, `combinations()`, `zip_longest()`, and `filterfalse()`. `filter()` is a built-in, but is "spiritually" part of `itertools`, as are `map()`, `range()`, `enumerate()`, and `zip()`. That list is not complete, but it's probably the ones I use most often. The excellent official documentation discusses everything in the module. Given that `itertools` in many ways extends several `itertools`-like functions already in `__builtins__`, using `from itertools import *` is one of the rare cases where I do not recommend against the *import* `*` pattern discussed elsewhere in this book.

Suppose that you have a FASTA source that might be large, and you wish to identify every (RNA) sequence where a long run of the same nucleotide occurs. But once you find one within a sequence, you don't want to spend extra work examining the rest of that sequence:

```
>>> for vaccine in read_fasta("data/COVID-19-vax-mRNA.fasta"):
...     long_seq = next(dropwhile(lambda run: run[1] < 8,
...         rle_encode(vaccine.Sequence)), None)
...     print(vaccine.Description)
...     print(f"First long nucleotide duplication: {long_seq}")
...
Spike-encoding_contig_assembled_from_BioNTech/Pfizer_BNT-162b2
```

```
First long nucleotide duplication: None
Spike-encoding_contig_assembled_from_Moderna_mRNA-1273
First long nucleotide duplication: ('A', 9)
```

To illustrate how concise and powerful iterator algebra can be, let's look at a somewhat famous mathematical series. The *alternating harmonic series* converges to the natural log of 2. It's not an especially fast convergence, but an elegant implementation can elegantly utilize several iterator-combining functions:

$$\sum_{n=1}^{\infty} \frac{(-1)^{n+1}}{n} = 1 - \frac{1}{2} + \frac{1}{3} - \frac{1}{4} + \frac{1}{5} - \cdots$$

```
>>> from math import log
>>> log(2)
0.6931471805599453

>>> from itertools import accumulate, cycle, islice
>>> alt_harm = accumulate(sign/denom
...          for (denom, sign) in enumerate(cycle([1, -1]), start=1))
>>> for approx in islice(alt_harm, 1_000_000, 1_000_003):    # ❶
...     print(approx)
...
0.6931476805592526
0.6931466805612526
0.6931476805582526
>>> for approx in islice(alt_harm, 4_000_000, 4_000_001):    # ❷
...     print(approx)
...
0.6931470805601476
```

❶ Consume the first million-and-three terms into the accumulator.

❷ Note that this is the *next* 4M terms, so 5M in total.

This section only presented a few uses of `itertools`. The functions inside the module can be combined in myriad ways, and being able to think in terms of such combinations is a valuable skill for any Python developer.

4.3.4 The `more-itertools` Third-Party Library

The third-party library `more-itertools` is a pleasant little gem that extends the building blocks of the standard library `itertools` discussed in the preceding section. Much as I have introduced other discussions within this section of this chapter, the problem is simply being unaware of a handy tool that will make a great many tasks you perform regularly easier.

> **Note**
>
> Readers who come from the world of JavaScript may be familiar with the brilliantly useful library Lodash (https://lodash.com/), which adds back into JavaScript many of the powerful features that I personally miss most when I have to venture into that language from my more familiar, and friendlier, Python. A great deal of what the Lodash library does, however, is implement functions similar to those provided by `itertools` and `more-itertools`.
>
>   This is a book about Python, however, and you need not have ever used JavaScript or Lodash to read this chapter.

I consider `more-itertools` to be, in a way, "the missing library in the batteries-included standard library." As an aside, I would put `requests` and `pytest` into a similar category (although I understand the good reasons why each of these are not actually included). One section in Chapter 8 discusses why using `requests` is almost always to be preferred; the entirety of the Appendix more or less simply assumes that `pytest` is the right choice rather than the standard library.

Even though I also have chapters in this book discussing NumPy and Pandas because they are so very widely used by Python programmers, I would not wish these to live in the standard library; those rightly occupy somewhat different domains, and are developed on a different cadence than Python itself. There are a few other libraries that are also nearly ubiquitously used among Python developers: Matplotlib (https://matplotlib.org/); scikit-learn (https://scikit-learn.org/stable/); Flask (https://flask.palletsprojects.com /en/2.2.x/) or FastAPI (https://fastapi.tiangolo.com/); and Pillow (PIL fork; https://pillow.readthedocs.io/en/stable/). Clearly, there are mistakes that could be made with all of these libraries as well; but they are outside the scope of this book.

An element of `more-itertools` that makes me give it a special place is that it is really not limited to any specific domain, as the other mentioned third-party libraries are. Nearly everything you will do in Python might plausibly be made just a little bit clearer and a little bit easier by using functions from `more-itertools`.

While I do not entirely object to Python programs that use `from itertools import *`, unfortunately I cannot write the same of `from more_itertools import *`. The functions therein are clearly well designed to work well together (and with those in `itertools` and with the handful of built-in functions dedicated to working with iterators). However, just a few of the names feel likely to conflict with names you are likely to use for reasonable and unrelated purposes. While you are unlikely to use the name `interleave_longest()` for unrelated purposes, `locate()`, `replace()`, `difference()`, `consume()`, `collapse()`, and a few others feel like they might very innocently serve unrelated purposes to the versions in `more-itertools`.

Most or all of the recipes in the documentation for `itertools` are directly included within `more-itertools` as directly importable functions. As well as providing those recipes without requiring you to copy and paste them into your own code, about 100 additional wonderful functions for advanced "iterator algebra" are included in the module. Clearly this book is not the place to repeat the documentation for all of those functions;

see https://more-itertools.readthedocs.io/en/stable/api.html for that documentation. However, let me show you just one (semi-random) example that I find particularly neat.

With the rise of JSON as an interchange format between different software systems, highly nested data structures have become more of a norm. However, in Python, "Flat is better than nested" (per line 5 of the *The Zen of Python*). Sometimes we'd like a painless way to traverse nested data without writing custom code. Such custom code usually uses recursion, which is an appropriate use. Sometimes, though, we'd just like a simple function to do it for us. Here is an example.

Recursively flattening a nested (concrete) data structure

```
>>> from more_itertools import collapse
>>> data = [
... [[[[['insures'], 'mostests', 'fugs', 'debouchments'],
...        'impostumated',
...        'astringe',
...        'mazeful'],
...        'handrails',
...        'floridean',
...        'oxymoron'],
...        'reprinter',
...        'confessionals',
...        'pornocracies'],
...     'wryly',
...     'lobotomizes',
...     'gelatinous',
...     'lipidoplast'],
...     'muscardines',
...     'contexts',
...     'orphanism',
...     'aftmost',
... ]
>>> collapse(data)
<generator object collapse at 0x7f5432ed49a0>
>>> list(collapse(data))
['insures', 'mostests', 'fugs', 'debouchments', 'impostumated',
 'astringe', 'mazeful', 'handrails', 'floridean', 'oxymoron',
 'reprinter', 'confessionals', 'pornocracies', 'wryly', 'lobotomizes',
 'gelatinous', 'lipidoplast', 'muscardines', 'contexts',
 'orphanism', 'aftmost']
```

This is nice, and we can see that the direct result of calling `collapse()` is a lazy iterator (which can thereby be combined and massaged using everything else within `itertools` and `more-itertools`).

What is even nicer is that this function works equally well on iterators that may themselves yield other iterators, without ever having to concretize more than one element at once.

Recursively flattening an iterator of iterators

```
>>> from random import random, randint, choice, seed
>>> def word_tree(words=None):
...     if words is None:
...         words = [word.rstrip() for word in open("sowpods")]
...     if random() < 0.75:
...         yield word_tree(words)
...     for _ in range(randint(1, 4)):
...         yield choice(words)
...
>>> seed(4)                                    # ❶
>>> wt = word_tree()
>>> wt
<generator object word_tree at 0x7f5432d0d990>
>>> next(wt)
<generator object word_tree at 0x7f5432d0f2e0>    # ❷
>>> seed(4)                                    # ❶
>>> for word in collapse(word_tree()):
...     print(word, end=" ")
...
insures mostests fugs debouchments impostumated astringe mazeful
handrails floridean oxymoron reprinter confessionals pornocracies
wryly lobotomizes gelatinous lipidoplast muscardines contexts
orphanism aftmost
```

❶ Using a seed creates reproducible randomness.

❷ The first value yielded by the iterator is an iterator itself.

Our familiar SOWPODS word list, utilized in a variety of other examples, is available at https://gnosis.cx/better.

4.4 Type Annotations Are Not Runtime Types

The use of type-checking tools has become popular among a significant segment of Python developers. As is mentioned in the Preface, this book is neither long enough nor appropriately focused to address the various mistakes that are possible within type annotations, even stipulating that you, or your team, have decided to utilize type annotations. Whether you *should* so decide is specifically not an opinion I will venture in this text.

Use of type annotations is significantly complex, although incremental or minimal use is possible, and tools like Mypy, Pytype, Pyright, and Pyre implement *gradual type annotations*.[3] As Python's standard library `typing` module and Python's syntax have grown new capabilities, both the sophistication of what can be expressed and the range of possible mistakes have grown enormously since 2014's PEP 484, titled "Type Hints."[4]

The main thing to keep in mind here is that *type annotations have zero effect on the runtime behavior* of Python. *Mostly.*

Note   Dynamic type evaluation in Python

As with most topics, certain caveats are needed. Annotations are available to Python programs at runtime, as is pretty much everything about Python that you might potentially introspect. For example:

```
>>> def add(a: int, b: int) -> int:
...     c: int = a + b  # Annotation of `c` not exposed directly
...     return c
...
>>> add.__annotations__
{'a': <class 'int'>, 'b': <class 'int'>, 'return': <class 'int'>}
>>> add.__code__.co_varnames
('a', 'b', 'c')
>>> import inspect
>>> inspect.getsource(add)
'def add(a: int, b: int) -> int:\n    c: int = a + b\n    return c\n'
>>> import typing
>>> typing.get_type_hints(add)
{'a': <class 'int'>, 'b': <class 'int'>, 'return': <class 'int'>}
```

While it is unusual for a "regular" Python developer to use this introspection, the library Pydantic (https://docs.pydantic.dev/) and some widely used libraries such as FastAPI (https://fastapi.tiangolo.com/) *do* use this kind of introspection, but wrap it in their own enhanced and useful interfaces.

---

3. The concept of gradual typing was introduced by Jeremy Siek and Walid Taha in 2006. See https://wphomes.soic.indiana.edu/jsiek/what-is-gradual-typing/ for background. A variety of programming languages and tools have implemented this concept, even beyond those in the Python ecosystem.
4. With a certain minor pride or vanity, I am fairly confident that my 2015 keynote at PyCon Belarus, "Python's (future) type annotation system(s)," was the first public conference presentation of these ideas within the Python world. That said, I have been no more than an observer of a trend, and have contributed nothing relevant to the specific directions typing has taken in Python.

4.4.1 Type Annotations Are Not Runtime Constraints

Suppose that we write a toy Python program that utilizes annotations.

Static and runtime type checking

```
# type-violations.py
from typing import TypeVar

Numeric = TypeVar("Numeric", float, complex, contravariant=True)

def fused_multiply_add(a: Numeric, b: Numeric, c: Numeric) -> Numeric:
    r: Numeric = (a * b) + c
    return r

print("fused_multiply_add(1, 2, 3)", end=" -> ")
try:
    print(fused_multiply_add(1, 2, 3))
except Exception as ex:
    print(type(ex))

print("fused_multiply_add('foo', 2, 'bar')", end=" -> ")
try:
    print(fused_multiply_add("foo", 2, "bar"))       # ❶
except Exception as ex:
    print(type(ex))

print("fused_multiply_add('foo', 2.0, 'bar)", end=" -> ")
try:
    print(fused_multiply_add("foo", 2.0, "bar"))     # ❷
except Exception as ex:
    print(type(ex))

print("fused_multiply_add(1+1j, 2.0, 3.0)", end=" -> ")
try:
    print(fused_multiply_add(1 + 1j, 2.0, 3.0))
except Exception as ex:
    print(type(ex))
```

❶ Line 20

❷ Line 26.

Using the static type analyzer Mypy, we can find certain problems in this script.

Mypy analysis of `type-violations.py`

```
[BetterPython]$ mypy type-violations.py
type-violations.py:20: error: Value of type variable "Numeric" of
  "fused_multiply_add" cannot be "object"
type-violations.py:26: error: Value of type variable "Numeric" of
  "fused_multiply_add" cannot be "object"
Found 2 errors in 1 file (checked 1 source file)
```

At runtime, the behavior is somewhat different.

Runtime exception catching of `TypeError`

```
[BetterPython]$ python type-violations.py
fused_multiply_add(1, 2, 3) -> 5
fused_multiply_add('foo', 2, 'bar') -> foofoobar
fused_multiply_add('foo', 2.0, 'bar) -> <class 'TypeError'>
fused_multiply_add(1+1j, 2.0, 3.0) -> (5+2j)
```

We can see that `type-violation.py` has typing issues both under static analysis and at runtime. However, the errors are somewhat different from each other. Most likely, from the name of the defined function, the developer did not intend for the function `fused_multiply_add()` to be used with strings, but we cannot know that for certain without either documentation or accurate annotations that are checked statically.

It is tempting to generalize by saying that static analysis is "more strict" than runtime type checking. However, while that happens to be true in this example, it is not true generally. Annotations might only be used gradually. As well, there are numerous edge cases where static checkers will not catch issues arising dynamically. The set of complaints—even strictly `TypeError` exceptions—can be more extensive *either* under static analysis *or* under runtime checking. Moreover, the details of this comparison depend on *which* static analysis tool is used, and in what version (which is very much outside the scope of this book).

We can see why this particular example encounters a runtime type error:

```
>>> "foo" * 2
'foofoo'
>>> "foo" * 2.0
Traceback (most recent call last):
[...]
TypeError: can't multiply sequence by non-int of type 'float'
```

It happens that the static analysis tool would be perfectly happy to allow `2` and `2.0` interchangeably as floating-point-like numbers. This is what `typing.SupportsFloat` is used for; it's also why `fused_multiply_add(1, 2, 3)` did not raise any complaint by the static analyzer. But in Python, while strings can be "multiplied" by an integer, they cannot be multiplied by a floating point number, even one whose value is equal to an integer.

If we removed *all* the type annotations from the preceding program, the runtime type checking and program behavior would not change whatsoever.

4.4.2 Mistaking `typing.NewType()` for a Runtime Type

This section singles out `NewType()`, but there are a number of objects within the `typing` module that are easy to confuse with features of runtime type checks. In fact, many of the same objects have dual roles that can confuse developers, especially those coming from other programming languages where type systems function differently (i.e., especially those with static typing, which annotations resemble).

An object like `typing.Sequence` is a good example of a dual-role object. Suppose you have a function that can only operate reasonably on a sequence. You might write something like this.

An annotated function to manipulate integer sequences

```
>>> from typing import Sequence
>>> def double_middle_element(seq: Sequence[int]) -> Sequence[int]:
...     if len(seq) > 0:
...         middle = len(seq)//2
...         item = seq[middle] * 2
...         new = seq[:middle] + type(seq)([item]) + seq[middle+1:]
...     return new
...
>>> double_middle_element([5, 8, 4, 6, 2, 3])
[5, 8, 4, 12, 2, 3]
>>> double_middle_element((5, 8, 4, 6, 2, 3))
(5, 8, 4, 12, 2, 3)
```

For experienced users of Python type annotations, this may be insufficiently constrained in the declaration since the declaration itself does not require that, for example, a tuple is returned if a tuple is passed as an argument (although that *is* the runtime behavior). However, that's not the topic of this particular section.

We might expect this code to catch some misuses that it seems obviously to declare improperly.

Annotations do not impose runtime constraints

```
>>> double_middle_element("abcde")
"ab['cc']de"
>>> double_middle_element({1: 'a', 2: 'b', 3: 'c'})
Traceback (most recent call last):
```

```
[...]
TypeError: unhashable type: 'slice'
```

The code accidentally "works" with a string as an argument. The result is likely not what we want, but no exception is raised. However, for the dictionary argument, the exception that occurs really is not related to the fact that the argument is *not a sequence of integers*.

If we wanted actual runtime checks, we could write something more like this.

A runtime-checked function to manipulate integer sequences

```
>>> def double_middle_element(seq):
...     "Double middle element in sequence of ints or return unchanged"
...     if not isinstance(seq, Sequence) or not seq:
...         return seq
...     if not all(isinstance(i, int) for i in seq):
...         return seq
...     middle = len(seq)//2
...     item = seq[middle] * 2
...     return seq[:middle] + type(seq)([item]) + seq[middle+1:]
...
>>> double_middle_element((5, 8, 4, 6, 2, 3))
(5, 8, 4, 12, 2, 3)
>>> double_middle_element([5, 8, 4, 6, 2, 3])
[5, 8, 4, 12, 2, 3]
>>> double_middle_element({1: 'a', 2: 'b', 3: 'c'})
{1: 'a', 2: 'b', 3: 'c'}
>>> double_middle_element("abcde")
'abcde'
```

Notice that the self-same object `Sequence` might play either a static or runtime role, but the code is structured differently for the two purposes. Using Pydantic might provide a path to unify these two roles, but the basic idea that "using the same object in different contexts does different things" isn't actually that hard to think about.

Some objects in `typing` definitely provide an attractive nuisance, however. For example, an actual colleague of mine—who admittedly primarily develops in C++, but has used Python on the side for more than a decade—wanted to have specialized integers against which he could perform an `isinstance()` check elsewhere in his program. This desire is eminently reasonable. Perhaps `UserId` is a special type of integer in the sense that we'd like to make sure a generic integer isn't used in certain places. Or maybe we want an integer for a thermometer temperature, or for a percentile ranking, or for a distance measure where we want to avoid confusing miles with kilometers. Knowing whether the wrong kind of unit/value has snuck in is quite useful.

With such a need in mind, here is an obvious—and wrong—solution to the requirement.

Failing program to convert temperatures to Kelvin

```
>>> from typing import NewType
>>> Fahrenheit = NewType("F", float)
>>> Celsius = NewType("C", float)
>>> roomF = Fahrenheit(70.0)
>>> roomC = Celsius(21.1)
>>> def to_Kelvin(t):
...     if isinstance(t, Celsius):
...         return t + 273.15
...     elif isinstance(t, Fahrenheit):
...         return 5 * (t-32)/9 + 273.15
...     else:
...         return temp
...
>>> to_Kelvin(roomF)
Traceback (most recent call last):
[...]
TypeError: isinstance() arg 2 must be a type, a tuple of types,
  or a union
```

At least this fails quickly. But why did that not work? If we read the `typing` documentation carefully, we discover that "these checks are enforced only by the static type checker."

The way we would actually solve this problem is with the plain-old, boring `class` statement that we've had since Python 1.0. Albeit, here I use a few more recent features for a more robust version.

Successful program to convert temperatures to Kelvin

```
>>> class Celsius(float):
...     def __new__(cls, deg):
...         if deg < -273.15:
...             raise ValueError("Colder than absolute zero")
...         return super().__new__(cls, deg)
...
>>> class Fahrenheit(float):
...     def __new__(cls, deg):
...         if deg < -459.67:
...             raise ValueError("Colder than absolute zero")
...         return super().__new__(cls, deg)
...
>>> def to_Kelvin(t):
...     if isinstance(t, Celsius):
...         return t + 273.15
...     if isinstance(t, Fahrenheit):
```

```
...          return 5 * (t-32)/9 + 273.15
...      return t
...
>>> to_Kelvin(Celsius(21.1))
294.25
>>> to_Kelvin(Fahrenheit(70.0))
294.26111111111106
>>> to_Kelvin(294.3)
294.3
>>> Celsius(-300)
Traceback (most recent call last):
[...]
ValueError: Colder than absolute zero
```

If you didn't care about the bounds checking, it would be sufficient simply to write, for example, class Celsius(float): pass.

4.5 Wrapping Up

In this chapter, we looked at a somewhat heterogeneous collection of mistakes, but still all within the domain we might call "generic Python concerns." Later chapters look at more specialized (but not less important) concerns with matters such as testing, data structures, security, and numeric computing.

Two mistakes here recapitulated the mistakes with good naming that started in Chapter 3, *A Grab Bag of Python Gotchas*. Good names—and following Pythonic conventions about naming—remain important as you become a more sophisticated programmer.

Several more mistakes discussed were mistakes of ignorance or forgetfulness. Python, in truth, has a few slightly obscure, yet enormously useful, corners within it. Knowing about some capabilities of the Python syntax or standard library can often make your work easier, and make your code friendlier for others to read.

A final two mistakes concerned a common confusion among newish Python developers, and especially those more familiar with statically typed programming languages. While the introductory material of this book discussed why this book does not specifically delve into the world of static type analysis in Python, the presence of type annotations can often mislead some programmers. This book itself, in fact, occasionally uses examples with annotations; but it only does so in order to highlight correct reader expectations; in other words, they are merely a form of documentation for most Python users (albeit an often useful form).

5

Just Because You Can,
It Doesn't Mean
You Should...

Python has a great many capabilities that exist for good reasons. However, many of these features create what jurists call an "attractive nuisance."[1] This chapter is a mixture of positive and negative advice, in truth. It presents some slightly unusual constructs that a new Python developer often learns and becomes excited about, before finally stumbling over the pitfalls those possibilities present. Hopefully, reading the mistakes here will facilitate the learning part but discourage the misuse follow-up. In some other mistakes, I simply discuss some techniques that people new to Python may not have known about (but which are mistakes not to avail yourself of); in one case (and another half case), people who have long used Python may also not be familiar with a newer feature.

5.1 Metaclasses

This section leans into slightly more arcane areas of Python's design. If you've seen metaclasses discussed, or if they are used in the codebases you work with, this is definitely for you. If you haven't, it's still worth reading, but treat the topic as an amusement or an enlightenment, rather than as a necessity. Libraries you use might use metaclasses, even if you are not aware of the fact; knowing more is always handy.

Metaclasses push at the edge of the highly dynamic nature of Python. Even class objects can themselves be created in different manners than their code describes by declaring a metaclass. Moreover, the choice of metaclass can itself, in principle, be dynamically chosen.

---

1. Attractive nuisance: "a legal doctrine which makes a person negligent for leaving a piece of equipment or other condition on property which would be both attractive and dangerous to curious children. These have included tractors, unguarded swimming pools, open pits, and abandoned refrigerators" (from https://dictionary.law.com). Some of the more obscure features in Python are certainly reminiscent of open pits and abandoned refrigerators.

Before we get to showing what metaclasses *can* do, and showing why doing those things is usually a mistake, let's think about a comment from the early 2000s (when metaclasses were introduced) that stands the test of 20 years:

> Metaclasses are deeper magic than 99% of users should ever worry about. If you wonder whether you need them, you don't (the people who actually need them know with certainty that they need them, and don't need an explanation about why).

> **— Tim Peters, Author of *The Zen of Python* (from the much-missed comp.lang.python Usenet newsgroup)**

Around the same time as Tim Peters' quote, and not too long after they were introduced to Python, I wrote a number of articles about Python metaclasses (often in collaboration with Michele Simionato). Unfortunately, I probably elicited the commission of many of the sins with metaclasses committed since.

Although I would almost universally advise against using metaclasses, there are some prominent Python frameworks that make broad use of them (*cough, cough,* Django: https://www.djangoproject.com/). Arguably, there *must be* occasions where they are the best approach to choose. However, it's probably informative that Python's standard library typing module initially used metaclasses widely but subsequently moved away from their use (the module is largely the creation of Python creator Guido van Rossum).

Let's take a look at a metaclass with an arguably good use. Suppose you have a large code base, particularly one with some sort of plugin system in which components are dynamically loaded. You'd like to be able to examine at runtime which classes have been created in this dynamic arrangement.

A metaclass to provide class registration and some plugins

```
from math import sqrt
import os
import logging

log_level = os.environ.get("APP_LOG_LEVEL", 20)
logging.basicConfig(filename='app.log', level=log_level)

class PluginLoggerMeta(type):                           # ❶
    def __init__(cls, name, bases, attrs):
        logging.info(f"Registering: {name}"
                    f"({', '.join(b.__name__ for b in bases)}): "
                    f"\n  contains: {', '.join(attrs.keys())}")

class Plugin(metaclass=PluginLoggerMeta):
    pass
```

```
if True:                                            # ❷
    class Point2d(tuple, Plugin):
        def __new__(self, x, y):
            return tuple.__new__(self, (x, y))

        @property
        def distance(self):
            return sqrt(self[0]**2 + self[1]**2)

if not False:                                       # ❷
    class Point3d(tuple, Plugin):
        def __new__(self, x, y, z):
            return tuple.__new__(self, (x, y, z))

        @property
        def distance(self):
            return sqrt(self[0]**2 + self[1]**2 + self[2]**2)

print(Point2d(4, 5).distance, Point3d(3, 5, 7).distance)
```

❶ Inherited from, not a metaclass of type

❷ In production, some other external condition

This arrangement *works*, and logging registered plugins is a perfectly reasonable goal. Let's take a look.

Running the source code of `metaclass.py`

```
[BetterPython]$ python code/metaclass.py
6.4031242374328485 9.1104335791443
[BetterPython]$ cat app.log
INFO:root:Registering: Plugin():
  contains: __module__, __qualname__
INFO:root:Registering: Point2d(tuple, Plugin):
  contains: __module__, __qualname__, __new__, distance
INFO:root:Registering: Point3d(tuple, Plugin):
  contains: __module__, __qualname__, __new__, distance
```

However, this use of metaclasses is simply *more fragile* than other approaches to accomplishing the same thing. Since our convention for plugins requires adding *something*, such as inheriting from `Plugin`, to work, we could just as easily require something else.

For example, a decorator like `@register_plugin` could just as well be required by the framework using plugins. All that decorator would need to do is log information about the class object, then return the class unchanged. For example:

> **Note   The guts of a metaclass**
>
> Usually, when you create a class in Python, what you are doing "behind the scenes" is calling the constructor `type()`. For example, here is a subclass of `tuple` (which needs to use `.__new__()` rather than `.__init__()` because immutable tuples cannot be modified during initialization, when the instance already exists):
>
> ```
> >>> from math import sqrt
> >>> class Point2d(tuple):
> ...     def __new__(self, x, y):
> ...         return tuple.__new__(self, (x, y))
> ...
> ...     def distance(self):
> ...         return sqrt(self[0]**2 + self[1]**2)
> ...
> >>> point = Point2d(3, 4)
> >>> point
> (3, 4)
> >>> point.distance()
> 5.0
> >>> point.__class__.__name__
> 'Point2d'
> ```
>
> The very useful `collections.namedtuple` creates dynamically generated classes similar to `Point2d`. We *could* write this instead:
>
> ```
> >>> Point2d = type("Point2d", (tuple,),
> ...                 {"__new__": lambda self, x, y:
> ...                     tuple.__new__(self, (x, y)),
> ...                 "distance": lambda self:
> ...                     sqrt(self[0]**2 + self[1]**2)})
> >>> point = Point2d(3, 4)
> >>> point.distance()
> 5.0
> >>> point.__class__.__name__
> 'Point2d'
> ```
>
> A metaclass is nothing but a class created using a subclass of `type` rather than `type` itself as the constructor of a class.[2] Or equivalently, every class definition (in regular format) could contain `metaclass=type` and retain the default behavior.

---

2. To be very pedantic, a metaclass does not strictly need to be a subclass of `type`. In principle, any callable that takes as arguments a name, a tuple of bases, and a dictionary of attributes/methods would work as a metaclass. This could even be a plain function if it returned a class object.

```
def register_plugin(cls):
    logging.info(f"Registering: {cls.__name__} ...")
    return cls
```

As used, we'd see something like this (depending on the configuration of `logging`):

```
>>> @register_plugin
... class TestClass: pass
Registering: TestClass ...
```

Likewise, if you wanted to use inheritance, rather than using a metaclass, you could simply include a logging .__new__() within the `Plugin` class. But why isn't this simply a minor style preference? Here's one of the numerous places where the fragility of metaclasses comes out:

```
>>> class NullMeta(type):
...         pass
...
>>> class NullBase(metaclass=NullMeta):
...         pass
...
>>> class MyStuff(Plugin, NullBase):
...         pass
...
Traceback (most recent call last):
      class MyStuff(Plugin, NullBase):
TypeError: metaclass conflict: the metaclass of a derived class must
      be a (non-strict) subclass of the metaclasses of all its bases
```

The error message is pretty good, but in essence the problem is that `Plugin` and `NullBase` imply different metaclasses to be used for class creation (`PluginLoggerMeta` and `NullMeta`, respectively), and Python cannot decide which one to use. There is a solution in creating a custom metaclass descending from both metaclasses, but this becomes thorny and arcane quickly.

If custom metaclasses become commonplace in your code, conflicts during multiple inheritance become almost inevitable. This is a danger that might be justified if it did something you couldn't do otherwise. However, as shown earlier, class decorators are almost always cleaner, more readable, and can accomplish either absolutely or very nearly *everything* that custom metaclasses can.

5.2 Monkeypatching

A powerful, and therefore easily misused, capability in highly dynamic languages like Python is that they allow *monkeypatching*. With monkeypatching, even existing modules and classes can be modified at runtime to exhibit different behaviors that might be better specialized for the needs of a specific project.

The programming language Ruby is, in many ways, quite similar to Python. It is even more dynamic, so a few things that are difficult to impossible to monkeypatch in Python are easy in Ruby (mainly the possibility of dynamically altering even built-in types, which Python does not allow). Partially as a consequence of such broad power, monkeypatching became much more deeply incorporated into Ruby's culture than it has in Python. In turn, this cultural trend also largely became seen as an antipattern among Ruby developers; however, a great deal of code (such as Ruby's biggest mover, the Rails web framework) included monkeypatching that could not be removed without breaking backward compatibility.

An influential article in that ecosystem was Avdi Grimm's 2008 "Monkey Patching Is Destroying Ruby" (https://avdi.codes/why-monkeypatching-is-destroying-ruby/). You can tell from the date that this discussion is not new. In fact, Grimm acknowledges Python as the source of the term, and a predecessor language in allowing it.

Already in 2008, monkeypatching was well-known in Python, but not especially widely used. In 2023, as I write this, that characterization remains true. You might certainly encounter Python code that uses monkeypatching, but only moderately often. Deciding to use monkeypatching in your own code is *usually* a mistake, but not *always*. Classes, instances, source code itself, and a few other objects can be monkeypatched in Python. For this example, though, I will present the most common use of the technique: monkeypatching modules.

For a slightly contrived example that nonetheless genuinely exemplifies the situations that tend to motivate Python developers to monkeypatch, suppose you have an application that processes CSV data that comes from a vendor. A sample data file might look like this.

Data in file *accounts.csv*

```
Balance,AccountNum,Owner
2913.94,3850234082,Omar
9102.53,0028382910,Sarita
5181.32,8213593023,David
...more rows...
```

Your application might look something like a more sophisticated version of this:

```
import re
import sys

def get_5k_balances(rows):
    for row in rows:
```

```
        if re.match(r"5\d{3}\.\d{2}", row):
            balance, account_num, owner = row.split(",")
            yield (f"Account: {account_num}\n"
                   f"  Owner: {owner.strip()}\n"
                   f"Balance: ${float(balance):,.2f}\n")

# ... many more functions ...

if __name__ == "__main__":
    for account in get_5k_balances(open(sys.argv[1])):
        print(account)
```

By stipulation, there are actually many places in this code where we perform a
re.match() against balance numbers. When we run this script, it will loop through the
specified file and yield formatted versions of some of the rows (i.e., Sarita's and Omar's
accounts do not have balances in the range of interest).

Running the source code of process-accounts.py

```
[BetterPython]$ python process-accounts.py accounts.csv
Account: 8213593023
  Owner: David
Balance: $5,181.32
```

After a while, our vendor introduces overdraft balances, and hence decides to change
the format so that balances are always shown with a leading plus or minus sign.

Data in file *accounts-new.csv*

```
Balance,AccountNum,Owner
+2913.94,3850234082,Omar
+9102.53,0028382910,Sarita
+5181.32,8213593023,David
-1002.26,4890094375,Juana
...more rows...
```

The program as written will not match any lines. So one might come up with a *clever*
idea to let all the re.match() calls look for the extra leading plus rather than change them
throughout the code. It's easy to do.

Source code of monkey_plus.py

```
import re
from re import match as _match
```

```
def match_positive(pat, s, flags=0):
    return _match(rf"\+{pat}", s, flags)


re.match = match_positive
```

If we add the single line `import monkey_plus` to the top of our script, creating `process-accounts2.py`, it now processes the new format (in *all* the hypothetical functions within the script that utilize `re.match()`, not only in `get_5k_balances()`).

Running the source code of `process-accounts2.py`

```
[BetterPython]$ python process-accounts2.py accounts-new.csv
Account: 8213593023
  Owner: David
Balance: $5,181.32
```

A clever programmer is tempted to notice that they control all of the code within `process-accounts2.py` and are confident that the only place where `re.match()` is used is in matching balances (or in any case, matching numbers preceded by a plus or a minus sign).

So far, nothing broke. But the clever programmer of this narration decides that they would like to add a switch to control which of the many functions available are used to process the data files that match the new vendor format. A reasonable program might be the following.

Source code of `process-accounts3.py`

```
import re
import monkey_plus
import argparse


def get_5k_balances(rows):
    # ... same as previously shown ...


# ... many more functions ...


if __name__ == "__main__":
    parser = argparse.ArgumentParser()
    parser.add_argument("datafile", type=str, help="CSV data file")
    parser.add_argument(
        "-f", "--function", action="store", default="get_5k_balances")
    args = parser.parse_args()
```

```
func = eval(args.function)
for account in func(open(args.datafile)):
    print(account)
```

Unfortunately, running this program gets us this.

Running the source code of `process-accounts3.py`

```
[BetterPython]$ python process-accounts3.py accounts-new.csv
usage: process-accounts3.py [-h] [-f FUNCTION] datafile
process-accounts3.py: error: the following arguments
    are required: datafile
```

It's easy at this point to start down a wild goose chase of trying to figure out how the arguments for `argparse` might be wrong. Or wonder whether the admittedly too clever `eval()` to get the function object from its name is amiss.

None of those issues is the mistake here, though. What has happened is that somewhere buried inside the "protected" (i.e., leading single underscore, and not exported) functions used to implement `argparse` there are uses of `re.match()`. One might even miss this looking at the source code since that module had used `import re as _re`, and therefore the calls are actually to `_re.match()`. Even so, the monkeypatching has badly broken a completely unrelated module—in this case, one in the standard library—in a way that is far from obvious, in code we did not necessarily even suspect would use our altered function. It's the same module *object* that is mutated by monkeypatching, it doesn't matter what name it happens to be bound to in different indirect imports.

The example provided in this discussion is a bit artificial. You probably would not be inclined to inject a new version of a function into a standard library module. However, you might be inclined to inject a function (or class attribute, or method, module constant, etc.) into a slightly obscure third-party library you are utilizing that does *almost but not quite* what you want. Quite likely you might inject a version derived from the provided version, as in the example. This risks unpleasant surprises when a completely different dependency turns out to also utilize that library, in ways that do not know about your alteration.

The actual best approach in situations of this sort is to bite the bullet and simply replace all relevant uses of, for example, `re.match()` in your code. If you decide to define a function such as `match_positive()` within your codebase, that can copy the signature of the original version and is a straightforward search-and-replace to utilize, whenever possible, and indeed *almost always*, it is better to leave the provided module function untouched.

5.3 Getters and Setters

In some programming languages—notably C++ and Java—a common pattern is to control access to private or protected variables, but to expose "getter" and "setter" methods.

In Python it is a mistake to use this pattern, although one sees such code written by programmers coming from other languages relatively often.

At first glance, my admonition against getters and setters might seem to contradict that in Chapter 4, *Advanced Python Usage*, in the section "Directly Accessing a Protected Attribute." There I advised against directly modifying pseudo-protected (i.e., one leading underscore) or pseudo-private (i.e., two leading underscores) instance attributes. I use "pseudo-" in the prior sentence because, of course, in Python you are never truly prevented from reading or modifying these (other than by convention and mild name mangling).

In so-called "bondage-and-discipline languages" like Java, the intention is to prevent users of a class from doing something they are not *supposed to*. In contrast, a common saying among Pythonistas is "We're all adults here." That is, the creator of a class may include *access advisories* by using single or double leading underscores, but these are not *access modifiers* in the style of C and Java (besides "protected" and "private", C—and Visual Basic also—includes "friend" as an end run around other access modifiers).

If an attribute of a Python instance contains one or two leading underscores, it is not because the creator of the class tries to guarantee you won't access it, but simply as a way of indicating that the attribute might disappear in the next version of their class, or its meaning or values might be altered in ways that are not guaranteed by documented and public APIs. Also, perhaps the meaning of that attribute with an access advisory might actually do something subtly different than what you might initially assume. The class author is making you no promises about that attribute.

Circling back to getters and setters, let's look at a quick example of such an antipattern in Python. The following *works*, of course; it merely feels non-idiomatic.

Writing Java in Python antipattern

```python
class GetterSetterExample:
    def __init__(self, value):
        self._value = value

    def get_value(self):
        return self._value

    def set_value(self, new_val):
        self._value = new_val
```

Even if these extra methods took additional actions, this would not feel like good Python. Yes, you should not muck with `._value`, but if an indirect mechanism to have guarded access to it is needed, *properties* provide a much more natural style.

For a slightly more fleshed out example than `GetterSetterExample`, let's suppose we want a `Rectangle` class, but with the special constraint that if we imagine the rectangle having a lower-left corner at the origin, no part of the rectangle falls outside a circle with a given radius. This is illustrated in Figure 5.1. In Pythonic style, we might write this as follows.

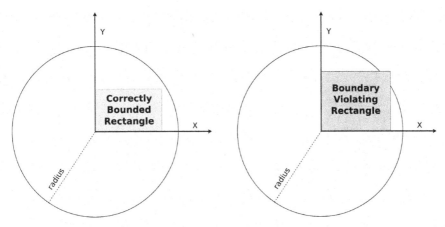

Figure 5.1   Valid and invalid rectangles according to diagonal length rule.

Writing Pythonic Python

```python
from sys import stderr
from math import sqrt

class BoundedRectangle:
    def __init__(self, x, y, radius=1):
        assert x > 0 and y > 0 and radius > 0      # ❶
        assert sqrt(x**2 + y**2) <= radius
        self._x = x
        self._y = y
        self._radius = radius                       # ❷

    @property
    def x(self):
        return self._x

    @x.setter                                       # ❸
    def x(self, new_x):
        if new_x < 0 or sqrt(new_x**2 + self._y**2) > self._radius:
            print("Rectangle bounds violated", file=stderr)
            return
        self._x = new_x

    @property
    def y(self):
        return self._y
```

```
    @y.setter
    def y(self, new_y):
        if new_y < 0 or sqrt(new_y**2 + self._x**2) > self._radius:
            print("Rectangle bounds violated", file=stderr)
            return
        self._y = new_y

    @property
    def area(self):
        return self._x * self._y
```

❶ Production code might do something more than assert invariants.

❷ By design, no mechanism is provided to change radius after initialization.

❸ A "setter" still has that name in its decorator, but not in its API.

It wouldn't be unreasonable to notice that we saved no code in defining the class, nor even did it become more readable or obvious. The Pythonic savings are for *users* of the class:

```
>>> from BoundedRectangle import BoundedRectangle
>>> rect = BoundedRectangle(0.65, 0.30)
>>> rect.x, rect.y, rect.area
(0.65, 0.3, 0.195)
>>> rect.y = 0.25
>>> rect.x, rect.y, rect.area
(0.65, 0.25, 0.1625)
>>> rect.y = 0.8
Rectangle bounds violated
>>> rect.x, rect.y, rect.area
(0.65, 0.25, 0.1625)
```

The quick summary of this section is that using properties—either read-only as with .area or read/write as with .x and .y—provides a simpler and more Pythonic API for users of classes. It remains the case that accessing "protected" attributes such as ._radius violates the *advice* of the class creator and might produce unpredictable behavior (i.e., in this particular class, the radius is intended to be set only on initialization).

5.4 It's Easier to Ask for Forgiveness Than Permission

Admiral Grace Hopper, who invented or popularized linkers, machine-independent programming languages, and the term *bug* in the programming sense, also famously commented: "It's easier to ask forgiveness than it is to get permission."

In the Python world—and to some degree within other programming language communities—the contrasting acronyms EAFP and LBYL (look before you leap) are commonly used. In fact, the official Python documentation describes this (https://docs.python.org/3/glossary.html#term-EAFP)[3]:

> Easier to ask for forgiveness than permission. This common Python coding style assumes the existence of valid keys or attributes and catches exceptions if the assumption proves false. This clean and fast style is characterized by the presence of many try and except statements. The technique contrasts with the LBYL style common to many other languages such as C.
>
> **— Python Documentation, Glossary**

In the main, this discussion is merely a moderate expansion of the official documentation. As with some other concerns of this book, preferring EAFP is merely a rough rule of thumb; using LBYL is certainly not *categorically* a mistake. However, if you find yourself writing an LBYL pattern, it is definitely worth asking yourself whether it might better be expressed in an EAFP style.

For a simple example, suppose that you have files with wordlists, one word per line. As often in this book, I've used the SOWPODS wordlist (https://gnosis.cx/better/data /sowpods) to randomly select words for the simple code shown. Specifically, I've variously run a command similar to shuf sowpods | head -50 > 50-words, in a separate terminal:

```
>>> def total_length(words_file):
...     total = 0
...     while word := words_file.readline():
...         total += len(word.strip())  # remove trailing LF
...     return total
...
>>> words1 = open("data/50-words")
>>> words2 = open("data/50-more-words")
>>> total_length(words1)
454
>>> total_length(words2)
444
```

It's a simple function, but it does something sensible. However, there are a lot of ways this function can go amiss:

```
>>> total_length(problem1)
Traceback (most recent call last):
```

---

3. My lovely colleague, and writer of this book's Foreword, Alex Martelli, contributed these lovely acronyms early in the evolution of Python's philosophy, perhaps a year or two on either side of 2000.

```
[...]
ValueError: I/O operation on closed file.

>>> total_length(problem2)
Traceback (most recent call last):
[...]
AttributeError: 'PosixPath' object has no attribute 'readline'

>>> total_length(problem3)
Traceback (most recent call last):
[...]
UnicodeDecodeError: 'utf-8' codec can't decode byte 0xe6 in
  position 2: invalid continuation byte

>>> total_length(problem4)
Traceback (most recent call last):
[...]
OSError: [Errno 5] Input/output error
```

An LBYL approach would be to check for the problems before attempting to call
total_length() with the object you have in hand. This might start as:

```
if not hasattr(words_file, "readline"):
    print("words_file is not a file-like object")
elif words_file.closed:
    print("words_file is a closed file")
else:
    print(f"Aggregate length is {total_length(words_file)}")
```

The problem here is that we have not even checked for those exceptions I have
specifically thought of and created in my REPL session, let alone all of those I have so far
failed to consider. I honestly do not know a mechanism other than trying to answer the
question of whether some unread bytes will be decodable as UTF-8 (nor from another
encoding, if specified in open()). Nor do I know how to ask in advance whether I/O
might fail. In the above REPL, I created that condition by putting a file on a thumb drive
and physically removing it; similar issues occur on network filesystems and in other
circumstances.

The EAFP approach is simply more flexible and more Pythonic here. For example:

```
try:
    print(f"Aggregate length is {total_length(words_file)}")
except AttributeError as err:
    print(f"words_file is not file-like: {type(words_file)}")
```

```
except ValueError as err:
    if hasattr(words_file, "closed") and words_file.closed:
        print("words_file is a closed file")
    else:
        print(f"ValueError encounted with message {type(err)}")
except UnicodeDecodeError as err:
    print(f"UnicodeDecodeError: {err}")
except OSError as err:
    print(f"OSError (probably I/O problem): {err}")
except Exception as err:
    print(f"Other error type: {err} {type(err)}")
```

This EAFP code handles *more* cases than does LBYL, but it also handles absolutely every failure with a generic fallback. We are able to provide different remediation of the problem for every exception that we know about, and some very general fallback for those problems we did not think about when first writing the code.

5.5 Structural Pattern Matching

Like a number of other sections of this book, this is a discussion of a sin of omission rather than a sin of commission. For a great many years before PEPs 384, 385, and 386, which introduced structural pattern matching to Python 3.10, beautiful and Pythonic code was written without this newish feature being available. In Chapter 1, *Looping Over the Wrong Things*, the discussion of the walrus operator (introduced in Python 3.8) similarly showed examples where code can simply be *better* by using newer constructs.

In the spirit of this chapter's title, you *could* use if, elif, and else statements to express everything that the match/case statements do. Indeed, if is certainly not going away, and it will remain the preferred pattern for a great many purposes. Let's look at a brief example where the structural pattern matching makes code more readable and shorter. For this, we will analyze some responses from the requests library (whose virtues are discussed in Chapter 8, *Security*).

Unpacking a response object

```
from requests.models import Response
def process_resp(resp):
    match resp:
        case Response(status_code=200, headers=headers) \
                if "json" in headers['Content-Type']:
            print("Received JSON response")
            match resp.json():
                case [*args]:
                    print(f" -> {', '.join(args[:5])}, ...")
                case {**kws}:
```

```
            print(f" -> {', '.join(kws.keys())}, ...")
        case str() as json:
            print(f" -> {json[:30]}...")
    case Response(status_code=200, text=text):
        print(f"Received {len(text.splitlines())} lines")
    case Response(status_code=404, text=text):
        print(f"Not Found with message {text.splitlines()[0]}...")
    case Response(status_code=status_code):
        print(f"Received status code {status_code}")
    case _:
        print("'Response' has no status code (wrong type?)")
```

It's easy enough to use this function, for example:

```
>>> import requests
>>> # Substitute some URL component path for RESOURCE below
>>> resp = requests.get("https://gnosis.cx/better/RESOURCE")
>>> process_resp(resp)                              # ❶
```

❶ Something will be printed here, depending on the response.

If you are not familiar with the syntax, it can be somewhat surprising. When we name the `Response` class and provide what looks like initialization parameters, we are actually *either* checking values *or* binding names within the nested block. For example, in the first clause, `Response(status_code=200, headers=headers)`, we first check whether the matched `resp` object has `resp.status_code == 200`; if that holds, we then bind `headers` to `resp.headers` within the block.

In the first case, we need to check additional features of the matched `resp`, which we can do with an extra `if` clause. If that case does not hold, including the `if` clause, then Python checks the next case, and if it is nonetheless a 200 status code, it binds `text` to `resp.text`. Following that, we consider 404 codes in a similar manner. If the first cases are not matched, we generically look for whatever status code was available; but we also fall back to a default case if the "response" lacks any status code at all.

Within the case that contains JSON data, we use another `match` against the actual type of the deserialized JSON. It might be either a JSON array (i.e., Python `list`) or a JSON object (i.e., Python `dict`). We match that by providing templates for what a list or dictionary looks like, capturing the contents as names `args` or `kws`. In the case a JSON string is the data, we can use the `as` clause to bind that to a name in the block scope (yes, this is strange that the empty string matches all strings; but it's convenient).

Let's see the function in use:

```
>>> import requests
>>> basename = "https://gnosis.cx/better/data"
>>> process_resp(requests.get(f"{basename}/sowpods"))
```

```
Received 267752 lines
>>> process_resp(requests.get(f"{basename}/sowpods.json"))
Received JSON response
 -> aa, aah, aahed, aahing, aahs, ...
>>> process_resp(requests.get(f"{basename}/sowpods.NOT_FOUND"))
Not Found with message <!DOCTYPE html>...
>>> process_resp(requests.get('http://localhost/unauthorized'))
Received status code 401                             # ❶
>>> process_resp(42)
'Response' has no status code (wrong type?)
```

❶ I created a local server and route to return a 401.

You *could*, of course, write equivalent code using only `if`-style switching. I leave it as an exercise for readers to actually write such code. You will most certainly find that such a version is considerably longer, more nested, and littered with `isinstance()` checks and assignments to temporary variables within blocks.

Per *The Zen of Python*, "Beautiful is better than ugly." It's a mistake to choose the latter.

5.6 Regular Expressions and Catastrophic Backtracking

Regular expressions can be extremely nuanced, and are often a concise and powerful way to express patterns in text. This book cannot get far into an explanation or tutorial on regular expressions, but my title *Regular Expression Puzzles and AI Coding Assistants* (Manning Publications, 2023) contains a tutorial introduction in its appendix; obviously I recommend that title.

Readers might have worked with regular expressions to a fair extent without having fallen into the trap of *catastrophic backtracking*. When you do hit this issue, it can be a very unpleasant surprise. Patterns that work well and quickly in many circumstances can start taking longer, and become worse at an exponential rate as the strings matched against grow longer.

For this example, suppose that we have a file in which each line contains a non-descending list of (two-digit) numbers, each separated by a space. We'd like to identify all the numbers up to, but not including, 90 from each line. Some lines will match and others will not. In this hypothetical file format, each line also has a label at its start. Let's look at an example of such a file (in the presentation here, some lines are wrapped because of book margins; in the file itself each labeled line is a physical line).

Data in file *numbers.txt*

```
A: 08 12 22 27 29 38 39 43 47 51 52 73 74 78 78 79 80 83 86 87 88 89
B: 03 04 04 05 16 18 23 26 30 31 33 34 35 36 52 61 63 68 69 72 75 80
   82 83 83 90 92 92 92 95 97
```

```
C: 01 07 14 19 27 30 34 36 36 38 44 47 47 50 51 54 58 60 61 62 82 83
   83 95
D: 05 10 13 17 30 31 42 50 56 61 63 66 76 90 91 91 93
E: 03 21 23 24 26 31 31 31 33 36 38 38 39 42 49 55 68 79 81
F: 04 08 13 14 14 16 19 21 25 26 27 34 36 39 43 45 45 50 51 62 66 67
   71 75 79 82 88
G: 03 10 27 49 51 64 70 71 82 86 94
H: 27 31 38 42 43 43 48 50 63 72 83 87 90 92
I: 12 16 18 19 38 39 40 43 54 55 63 73 74 74 75 77 78 79 88
```

As a naive version of this program, we might try defining the pattern:

```
pat = re.compile(r"^(.+: )(.+ )+(?=9.)")
```

Now let's try to process this file using this pattern. Presumably in real code we would take some action using the groups in the match, beyond printing out the fact it matched or failed.

Timing the regular expression matching

```
>>> from time import monotonic
>>> for line in open("data/numbers.txt"):
...     start = monotonic()
...     if match := re.search(pat, line):
...         print(f"Matched line {line.split(':')[0]} "
...             f"in {monotonic()-start:0.3f} seconds")
...     else:
...         print(f"Fail on line {line.split(':')[0]} "
...             f"in {monotonic()-start:0.3f} seconds")
...
Fail on line A in 0.226 seconds
Matched line B in 0.000 seconds
Matched line C in 0.000 seconds
Matched line D in 0.000 seconds
Fail on line E in 0.026 seconds
Fail on line F in 6.738 seconds
Matched line G in 0.000 seconds
Matched line H in 0.000 seconds
Fail on line I in 0.025 seconds
```

We can notice a few things. In the first place, the actual matches always take little time (less than a millisecond), while most failures take a moderate fraction of a second. Except in the case of line F, which took almost 7 seconds. It may not be obvious, but in fact if line F had one more number less than 90, it would take twice as long. And one more number after that, another doubling. Exponential behavior gets bad quickly.

Note   Visualizing backtracking

Understanding what regular expression engines are doing can certainly be confusing. In particular, NFAs (nondeterministic finite automata) that perform backtracking match in ways that are not immediately intuitive. Let's look at a simpler and non-catastrophic example, step by step (in Figure 5.2).

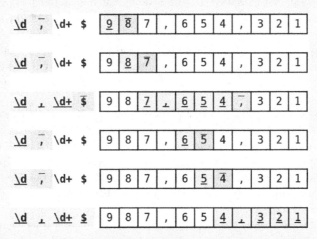

Figure 5.2   Matching thousands of a comma-separated longer number.

We might have a long number string that uses commas to separate at the thousands, millions, billions, etc., according to a Western convention of grouping by three digits. The pattern r"\d,\d+$" should satisfy this.

In the illustration, characters and regex subpatterns that match appear underlined and with a green background. Characters and regex subpatterns that fail appear overlined and with a red background.

In order to match, the regex engine scans forward to find a digit, then expects a comma to follow. When that fails, it abandons the partial match, and scans again for a later digit. Once it finds a digit-comma sequence, it looks for repeated digits. Initially, it finds a subsequence of the match, but fails when the end-of-string is not reached. So back to scanning for the initial digit again, *giving back* part of the match.

Let's think about what is happening in the number sequences example. Since the subpattern r"(.+)+" can actually match any characters, it first tries to match the entire string, then finding no lookahead of r"(?=9.)" it *backtracks* to consider a bit less. Perhaps after that backtracking, it finds that the next unmatched characters are "9.". If not, it tries backtracking more as the *one-or-more* quantifier allows taking fewer repetitions. However, after each backtracking, the pattern tries to search forward with more repetitions, keeping the place of the last backtrack. When that doesn't succeed, we unwind the tail, and backtrack more on the head.

In a manner similar to the famous Tower of Hanoi puzzle (https://en.wikipedia.org /wiki/Tower_of_Hanoi), every possible state of head versus tail needs to be explored before the pattern can ultimately fail. One might have an intuition that the problem can be solved by using a non-greedy repeating group. Intuitively, it feels like maybe the pattern will try to backtrack less hard if we aren't greedy in matching as much as possible with the +. However, if we set the pattern to r"^(.+:)(.+?)+(?=9.)", the time actually gets a little bit worse (about 10 seconds on my machine; but an exponential increase with length either way). If you think again about the problem, you'll realize that matching as little as possible instead of as much as possible doesn't actually prevent backtracking since a non-match overall remains "not possible" for the regex engine. The same possibility space still needs to be explored.

In this exact problem, there is actually an easy solution. If we use the pattern r"^(.+:)(\d+?)+(?=9\d)", all the times become negligible. We match *some digits* followed by space rather than *any sequence including space*. However, most of the time when you hit this problem it is not as simple as the example. Rather, the most typical situation is when you consider alternative sub-patterns but do not realize that they can sometimes actually match the same strings (which is effectively what we did with the (.+) in which the dot can also be a space).

The general form of the "overlapping-alternatives" problem is (meta-syntactically) («pat1»|«pat2»|«pat3»)+ where each of the patterns might themselves be complex and not make it obvious they can match the same thing. As a simple example, consider a subpattern like \b(a\S*|\S*f\S*|\S*z)\b; that is, words that start with "a", words that have an "f" in the middle, and words that end with "z". Writing it in English it's easy to see that "alferez" (a high-ranking official in medieval Iberia) matches every alternative. If the string contains many repetitions of that word, a full match would backtrack across all the options.

There is not one completely general solution to these kinds of problems or mistakes. Sometimes a lookahead for an easier-to-match but less specific pattern can precede the real search and allow it to fail quickly. For example, in the current goal, we might simply generically assert a space-9 occurs somewhere before really matching: ^(?=.* 9)(.+:) (.+)+(?=9\d). This produces the correct answers and match groups, but always in a few microseconds for each line.

In Python 3.11, a very nice new feature was introduced to the re module. Actually, two closely related features: possessive quantifiers and atomic groups. In both cases, the meaning is "match or fail once, but don't backtrack." Despite the related purpose of these constructs, it's not obvious that they lend themselves to the current goal. But becoming aware of them will benefit you in rewriting many problem patterns.

5.7 Wrapping Up

There is heterogeneity in the mistakes of this chapter. Python allows and enables you to do a great many things, even some that are generally unwise. Some of these techniques are particularly tempting to *advanced* Python programmers, or at least those on the edge of being advanced; these are not generally beginners' mistakes. Give someone a new hammer, and every problem starts to look like a thumb.

The ability to utilize metaclasses is certainly an advanced feature. Moreover, it is even an advanced feature that has dedicated syntax rather than simply emerging from the object model of Python *accidentally*. In contrast, monkeypatching is a somewhat advanced capability, but one that more or less follows automatically from what it means to be an object in Python. In that case, the capability exists mostly because Python's developers did not take large efforts to prevent it more than because they designed the language *for* it. Either way, either of these techniques should be used rarely, at most.

Writing getters and setters is not an especially advanced technique. They are rather ordinary methods. But the habit of using them is almost always the result of vestiges of other languages carrying over to the detriment of idiomatic Python. Properties, or just direct attribute access, are always more clear and more beautiful. To some degree, the same can be said of the choice between LBYL and EAFP coding styles. I will confess that an attitude characterized by an old saying, "Exceptions are not that exceptional," is not as clear a consensus among experienced Pythonistas as I think it should be. While I fall on one side of a possible divide, there are a great many situations where checking *everything* in advance is infeasible and fragile, and both local- and outer-scope exception handling are essential.

The remaining mistakes here are first one of not taking advantage of a feature new to Python 3.10. Structural pattern matching with `match` and `case` is concise and expressive, and very often now just much more clear in expression of intent. It's often a little bit faster than walls of `elif` clauses. The final mistake about backtracking in regular expressions is just tricky. Using regular expressions wisely, but moderately, is extremely powerful; not being aware of when they become dramatically slower is a lurking danger, but not one with a simple and categorical solution. The mistake discussion gives pointers on what to be conscious of when creating this potential hazard.

Picking the Right Data Structure

This chapter hopes to save its readers from unnecessarily difficult code by drawing attention to a number of useful data structures that Python beginners, and even many advanced language users, may be unaware of or merely tend to forget. Four of these data structures are contained in the Python standard library, in `collections`, and another is in `dataclasses` (sort of—we'll discuss that). The last mistake discussed looks at several additional, closely related, sequence (i.e., `list`-like) data structures that can sometimes be more efficient than lists. These are all built-ins or in standard library modules.

This book's longest discussion of mistakes comes in Chapter 7, *Misusing Data Structures*, in the section "Rolling Your Own Data Structures." That more advanced mistake goes into a great many pros and cons of creating custom data structures. Until you've *considered* all the standard library collections discussed in this chapter, and also the third-party libraries sortedcontainers (https://grantjenks.com/docs/sortedcontainers/) and pyrsistent (https://pyrsistent.readthedocs.io/en/latest/), you are most certainly premature in creating your own custom data structures.

Some of the discussions in this chapter—each about one particular data structure available in the Python standard library—are arranged a bit differently than other sections in this book. For each of them, a simple task using one of these simple data structures is shown; following that is the *mistake* represented by the longer, less readable, and sometimes notably slower code that would be needed to achieve the same goal without these data structures.

6.1 `collections.defaultdict`

In the very ancient history of Python (before 2.7), `collections.defaultdict` was available but `collections.Counter` was not; the use case that `Counter` has addressed since 2010 was met with a recommendation of "use `defaultdict`."

Both of these collections are subclasses of `dict` that add specialized capabilities. A default dictionary is only narrowly specialized, and in that sense is more general than `collections.Counter`, `collections.OrderedDict`, or `collections.UserDict`. The

latter two of these are worth reading about in the Python documentation
(https://docs.python.org/3/library/collections.html), but this book does not specifically
address them.

The "mistake" fixed by using `defaultdict` is simply that of using a repetitive and
overly verbose pattern that can be simplified. I often make this mistake of inelegance, and
hence feel the reminder is worthwhile.

When you work with plain dictionaries you often want to modify a mutable value
associated with a key. But before you can perform that modification, you need to check
whether the dictionary *has* the needed key in the first place. For example, let's work with
the SOWPODS wordlist used in various examples, and create a dictionary that maps first
letters to a collection of words starting with that letter:

```
>>> from random import choice, seed
>>> from pathlib import Path
>>> words = Path("data/sowpods").read_text().split()
>>> seed("first-letter")                             # ❶
>>> for _ in range(100):
...        word = choice(words)
...        first_letter = word[0]
...        if first_letter not in by_letter:
...            by_letter[first_letter] = set([word])
...        else:
...            by_letter[first_letter].add(word)
...
>>> by_letter.get("g", set())
set()
>>> by_letter.get("r", set())
{'repositors', 'rotating', 'resectional', 'reflectometry'}
```

❶ A seed is used simply so readers can replicate specific choices.

A similar pattern is also often used with `list` and `.append()`, and sometimes with
other collections and their corresponding method for including more items.

This pattern is perfectly workable, but is made better with `defaultdict`:

```
>>> first_letter = defaultdict(set)
>>> seed("first-letter")
>>> by_letter = defaultdict(set)
>>> for _ in range(100):
...        word = choice(words)
...        by_letter[word[0]].add(word)
...
>>> by_letter['g']
set()
```

```
>>> by_letter['r']
{'repositors', 'rotating', 'resectional', 'reflectometry'}
```

Not only collections can be used, but any callable. For example, recall the fanciful numerological function `word_number()` defined in Chapter 1, *Looping Over the Wrong Things*, in the section "(Rarely) Generate a List for Iteration." But here let's pretend that this function is actually computationally expensive and we'd like to avoid running it more often than needed (`@functools.lru_cache` and `@functools.cache` decorators also provide a useful way of achieving this task):

```
>>> def word_number(word):
...     magic = 0
...     for letter in word:
...         magic += 1 + ord(letter) - ord("a")
...     return magic
...
>>> word_magic = defaultdict(lambda: "<unknown>")
>>> word_magic["chillier"] = word_number("chillier")
>>> word_magic["snicker"] = word_number("snicker")
>>> word_magic["bonesetter"] = word_number("bonesetter")
>>> word_magic["overboiled"]
'<unknown>'
>>> word_magic["chillier"]
76
>>> word_magic
defaultdict(<function <lambda> at 0x7fab522b9bc0>, {'chillier': 76,
'snicker': 79, 'bonesetter': 123, 'overboiled': '<unknown>'})
```

In this particular example, however, we might want to go ahead and perform the calculation once to actually save the expensive calculation into the dictionary (the next example works with a regular `dict` as well):

```
>>> word_magic.setdefault("sternitic", word_number("sternitic"))
117
>>> word_magic
defaultdict(<function <lambda> at 0x7fab522b9bc0>, {'chillier': 76,
'snicker': 79, 'bonesetter': 123, 'overboiled': '<unknown>',
'sternitic': 117})
>>> word_magic.setdefault("overboiled", word_number("sternitic"))
'<unknown>'
```

Related to `defaultdict`, the standard, but largely overlooked, `dict.setdefault()` also provides a mechanism to retrieve a key if it exists, but set (and retrieve) it if it hadn't already. To circle back to the first paragraph of this discussion, a `Counter` resembles a `defaultdict` with the factory set to `int`, but adding additional methods.

6.2   `collections.Counter`

One of the loveliest collections in the `collections` module of the Python standard library is `Counter`. This is an implementation of a concept sometimes called a *multiset*, *bag*, or *mset* (https://en.wikipedia.org/wiki/Multiset). A very common use for counters is in conveniently creating what are often informally called histograms.[1] For this section and the next few, I present the solution (i.e., a Pythonic example) first, then the mistake.

6.2.1   The Solution

On my personal system, I have a small Python script called `histogram` that I use relatively frequently. Let's look at that entire script.

Source code of `histogram`

```
#!/usr/bin/env python
import re
from sys import argv, stdin
from collections import Counter

if '-w' in argv or '--word' in argv:               # ❶
    # Word histogram
    cleaned = re.sub(r'[^\w]', ' ', stdin.read())
    hist = Counter(cleaned.lower().split())
else:
    # Letter histogram
    cleaned = re.sub(r'[^\w]', ", stdin.read())
    hist = Counter(cleaned)

for item, count in hist.most_common():
    print(f"{count}\t{item}")
```

❶ `argparse`, `click`, `docopt`, or `typer` would allow more versatile switch handling.

I use this utility in manners such as the following (here combined with other shell utilities, such as `head`):

---

1. To be technical, a histogram is a representation of continuous data divided into *bins* by numeric value ranges (most commonly uniformly sized bins). Similar, but not identical, is a bar chart of the count or frequency of categorical data. The utility shown in this chapter is the latter.

```
[BetterPython]$ histogram < frontmatter | head -8
895     e
807     t
766     o
641     n
626     i
618     a
579     s
465     r
[BetterPython]$ histogram --word < frontmatter | head -8
65      the
52      of
47      to
43      a
42      in
42      python
29      and
26      i
```

I might even create a visualization this way, as in Figure 6.1 (the similarly small barchart utility, which uses matplotlib, is available from the book's website):

```
[BetterPython]$ histogram -w < frontmatter | head -8 | barchart
```

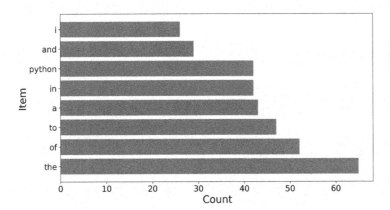

Figure 6.1   Word counts of this book's frontmatter.

The data shown will not be precisely accurate for the final version of this book's frontmatter, but it will be similar. In my script, I merely initialize a counter with iterables (either of letters or of words), and use the .most_common() method to order the objects being counted. In larger programs, you are likely to call the method .update() repeatedly on an existing counter, each time increasing the count for each object in the passed-in iterable. The .subtract() method decrements these counts. For example:

```
>>> from collections import Counter
>>> count = Counter()
>>> count.update("gildings")
>>> count.update("delated")
>>> count.most_common()
[('d', 3), ('g', 2), ('i', 2), ('l', 2), ('e', 2), ('n', 1),
('s', 1), ('a', 1), ('t', 1)]
>>> count.subtract("antennas")
>>> count.most_common()
[('d', 3), ('g', 2), ('i', 2), ('l', 2), ('e', 1), ('s', 0),
('t', 0), ('a', -1), ('n', -2)]
>>> del count["n"]
>>> count.most_common()
[('d', 3), ('g', 2), ('i', 2), ('l', 2), ('e', 1), ('s', 0),
('t', 0), ('a', -1)]
>>> count.most_common(4)
[('d', 3), ('g', 2), ('i', 2), ('l', 2)]
```

All the letters (or any hashable objects) that have never been seen are not present, but each one that has been seen indicates the number of times it has been seen. Because the code uses .subtract(), we might reach a zero or negative count. Since Counter is a subclass of dict it still has all the usual dictionary behaviors, such as deleting a key, if we wish to use those.

6.2.2 The Mistake

If you didn't know about collections.Counter you could still implement the same program, of course. It would merely be less elegant. For example:

```
>>> import re
>>> from pathlib import Path
>>> from operator import itemgetter
>>> frontmatter = Path("frontmatter").read_text()
>>> hist = {}
>>> for word in cleaned.split():
...     if word in hist:
...         hist[word] += 1
...     else:
...         hist[word] = 1
...
```

```
>>> counts = sorted(hist.items(), key=itemgetter(1), reverse=True)
>>> counts[:8]
[('the', 65), ('of', 52), ('to', 47), ('a', 43), ('in', 42),
('python', 42), ('and', 29), ('i', 26)]
```

The result we want is definitely achievable without `collections.Counter`. However, we need to get more clever with comprehensions, custom sort order, slicing, and so on than if we use a counter. The non-counter approach also requires two to five lines for each operation that is a one-method call on a counter.

6.3 collections.deque

A deque is a thread-safe generalization of stacks and queues. That is to say, while a `collections.deque` has almost the same API as does the built-in `list`, it adds `.*left()` versions of several methods of lists. Crucially, even though lists *can* do these same things—for example, `list.pop(0)` does the same thing as `deque.popleft()`, and `list.insert(0, x)` does the same thing as `deque.appendleft()`—a deque does them *efficiently*. Both FIFO (first in, first out) and LIFO (last in, first out) operations work well with deques.

In Chapter 7, *Misusing Data Structures*, the first two sections treat situations in which ill-advised uses of lists can have quadratic complexity (see the note in the first section of Chapter 3, *A Grab Bag of Python Gotchas*, and https://en.wikipedia.org/wiki /Big_O_notation for discussions of "quadratic"). This section foreshadows those discussions.

Underneath the implementation of `collection.deque` is a *doubly linked list* rather than an *array of references* (as with `list`). This makes appending or popping from both ends efficient, but it also makes indexing less efficient than on lists, and slices are unavailable (because providing them would falsely imply efficiency in the eyes of the `deque` designer, Raymond Hettinger). However, `deque` provides an interesting `.rotate()` method that lists lack (also because they are inefficient there). Neither `deque` nor `list` is a "pure win," but rather provides a trade-off. The complexity of some common operations is presented in Table 6.1.

Table 6.1   Efficiency of common operations on deque and list.

Operation	deque	list
Indexing at a position (`stuff[p]`)	O(N)	O(1)
Popping/appending item at left side	O(1)	O(N)
Popping/appending item at right side	O(1)	O(1) amortized
Inserting/deleting from middle	O(N)	O(N)

For this section and the few around it, I present the solution (i.e., a Pythonic example) first, then the mistake.

6.3.1   The Solution

An example given in the Python documentation (https://docs.python.org/3/library/collections.html) shows using a deque for a moving average. This is a good, simple case where we'd like to be able to append to one end and pop from the other. Astute readers will notice that for the narrow task of the script shown, we do not actually need a collection at all; imagine, however, that other operations are also performed within the script and that you hence need the concrete collection rather than only the total.

Source code of code/moving-average-deque

```
#!/usr/bin/env python
from sys import stdin, argv
from collections import deque

window = int(argv[1]) if len(argv) > 1 else 5
nums = deque()

# Pre-populate deque with first window of numbers
for n, num in zip(range(window), stdin):
    nums.append(int(num.rstrip()))

# Calculate initial sum and mean
total = sum(nums)
print(total/window)

# For each new number read, print the moving average
for num in stdin:
    total -= nums.popleft()
    nums.append(int(num.rstrip()))
    total += nums[-1]
    print(total/window)
```

Using this utility is simple:

```
[BetterPython]$ echo "4 6 2 1 3 10 11 35 32" |
                tr ' ' '\n' |                    # ❶
                moving-average-deque
3.2
4.4
```

```
5.4
12.0
18.2
```

❶ The tr shell utility here converts spaces to newlines.

6.3.2 The Mistake

You *could* implement this program using lists with only a few characters' difference, and the utility would become dramatically worse.

Source code of code/moving-average-list

```
#!/usr/bin/env python
from sys import stdin, argv

window = int(argv[1]) if len(argv) > 1 else 5
nums = []

# Pre-populate deque with first window of numbers
for n, num in zip(range(window), stdin):
    nums.append(int(num.rstrip()))

# Calculate initial sum and mean
total = sum(nums)
print(total/window)

# For each new number read, print the moving average
for num in stdin:
    total -= nums.pop(0)
    nums.append(int(num.rstrip()))
    total += nums[-1]
    print(total/window)
```

For small inputs, this is not important, and the behavior is the same:

```
[BetterPython]$ echo "4 6 2 1 3 10 11 35 32" |
                tr ' ' '\n' |
                moving-average-list
3.2
4.4
5.4
12.0
18.2
```

The four-line script `numbers` is available at the book's website, as is `moving-average-deque`. The argument to `numbers` is the number of numbers in the [1, 1000] interval to generate randomly:

```
% numbers 7 | moving-average-list
510.0
571.2
670.8
```

However, looking at a larger window and more data, we notice an important difference in the two implementations of a moving average algorithm:

```
[BetterPython]$ time numbers 1_000_000 |          # ❶
                   moving-average-deque 100_000 >/dev/null

real    0m0.869s

[BetterPython]$ time numbers 1_000_000 |
                   moving-average-list 100_000 >/dev/null

real    0m18.025s
```

❶ The Unix-isms of `time` and `/dev/null` are incidental; we just want to time the script, but don't care about output.

Increasing efficiency by 20x is wonderful, of course. Along with it, though, we get thread safety, which is very often important in a context of queues and stacks. When, for example, we pop a value from a collection, a Python `list` does not guarantee that two threads don't pop the same item, whereas a `deque` does. When you write multithreaded code, you need to think carefully about whether the data structures shared among threads enable deadlocks, race conditions, and other concurrency pitfalls; picking the right data structure does not eliminate these concerns, but picking the wrong one almost guarantees them. Broader concerns around concurrency are outside the scope of this book, but the appendix, *Topics for Other Books*, provides a very brief recap of the Python concurrency ecosystem.

6.4   `collections.ChainMap`

The lovely object `collections.ChainMap` is a sort of *virtual mapping*. It provides an abstraction for looking through multiple dictionaries (or other mappings) successively. When using a `ChainMap` we avoid needing to copy any data and also avoid modification of the underlying dictionaries outside of the proper context for doing so.

For this section, as with the last few, we will look at a Python solution first, followed by the mistake it fixes.

6.4.1 The Solution

A common pattern for configuration options is to have multiple dictionaries that could potentially contain information, with each overriding a previous one according to the business logic of an application. Using ChainMap we can accomplish exactly that:

```
>>> from collections import ChainMap
>>> default = {
...     "timeout-secs": 30,
...     "environment": "development",
...     "env-file": "/opt/.env-default"
... }
>>> application = {
...     "timeout-secs": 15,
...     "application-name": "FooBarMaker",
...     "env-file": "/user/local/foobar/.env"
... }
>>> user = {
...     "timeout-secs": 60,
...     "env-file": "/home/david/.env-foobar",
...     "username": "David"
... }

>>> settings = ChainMap(user, application, default)
>>> settings["timeout-secs"]                        # ❶
60
>>> settings["username"]                            # ❷
'David'
>>> settings["environment"]                         # ❸
'development'
>>> settings.get("application-name", "app")         # ❹
'FooBarMaker'
>>> settings.get("session", "Unknown")              # ❺
'Unknown'
```

❶ First mapping provides the key, others ignored

❷ Only first mapping has the key

❸ Last mapping has the key

❹ Middle mapping has the key, so return value

❺ No mappings have the key, fall back to argument

This becomes even more useful if some of the mappings might change at runtime. For example:

```
>>> user['username'] = "Dr. Mertz"
>>> settings["username"]
'Dr. Mertz'
>>> user['application-name'] = "DavidMaker"
>>> settings["application-name"]
'DavidMaker'
```

The mappings included in a `ChainMap` are dynamically referenced. We can examine which they are:

```
>>> settings.maps
[{'timeout-secs': 60, 'env-file': '/home/david/.env-foobar',
'username': 'Dr. Mertz', 'application-name': 'DavidMaker'},
{'timeout-secs': 15, 'application-name': 'FooBarMaker', 'env-file':
'/user/local/foobar/.env'}, {'timeout_secs': 30, 'environment':
'development', 'env-file': '/opt/.env-default'}]
```

The method `collections.ChainMap.new_child()` also allows you to add additional maps to the beginning of the search sequence. In principle, the `.maps` attribute can be modified as well, but it is usually less clean to do so (creating a new `ChainMap` is nearly free).

6.4.2 The Mistake

Doing what `ChainMap` does "manually" is possible, but cumbersome. For example, we might write a function to accomplish the same purpose:

```
def search_dicts(key, default, *dicts):
...     for dict_ in dicts:
...         if key in dict_:
...             return dict_[key]
...     return default
...
>>> search_dicts("timeout-secs", 120, user, application, default)
60                                              # ❶
>>> search_dicts("environment", "prod", user, application, default)
'development'                                   # ❷
>>> search_dicts("session", "Unknown", user, application, default)
'Unknown'                                       # ❸
```

❶ Located value from user

❷ Located value from `default`

❸ Fall back to argument

This isn't a large amount of code, but you need to call it each time, rather than carrying the sequence of mappings around in a single object. Moreover, this is effectively only `collections.ChainMap.get()` and not the full collection of `dict`-like methods a `ChainMap` provides.

Worse than a utility function such as the one shown is manually updating dictionaries. For example, if we were to do this, we would indeed get a mapping with the collection of values we wish to use:

```
>>> default.update(application)
>>> default.update(user)
>>> default
{'timeout-secs': 60, 'environment': 'development', 'env-file':
'/home/david/.env-foobar', 'application-name': 'DavidMaker',
'username': 'Dr. Mertz'}
```

However, after merging `application` and `user` into `default`, we have lost a record of what might have earlier been inside `default` and what might have been absent. For many applications, retaining that information is valuable.

One might try to remedy this by using a brand-new name (assume all the initial mappings are reset to the initial values shown earlier):

```
>>> settings = default.copy()
>>> settings is default
False
>>> settings.update(application)
>>> settings.update(user)
>>> settings
{'timeout-secs': 60, 'environment': 'development', 'env-file':
'/home/david/.env-foobar', 'application-name': 'FooBarMaker',
'username': 'David'}
```

This is perhaps better than the last mistaken version since `default` has its initial configuration maintained. Still, if the application updates one or more of the collected mappings, that is not reflected in `settings` unless we use the same few lines each time before checking `settings`.

6.5 Dataclasses and Namedtuples

Python's standard library includes two very useful data structures for storing "records" of related data elements. The first is namedtuples, which under the hood are simply subclasses of tuples, but with named fields. The second is dataclasses, which are simply Python classes with many dunders and other useful behaviors generated automatically in a concise way.

The things we can do with dataclasses and namedtuples can also be accomplished with the built-in types `dict` and `tuple`. Indeed, every `namedtuple` is simply a subclass of `tuple`, so it is genuinely the same type. However, using datatypes that allow readers to frame code very clearly as "records" improves readability and makes reasoning easier.

Very often, it is useful to work with a collection of data where each item has a fixed collection of fields, but we work with many such items (comparing, sorting, aggregating, etc.). Namedtuples and dataclasses have more parts than simple scalars—such as `float`, `int`, `str`, or `decimal.Decimal` or other special types—but are more similar to *datatypes* than to *data structures*. The most obvious difference between the two types this section discusses is that dataclasses are mutable while namedtuples are immutable.

Let's look at an example of record-oriented data. We often encounter such data in relational database tables, in CSV or fixed-width files, in formats like Apache Parquet or Apache Arrow, in JSON serialized records, and elsewhere. For extensive numeric analysis especially, a dataframe library such as Pandas or Polars is often useful. However, for this discussion we remain in pure-Python land.

The standard library module `csv` is often very useful for reading line-oriented, delimited textual data files. Despite the acronym standing for "comma-separated values" the module is perfectly happy to work with any delimiter you might have in your data files. The `csv` module is especially useful when character escaping is needed (the delimiter, and the escape and quoting characters themselves, have to be treated nonliterally). For the example in this discussion, we avoid that concern, by stipulation and by the actual format of the example file. In the archive for the book (https://gnosis.cx/better) we have a file with some information on per-nation demographics:

```
[data]$ wc -l population-data.txt
236 population-data.txt
[data]$ head -5 population-data.txt
Name|Population|Pct_Change_2023|Net_Change|Density_km3|Area_km2
China|1,439,323,776|0.39|5,540,090|153|9,388,211
India|1,380,004,385|0.99|13,586,631|464|2,973,190
United States|331,002,651|0.59|1,937,734|36|9,147,420
Indonesia|273,523,615|1.07|2,898,047|151|1,811,570
```

6.5.1 Using Namedtuples

Each line represents some sort of object with the various attributes on it, and the collection of lines should live in a collection such as `list` or `set` to perform group operations. Let's try one approach using `collections.namedtuple`:

```
>>> from collections import namedtuple
>>> from operator import attrgetter
```

```
>>> from statistics import mean

>>> with open("population-data.txt") as pop:
...     fields = pop.readline().strip().split("|")
...     Nation = namedtuple("Nation", fields)
...     world_data = []
...     for line in pop:
...         line = line.replace(",", "")  # integers without sep
...         data = line.split("|")
...         typed_data = [data[0]] + [float(v) for v in data[1:]]
...         world_data.append(Nation(*typed_data))
...

>>> max(world_data, key=lambda rec: rec.Density_km3)  # ❶
Nation(Name='Monaco', Population=39242.0, Pct_Change_2023=0.71,
Net_Change=278.0, Density_km3=26337.0, Area_km2=1.0)

>>> for nation in sorted(                             # ❷
...         world_data,
...         key=attrgetter("Net_Change"),
...         reverse=True)[:4]:
...     print(nation)
...
Nation(Name='India', Population=1380004385.0, Pct_Change_2023=0.99,
Net_Change=13586631.0, Density_km3=464.0, Area_km2=2973190.0)
Nation(Name='China', Population=1439323776.0, Pct_Change_2023=0.39,
Net_Change=5540090.0, Density_km3=153.0, Area_km2=9388211.0)
Nation(Name='Nigeria', Population=206139589.0, Pct_Change_2023=2.58,
Net_Change=5175990.0, Density_km3=226.0, Area_km2=910770.0)
Nation(Name='Pakistan', Population=220892340.0, Pct_Change_2023=2.0,
Net_Change=4327022.0, Density_km3=287.0, Area_km2=770880.0)

>>> f"{mean(nation.Population for nation in world_data):,.0f}"
'33,171,203'                                          # ❸
```

❶ Highest population density

❷ First four by population increase

❸ Average population of countries

As namedtuples are a kind of tuple, we can equally reference the data inside them by index as well. It's just that names are usually friendlier. We can introspect the fields used and convert the structure to a dictionary as well:

```
>>> world_data[37][5]
306230.0
>>> world_data[37].Area_km2
306230.0
>>> world_data[37]._fields
('Name', 'Population', 'Pct_Change_2023', 'Net_Change',
'Density_km3', 'Area_km2')
>>> world_data[37]._asdict()
{'Name': 'Poland', 'Population': 37846611.0,
'Pct_Change_2023': -0.11, 'Net_Change': -41157.0,
'Density_km3': 124.0, 'Area_km2': 306230.0}
```

6.5.2 Static versus Dynamic

Readers will note that the prior example is probably a bit *too clever* for most uses. We dynamically created the attributes of the namedtuple, and yet we used those names in subsequent code under the assumption we knew which field names were dynamically determined.

Of course, we do not *need to* rely on dynamic creation of field names. The constructor will accept a static sequence or even a static space-separated string of field names. This is the more usual case, although the dynamic case certainly has some uses; for example, if you *know* the files you read will have a few field names, but they might vary in other fields.

In order to emphasize the static declaration, some Pythonistas prefer a class-style spelling of typing.NamedTuple. Note in the following code that the annotations are merely documentation of intention; they *do not* perform any casting of types or checking that annotations match (unless third-party type checkers are used). For example:

```
from typing import NamedTuples
>>> class Nation(NamedTuple):
...        Name: str
...        Population: int
...        Pct_Change: float
...        Net_Change: int
...        Density: float
...        Area: float
...
>>> poland = Nation(
...        "Poland",
...        37_846_611,
...        -0.11,
...        -41_157,
...        Density=124.0,
```

```
...       Area=306_230
... )
...
>>> poland
Nation(Name='Poland', Population=37846611, Pct_Change=-0.11,
Net_Change=-41157, Density=124.0, Area=306230)
```

We can use either positional or named parameters to create a new `Nation` object, so the example uses a mixture (positional first, of course). As promised, the type declarations are not enforced; for example, `poland.Area` is an integer (as in the actual source data) even though it conceptually could be nonintegral as "declared."

6.5.3 Data Classes

Using data classes is very similar to using `typing.NamedTuple` in syntax. However, data classes allow you to mutate fields, and also allow you to add methods that are useful for working with the data within fields. Let's create a `dataclass` version of our `Nation` object.

Mutability is the overriding difference between `typing.NamedTuple` and `@dataclasses.dataclass`, but `collections.namedtuple` has the advantage of feeling much more lightweight when used in code (for human readers, not in underlying resource utilization). In speed and memory usage, the options are roughly equivalent; the main difference is in expressing an intent. Likewise, in almost all of your plain classes, you *could* decorate them as data classes and cause no harm to your program operation; but if a class really doesn't have a record-oriented purpose, such a decorator would be confusing and mislead later developers:

```
>>> from dataclasses import dataclass
>>> from copy import copy                              # ❶

>>> @dataclass
... class DataNation:
...       Name: str
...       Population: int = 0
...       Pct_Change: float = 0
...       Net_Change: int = 0
...       Density: float = 0
...       Area: float = 0
...
...       def project_next_year(self, new_people):
...           self.Population += new_people
...           self.Net_Change = new_people
...           self.Pct_Change = new_people / self.Population
```

```
...            self.Density = self.Population / self.Area
...            return self
...

>>> peru_2023 = DataNation(
...     "Peru",
...     32_971_854,
...     Pct_Change=1.42,
...     Net_Change=461_401,
...     Density=26,
...     Area=1_280_000                              # ❷
... )

>>> peru_2023
DataNation(Name='Peru', Population=32971854, Pct_Change=1.42,
Net_Change=461401, Density=26, Area=1280000)
>>> peru_2023.Density, peru_2023.Population
(26, 32971854)

>>> peru_2024 = copy(peru_2023).project_next_year(500_000)
>>> peru_2024.Density, peru_2024.Population
(26.1498859375, 33471854)
```

❶ For the example, we wish to retain the old record.

❷ The round number suggests the source data is imprecise.

As with the documentary annotations in `typing.NamedTuple` the annotations in a dataclass are not enforced in any way by Python itself. While conventional, the annotations are not even required to be types by Python.

Data classes have a few more "advanced" features, such as `dataclasses.field()` which allows you to specify a mutable default that is specific to the instance. `dataclasses.fields()`, `dataclasses.asdict()`, and `dataclasses.astuple()` provide means to introspect and transform data classes.

When you define a data class, you use a decorator rather than, for example, inheriting from a base class. This is used because the construction somewhat dynamically adds attributes and methods to the created class that would not be possible with inheritance. You don't need to worry about this, just remember the syntax. However, if you really need to know whether an object is a dataclass, you can ask `dataclasses.is_dataclass(obj)`.

6.6   Efficient Concrete Sequences

Python has a few data structures that are virtual subclasses of `collections.Sequence` but that avoid most of the indirection and value boxing that Python `list` requires. These types include bytes, bytearray, and array.array. The last of these is a family of data structures, in the sense that it can be configured to hold a variety of identical bit-sized elements of the same numeric datatype.

There is a relatively narrow domain where it makes sense to use Python's standard library array module rather than "taking the next step" to use NumPy, but within that narrow range of use cases, it is nice to have array.array available to avoid external dependencies. Conceptually, bytearray is very similar to array.array("B") in that both are mutable unboxed sequences of integer values between 0 and 255 (i.e., bytes). However, the collection of methods each provides are distinct. bytearray has most of the same methods as str, and is deliberately string-like; in contrast array.array (of every datatype) has methods much closer to those in list.

Just as tuple is, in some sense, a "mutable version of list," bytes is "an immutable version of bytearray." The analogy isn't perfect. Tuples have a starkly constrained collection of methods (i.e., exactly two, .count() and .index()) but bytes has many methods, most in common with str. The built-in type bytearray in turn essentially has a superset of the methods of bytes (some methods relevant to mutable sequences are only in bytearray):

```
>>> set(dir(bytearray)) - set(dir(bytes))          # ❶
{'copy', 'clear', 'remove', 'append', '__alloc__', '__delitem__',
'__setitem__', 'reverse', 'pop', '__iadd__', 'insert', '__imul__',
'extend'}
```

❶ A few sensible things to do with mutable sequences

Let's look at a few cases where notable (but constant rather than big-O) speed differences occur. For these quick examples, we just use random data; more realistically, these bytes might instead be meaningful content in a binary format. Analyzing or transforming such binary data is often an important goal:

```
>>> from array import array
>>> with open("/dev/urandom", "rb") as r:
...     rand_bytes = r.read(2**29)  # 512 MiB
...
>>> type(rand_bytes)
<class 'bytes'>
>>> rand_bytearray = bytearray(rand_bytes)
>>> rand_array = array("B", rand_bytes)
>>> rand_list = list(rand_bytes)
>>> for a, b, c, d in zip(
...         rand_bytes, rand_bytearray, rand_array, rand_list
...     ):
...     assert a == b == c == d
...
```

```
>>> rand_list[:3]
[201, 217, 132]
```

Superficially, these four types of sequences seem similar. It took a while to run the loop to make sure they have equal elements, but indeed they do. A first notable difference among them is their memory usage. For the first three objects, we can ask about the memory usage in a simple way:

```
>>> import sys
>>> f"{sys.getsizeof(rand_bytes):,}"
'536,870,945'
>>> f"{sys.getsizeof(rand_bytearray):,}"
'536,870,969'
>>> f"{sys.getsizeof(rand_array):,}"
'570,425,427'
```

These sizes are not quite identical since their headers vary (and `array.array` uses a modest overallocation strategy, similar to `list`). However, all of these are close to the 536,870,912 bytes that are the minimal possible size to represent all of these random bytes.

The question is somewhat more complicated for `rand_list`. Lists use a relatively aggressive overallocation of slots; but even apart from such overallocation of memory, each slot is a pointer to an internal data structure used to represent a Python integer. For byte-sized integers (i.e., between 0 and 255), this structure occupies 28 bytes. For larger integers or wider floating point numbers, the size of the *boxed number* increases somewhat, albeit slowly. In concept, a list of integers needs to contain *both* an array of pointer slots (probably 64-bit on modern systems), of roughly the length of the array, and *also*, at a different memory address, the underlying boxed number.

However, this is further complicated in the current example by the fact that *small integers are interned* in CPython. This is discussed briefly at the start of Chapter 2, *Confusing Equality with Identity*. It means that all the pointers to 8-bit integers have already been allocated when Python starts up, and these pointers are simply reused for repeating list slots. If we were working with larger numbers, we would have to multiply the number of (non-duplicated) items by the size of the boxed number, and add that to the size of the pointer array itself:

```
>>> sys.getsizeof(2)
28
>>> sys.getsizeof(2**31)
32
>>> sys.getsizeof(2**63)
36
>>> sys.getsizeof(2**200)
52
```

```
>>> f"{sys.getsizeof(rand_list):,}"
'4,294,967,352'
```

As a ballpark figure, the list version takes about 4 GiB, since 64-bit pointers are eight times as large as 8-bit numbers. If we were dealing with non-interned numbers, the memory story would lean much more heavily against `list`.

Often much more important than memory usage is runtime:

```
>>> assert (rand_bytes.count(42) ==                    # ❶
...          rand_bytearray.count(42) ==
...          rand_array.count(42) ==
...          rand_list.count(42))
>>> %timeit rand_bytes.count(42)
178 ms ± 501 µs per loop (mean ± std. dev. of 7 runs, 10 loops each)
>>> %timeit rand_bytearray.count(42)
179 ms ± 1.49 ms per loop (mean ± std. dev. of 7 runs, 10 loops each)
>>> %timeit rand_array.count(42)
5.5 s ± 33.6 ms per loop (mean ± std. dev. of 7 runs, 1 loop each)
>>> %timeit rand_list.count(42)
4.88 s ± 17.3 ms per loop (mean ± std. dev. of 7 runs, 1 loop each)
```

❶ Sanity check that the counts will be identical

It's impressive how much faster counting on `bytes` or `bytesarray` is than on `list`. It's disappointing that the similar data structure `array.array` doesn't achieve similar results (even coming in slightly worse than `list`). The reason for this is that in CPython, `array.array.count()` still uses the same indexing machinery as other pure-Python sequences. This has been a "known issue" in CPython since at least 2015 and Python 3.7—no core developers have felt it is one that needs to be fixed, however, since as soon as you start asking this question, the answer is *almost always* "use NumPy" (which solves an enormous number of other problems at the same time).

Of course, the example only used 8-bit unsigned integers. If you wanted to store 16-, 32-, or 64-bit signed or unsigned integers, or floating point numbers of system width (usually 64-bit nowadays), `bytearray` would clearly not be an option. Also, in these cases, `array.array` would pull modestly ahead of `list` because of interning. As a redemption for `array.array`, we can notice that it *is* still much faster than `list` in a range of other situations where we work with sequences of numbers of the same underlying machine type. For example:

```
>>> rand_arr2 = rand_array[:-1]
>>> rand_arr3 = rand_array[:-1]
>>> rand_arr2 is rand_arr3                             # ❶
False
```

```
>>> rand_arr2 == rand_arr3                          # ❷
True
>>> %timeit rand_arr2 == rand_arr3
196 ms ± 2.42 ms per loop (mean ± std. dev. of 7 runs, 1 loop each)
>>> rand_list2 = rand_list[:-1]
>>> rand_list3 = rand_list[:-1]
>>> %timeit rand_list2 == rand_list3
886 ms ± 12.4 ms per loop (mean ± std. dev. of 7 runs, 1 loop each)
```

❶ Slices create genuinely new objects, copying the old ones.

❷ These distinct objects remain equal.

The speedup from `list` isn't as dramatic as the 30x difference in counting on `bytes`, but 4.5x is a worthwhile speedup if the underlying operation matters in your application.

There are a lot of corners where non-`list` sequences will speed things up, where they won't, and where they simply are not suitable for the purpose at hand. For many cases where you need to work with sequences of numbers, however, it is very much worth keeping these other sequences in mind as options.

6.7 Wrapping Up

I will, in fact, claim that the difference between a bad programmer and a good one is whether he considers his code or his data structures more important. Bad programmers worry about the code. Good programmers worry about data structures and their relationships.

— **Linus Torvalds, Creator of Linux**

Choosing a data structure well suited to your tasks is one of the most important tasks in programming. Python provides both ubiquitously used data structures—mainly `dict`, `list`, `tuple`, and `set` built-in types—and some others that are more often overlooked. Many of these overlooked gems live inside the `collections` module of the standard library. A few live in other modules, or simply as less used built-ins.

On the Python Package Index (https://pypi.org/) you can probably find hundreds of very specialized data structure modules. There are definitely times when one of these is exactly what you need; however, much of what lives on PyPI is somewhat preliminary or partial, being the hobby of one or a few programmers. The libraries sortedcontainers and pyrsistent mentioned in the introduction to this chapter are definitely worth being aware of. I've found specific use for pygtrie (https://pypi.org/project/pygtrie/) and R-tree (https://pypi.org/project/Rtree/) as well, for example.

A good strategy when choosing a data structure for your project is to first think about whether any of the "big four" listed in the preceding paragraph accomplish exactly what you need (including good big-O behavior). Very often the answer is yes. If you feel like there may be drawbacks to using those, consider using one of the other data structures in the standard library `collections`, `array`, `enum`, `dataclasses`, or perhaps `queue` and a few others. If it still feels like something is missing, think about sortedcontainers, pyrsistent, NumPy, and Pandas. If that still falls short—and if it does, think very carefully about whether you are genuinely asking the right questions—look for other data structure projects in the open source world. And in the rare, but not nonexistent, circumstance those earlier steps don't satisfy your needs, think about creating custom data structures (after reading the next chapter).

7

Misusing Data Structures

Python has extremely well-designed data structures and data representations, many of which are discussed in the prior chapter. However, a few antipatterns, that are unfortunately common, can make the use of data structures dramatically inefficient or lead to unintended behavior in your code.

7.1 Quadratic Behavior of Repeated List Search

In Python, the in keyword is a very flexible way of looking for "membership" in an object, most often some sort of container. Behind the scenes, the keyword in is calling the .__contains__(self, elem) method of the object that potentially has something "inside" it.

Bear with me for a few paragraphs while I discuss the behavior of in, and before I get to the quadratic behavior gotcha one can encounter using lists. I believe a deeper understanding of the mechanisms of "containment" will help many developers who might have only an approximate mental model of what's going on.

A great many kinds of objects—some that might seem unexpected—respond to in. Here is an example.

RegexFlag can check for membership

```
>>> import re
>>> flags = re.VERBOSE | re.IGNORECASE | re.DOTALL | re.UNICODE
>>> type(flags)
<flag 'RegexFlag'>
>>> re.U in flags
True
>>> type(re.M)
<flag 'RegexFlag'>
```

In a commonsense way, the flag re.U (which is simply an alias for re.UNICODE) is *contained* in the mask of several flags. A single flag is simply a mask that indicates only one operational `re` modifier. Moreover, a few special objects that are not collections but iterables also respond to `in`. For example, `range` is special in this way.

Exploring what a range is

```
>>> import collections
>>> r = range(1_000_000_000_000)              # ❶
>>> isinstance(r, collections.abc.Collection)
True
>>> r[:10]                                    # ❷
range(0, 10)
>>> r[999_999_999_990:]
range(999999999990, 1000000000000)
>>> f"{r[999_999_999_990:][5]:,}"             # ❷
'999,999,999,995'
```

❶ Ostensibly, this is a very large collection; in truth it is a very compact representation that doesn't actually *contain* a trillion integers, only the endpoints and step of the range.

❷ A number of clever shortcuts exist in the implementation of the `range` object, generally producing what we "expect."

Part of the cleverness of `range` is that it does not need to do a linear search through its items, even though it is in many respects list-like. A `range` object behaves like a realized list in most ways, but only *contains* anything in a synthetic sense. In other words, `range(start, stop, step)` has an internal representation similar to its call signature, and operations like a slice or a membership test are calculated using a few arithmetic operations. For example, `n in my_range` can simply check whether $start \leq n < stop$ and whether $(n - start) \% step = 0$.

Timing the efficiency of range

```
>>> %timeit 10 in r
54 ns ± 0.85 ns per loop (mean ± std. dev. of 7 runs, 10,000,000
loops each)
>>> %timeit 999_999_999_995 in r
77 ns ± 0.172 ns per loop (mean ± std. dev. of 7 runs, 10,000,000
loops each)
```

The time to check for membership of an element near the "start" of a range is almost identical to that for membership of an element near the "end" because Python is not actually *searching* the members.

Lists are a concrete and ordered collection of elements that can be appended to very quickly, and have a few other internal optimizations. However, we have to watch where the *ordered* part might bite us. The only generic way to tell if an element is contained in a list is to do a linear search on the list. We might not find it until near the end of the search, and if it isn't there, we will have had to search the entire list.

> **Note   When you want your lists sorted**
>
> We can use the `bisect` module in the standard library if we wish to speed this greatly for lists we are happy to keep in sorted order (which is not all of our lists, however). The `sortedcontainers` third-party library (https://grantjenks. com/docs/sortedcontainers/) also provides a similar speedup when we can live with the mentioned constraint.

We can see where checking containment within a list becomes unwieldy with a simple example. I keep a copy of the 267,752-word SOWPODS (https://en.wikipedia.org/wiki /Collins_Scrabble_Words) English wordlist on my own system. We can use that as an example of a moderately large list (of strings, in this case).

Searching the SOWPODS wordlist

```
>>> words = [w.rstrip() for w in open('data/sowpods')]
>>> len(words)
267752
>>> import random
>>> random.seed(42)
>>> most_words = random.sample(words, k=250_000)     # ❶
>>> %timeit "zygote" in most_words
2.8 ms ± 147 µs per loop (mean ± std. dev. of 7 runs, 100 loops each)
>>> %timeit "zebra" in most_words
200 µs ± 12.2 µs per loop (mean ± std. dev. of 7 runs, 1,000 loops
each)
>>> %timeit "aardvark" in most_words
172 µs ± 776 ns per loop (mean ± std. dev. of 7 runs, 10,000 loops
each)
>>> %timeit "coalfish" in most_words
10.7 ms ± 163 µs per loop (mean ± std. dev. of 7 runs, 100 loops each)
```

❶ The words are genuinely shuffled in the random sampling.

We can see that both "aardvark" and "zebra" take a fairly modest 200 microseconds to search. Showing that the `most_words` list really is not ordered alphabetically, "zygote" takes over 10 times as long to find (but it *is* found).

However, "coalfish" (a genuine word in the full dictionary, closely related in the Linnaean classification system to pollock) takes over 10 milliseconds because it is never found in the sampled list.

For a one-off operation, 10 milliseconds is probably fine. But imagine we want to do something slightly more complicated. The example is somewhat artificial, but one can realistically imagine wanting instead to compare lists of people's names or addresses for a degree of duplication—or, for example, of shotgun-sampled nucleotide fragments from soil—in a real-world situation.

Finding words from one collection in another collection

```
>>> random.seed(13)
>>> some_words = random.sample(words, k=10_000)
>>> sum(1 for word in some_words if word not in most_words)
649
>>> %timeit sum(1 for word in some_words if word not in most_words)
55.2 s ± 1.26 s per loop (mean ± std. dev. of 7 runs, 1 loop each)
```

Taking a full minute for this simple operation is terrible, and it gets worse quickly—at approximately an $O(N^2)$ rate (to be precise, it is $\Omega(N{\times}M)$ since it gets even worse as the hit rate goes down for specific data).[1]

What we've shown is concise and superficially intuitive code to perform one linear scan of most_words for every word in some_words. That is, we perform an $O(N)$ scan operation M different times (where N and M are the sizes of the respective lists). A quick clue you can use in spotting such pitfalls is to look for multiple occurrences of the in keyword in an expression or within a suite. Whether in an if expression or within a loop, the complexity is similar.

Fortunately, Python gives us a very efficient way to solve exactly this problem by using sets.

Efficiently finding words from one collection in another collection

```
>>> len(set(some_words) - set(most_words))
649
>>> %timeit len(set(some_words) - set(most_words))
43.3 ms ± 1.31 ms per loop (mean ± std. dev. of 7 runs, 10 loops each)
```

That's better than a 1000x speedup. We can see that the result is exactly the same. Even assuming we needed to concretely look at where those words occur within our lists rather

---

1. The so-called big-O notation is commonly used in computer science when analyzing the complexity of an algorithm. Wikipedia has a good discussion at https://en.wikipedia.org/wiki/Big_O_notation. There are multiple symbols used for slightly different characterizations of asymptotic complexity: O, o, Ω, ω, and Θ. Big-O is used most commonly, and indicates a worst-case behavior; Big-Theta indicates an asymptote for both worst case and best case; Big-Omega indicates a best-case behavior. Small-o and Small-omega are used to express the somewhat more complex concepts of one function *dominating* another rather than *bounding* another.

than merely count them or see what they are, 649 operations of `some_words.index(word)` is *comparatively* cheap relative to the three-orders-of-magnitude difference encountered (looking through the shorter list is far faster, and typically we find the different word after searching halfway).

> **Note   Trie structures for fast prefix search**
>
> If the particular problem discussed is genuinely close to the one you face, look towards the third-party module `pygtrie` (https://pypi.org/project/pygtrie/), which will probably get you even faster and more flexible behavior. For the precise problem described, `CharTrie` is the class you'd want. In general, the *trie* data structure (https://en.wikipedia.org/wiki/Trie) is very powerful for a class of string search algorithms.

7.2 Deleting or Adding Elements to the Middle of a List

An early discussion in this book, in Chapter 3, *A Grab Bag of Python Gotchas*, addresses how naive string concatenation within a loop might encounter quadratic complexity. That is to say, the overall time and computation needed to perform a sequence of N operations is $O(N^2)$.[2]

Although in many situations the solution to a slowdown in (certain) string operations is to simply "use a list instead" (perhaps followed by a final `"".join(thelist)` to get back a string), lists have their own very similar danger. The problem here is in not understanding what is "cheap" and what is "expensive" for lists. Specifically, inserting or removing items from a list anywhere other than at the end is *expensive*.

We first explore some details of exactly how lists are implemented in Python, then look at which other data structures would be good choices for which actual use cases.

Python gives you the ability to insert or remove items from anywhere within a list, and for some purposes it will seem like the obvious approach. Indeed, for a few operations on a relatively small list, the minor inefficiency is wholly unimportant.

---

2. *Ibid.*

Note   Cost and amortized cost

For lists, accessing an item at a given numeric position is O(1). Changing the value at a numeric position is O(1). Perhaps surprisingly, `list.append()` and `list.pop()` are also *amortized* O(1).

That is, adding more items to a list will intermittently require reallocating memory to store their object references; but Python is clever enough to use pre-allocated reserve space for items that might be added. Moreover, as the size of a list grows, the pre-allocation padding also grows. The overall effect is that reallocations become rarer, and their relative cost averages out to 0% asymptotically. In CPython 3.11, we see the following behavior on an x86-64 architecture (but these details are not promised for a different Python implementation, version, or chip architecture):

```
>>> from sys import getsizeof
>>> def pre_allocate():
...     lst = []
...     size = getsizeof(lst)
...     print(" Len   Size  Alloc")
...     for i in range(1, 10_001):
...         lst.append('a')
...         newsize = getsizeof(lst)
...         if newsize > size:
...             print(f"{i:>4d}{newsize:>7d}{newsize-size:>6d}")
...             size = newsize
...
>>> pre_allocate()                                      # ❶
 Len   Size  Alloc  |   Len   Size  Alloc
   1     88    32   |   673   6136   704
   5    120    32   |   761   6936   800
   9    184    64   |   861   7832   896
  17    248    64   |   973   8856  1024
  25    312    64   |  1101  10008  1152
  33    376    64   |  1245  11288  1280
  41    472    96   |  1405  12728  1440
  53    568    96   |  1585  14360  1632
  65    664    96   |  1789  16184  1824
  77    792   128   |  2017  18232  2048
  93    920   128   |  2273  20536  2304
 109   1080   160   |  2561  23128  2592
 129   1240   160   |  2885  26040  2912
 149   1432   192   |  3249  29336  3296
 173   1656   224   |  3661  33048  3712
 201   1912   256   |  4125  37208  4160
 233   2200   288   |  4645  41880  4672
```

```
269    2520    320   |   5229   47160   5280
309    2872    352   |   5889   53080   5920
353    3256    384   |   6629   59736   6656
401    3704    448   |   7461   67224   7488
457    4216    512   |   8397   75672   8448
521    4792    576   |   9453   85176   9504
593    5432    640
```
❶ Printed output modified to show two columns of `len/size/alloc`

This general pattern of pre-allocating a larger amount each time the list grows, roughly in proportion to the length of the existing list, continues for lists of millions of items.

Inserting and removing words from middle of list

```
>>> words = [get_word() for _ in range(10)]
>>> words
['hennier', 'oughtness', 'testcrossed', 'railbus', 'ciclatoun',
'consimilitudes', 'trifacial', 'mauri', 'snowploughing', 'ebonics']
>>> del words[3]                                          # ❶
>>> del words[7]
>>> del words[3]                                          # ❶
>>> words
['hennier', 'oughtness', 'testcrossed', 'consimilitudes', 'trifacial',
'mauri', 'ebonics']
>>> words.insert(3, get_word())
>>> words.insert(1, get_word())
>>> words                                                 # ❷
['hennier', 'awless', 'oughtness', 'testcrossed', 'wringings',
'consimilitudes', 'trifacial', 'mauri', 'ebonics']
```

❶ The word deleted at initial index 3 was *railbus*, but on next deletion *ciclatoun* was at that index.

❷ The word *wringings* was inserted at index 3, but got moved to index 4 when *awless* was inserted at index 1.

Note   Focus on concepts, but code available at book website

The specific implementation of the `get_word()` function used here is not important. However, as with other examples ancillary to the main point of a section, or requiring larger datasets, the source code and data file can be found at https://gnosis.cx/better. All that matters for the current section is that `get_word()` returns some string each time it is called.

For the handful of items inserted and removed from the small list in the example, the relative inefficiency is not important. However, even in the small example, keeping track of *where* each item winds up by index becomes confusing.

As the number of operations gets large, this approach becomes notably painful. The following toy function performs fairly meaningless insertions and deletions, always returning five words at the end. But the general pattern it uses is one you might be tempted towards in real-world code.

Asymptotic timing for insert-and-delete from list middle

```
>>> from random import randrange
>>> def insert_then_del(n):
...     words = [get_word() for _ in range(5)]
...     for _ in range(n):
...         words.insert(randrange(0, len(words)), get_word())
...     for _ in range(n):
...         del words[randrange(0, len(words))]
...     return words
...
>>> insert_then_del(100)
['healingly', 'cognitions', 'borsic', 'rathole', 'division']
>>> insert_then_del(10_000)
['ferny', 'pleurapophyses', 'protoavis', 'unhived', 'misinform']
>>> %timeit insert_then_del(100)
109 µs ± 2.42 µs per loop (mean ± std. dev. of 7 runs, 10,000 loops
each)
>>> %timeit insert_then_del(10_000)
20.3 ms ± 847 µs per loop (mean ± std. dev. of 7 runs, 10 loops each)
>>> %timeit insert_then_del(1_000_000)
1min 52s ± 1.51 s per loop (mean ± std. dev. of 7 runs, 1 loop each)
```

Going from 200 operations (counting each of insertion and deletion) to 20,000 operations takes on the order of 200x as long. At these sizes the lists themselves are small enough to matter little; the time involved is dominated by the number of calls to get_word(), or perhaps a bit to randrange(), although we still see a 2x proportional slowdown from the list operations.

However, upon increasing the number of operations by another 100x, to 2 million, linear scaling would see an increase from 20 ms to about 2 seconds. Instead it jumps to nearly 2 minutes, or about a 55x slowdown from linear scaling. I watched my memory usage during the 15 minutes that %timeit took to run the timing seven times, and it remained steady.

It's not that these operations actually use very much memory; rather, every time we insert one word near the middle of a 1 million word list, that requires the interpreter to move 500,000 pointers up one position in the list. Likewise, each deletion near the middle of a 1 million word list requires us to move the top 500,000 pointers back down. This gets much worse very quickly as the number of operations increases further.

7.2.1 More Efficient Data Structures

There is no one solution to the problem described here. On the other hand, there is exceedingly rarely an actual use case for the exact behavior implemented by code such as the preceding example. Trust me, code like that is not purely contrived for this book—I have encountered a great much like it in production systems (with the problem buried beneath a lot of other functionality in such code).

If you merely need to be able to insert and delete from *either* the end *or* the beginning of a concrete sequence, `collections.deque` gives you exactly what you need. This is not an arbitrary middle for insertion and deletion, but very often all you actually want is `.appendleft()` and `.popleft()` to accompany `.append()` and `.pop()`.

In some cases, `sortedcontainers` or `pyrsistent` may have closer to the performance characteristics you need, while still offering a *sequence* datatype. Generally, using these third-party containers is still only going to get you to $O(N \times \log N)$ rather than $O(N)$, but that remains strikingly better than $O(N^2)$.

Later in this chapter, in the section "Rolling Your Own Data Structures," I show an example where creating a custom data structure actually *can* make sense. My pure-Python implementation of `CountingTree` is able to do exactly the "insert into the middle" action that is described in this section, and remains relatively efficient. For this narrow and specific use case, my custom data structure is actually pretty good.

However, instead of reaching for the abovementioned collections—as excellent as each of them genuinely is—this problem is probably one in which you (or the developer before you) misunderstood what the underlying problem *actually* requires.

For example, a somewhat plausible reason you might *actually* want to keep an order for items is because they represent some sort of *priority* of actions to be performed or data to be processed. A wonderful data structure in which to maintain such priorities is simply a Python `dict`. A plausible way of using this fast data structure is to keep your "words" (per the earlier example) as keys, and their priority as values.

A priority is not exactly the same thing as an index position, but it *is* something that very quickly allows you to maintain a sequence for the data you wish to handle, while keeping insertion or deletion operations always at $O(1)$. This means, of course, that performing N such operations is $O(N)$, which is the best we might plausibly hope for. Constructing a sequence *at the end* of such operations is both cheap and easy, as the following example shows.

A collection of items with a million possible priorities

```
>>> from pprint import pprint
>>> from functools import partial
>>> priority = partial(randrange, 1, 1_000_000)
>>> words = {get_word():priority() for _ in range(100_000)}
>>> words_by_priority = sorted(words.items(), key=lambda p: p[1])
>>> pprint(words_by_priority[:10])
[('badland', 8),
 ('weakliest', 21),
```

```
     ('sowarry', 28),
     ('actinobiology', 45),
     ('oneself', 62),
     ('subpanel', 68),
     ('alarmedly', 74),
     ('marbled', 98),
     ('dials', 120),
     ('dearing', 121)]
>>> pprint(words_by_priority[-5:])
[('overslow', 999976),
 ('ironings', 999980),
 ('tussocked', 999983),
 ('beaters', 999984),
 ('tameins', 999992)]
```

It's possible—even likely—that the same priority occurs for multiple words, occasionally. It's also very uncommon that you *actually* care about *exactly* which order two individual items come in out of 100,000 of them. However, even with duplicated priorities, items are not dropped, they are merely ordered arbitrarily (but you could easily enough impose an order if you have a reason to).

Deleting items from the words data structure is just slightly more difficult than was del words[n] where it had been a list. To be safe, you'd want to do something like:

```
>>> for word in ['producibility', 'scrambs', 'marbled']:
...     if word in words:
...         print("Removing:", word, words[word])
...         del words[word]
...     else:
...         print("Not present:", word)
...
Not present: producibility
Removing: scrambs 599046
Removing: marbled 98
```

The extra print() calls and the else clause are just for illustration; presumably if this approach is relevant to your requirements, you would omit them:

```
>>> for word in ['producibility', 'scrambs', 'marbled']:
...     if word in words:
...         del words[word]
...
```

This approach remains fast and scalable, and is quite likely much closer to the actual requirements of your software than was misuse of a list.

7.3   Strings Are Iterables of Strings

Strings in Python are strange objects. They are incredibly useful, powerful, and well designed. But they are still strange. In many ways, strings are *scalar* objects. They are immutable and hashable, for example. We usually think of a string as a *single value*, or equivalently call it *atomic*.

However, at the same time, strings are iterable, and every item in their iteration is also a string (which is itself iterable). This oddity often leads to mistakes when we wish to decompose or flatten nested data. Sometimes in related contexts as well, as shown in the following example.

Naive attempt at `flatten()` function

```
>>> def flatten(o, items=[]):
...     try:
...         for part in o:
...             flatten(part, items)
...     except TypeError:
...         items.append(o)
...     return items
```

If you prefer LBYL (look before you leap) to EAFP (easier to ask forgiveness than permission) you could write this as follows.

Naive attempt at `flatten2()` function

```
>>> from collections.abc import Iterable
>>> def flatten2(o, items=[]):
...     if isinstance(o, Iterable):
...         for part in o:
...             flatten2(part, items)
...     else:
...         items.append(o)
...     return items
```

Either way, these are perfectly sensible functions to take a nested data structure with scalar leaves, and return a linear sequence from them. These first two functions return a concrete list, but they could equally well be written as a generator function such as the following.

Naive attempt at `flatten_gen` function

```
>>> def flatten_gen(o):
...     if isinstance(o, Iterable):
...         for part in o:
...             yield from flatten_gen(part)
```

```
...        else:
...            yield o
```

Using this function often produces what we'd like:

```
>>> nested = [
...     (1, 2, 3),
...     {(4, 5, 6), 7, 8, frozenset([9, 10, 11])},
...     [[[12, 13], [14, 15], 16], 17, 18]
... ]
>>> flatten(nested, [])                              # ❶
[1, 2, 3, 8, 9, 10, 11, 4, 5, 6, 7, 12, 13, 14, 15, 16, 17, 18]
>>> flatten2(nested, [])                             # ❶
[1, 2, 3, 8, 9, 10, 11, 4, 5, 6, 7, 12, 13, 14, 15, 16, 17, 18]
>>> for item in flatten_gen(nested):
...     print(item, end=" ")
... print()
1 2 3 8 9 10 11 4 5 6 7 12 13 14 15 16 17 18
```

❶ To avoid mutable-default issues, pass in initial `items` to expand.

In the examples, the iterable but unordered set in the middle happens to yield the `frozenset` first, although it is listed last in the source code. You are given no guarantee about whether that accident will hold true in a different Python version, or even on a different machine or different run.

This all breaks down terribly when strings are involved. Because strings are iterable, every item in their iteration is also a string (which is itself iterable).

How strings break recursion

```
>>> import sys
>>> sys.setrecursionlimit(10)                        # ❶
>>> flatten(nested, [])
[1, 2, 3, 8, 9, 10, 11, 4, 5, 6, 7, 12, 13, 14, 15, 16, 17, 18]
>>> flatten('abc', [])
Traceback (most recent call last):
  File "<stdin>", line 1, in <module>
  File "<stdin>", line 4, in flatten
  File "<stdin>", line 4, in flatten
  File "<stdin>", line 4, in flatten
  [Previous line repeated 6 more times]              # ❷
RecursionError: maximum recursion depth exceeded
```

❶ The same breakage occurs with a default depth of 1000, it just shows more lines of traceback before doing so.

❷ Recent `python` shells simplify many tracebacks, but `ipython` does not by default.

Using `flatten2()` or `flatten_gen()` will produce very similar tracebacks and exceptions (small details of their tracebacks vary, but `RecursionError` is the general result in all cases). If strings are nested within other data structures rather than top level, the result is essentially the same:

```
>>> flatten2(('a', ('b', 'c')), [])
Traceback (most recent call last):
  File "<stdin>", line 1, in <module>
  File "<stdin>", line 4, in flatten2
  File "<stdin>", line 4, in flatten2
  File "<stdin>", line 4, in flatten2
  [Previous line repeated 2 more times]
  File "<stdin>", line 2, in flatten2
  File "<frozen abc>", line 119, in __instancecheck__
RecursionError: maximum recursion depth exceeded in comparison
```

The solution to these issues is to add some unfortunate ugliness to code, as in the examples shown here.

Ugly but safe flatten function

```
>>> def flatten_safe(o, items=[]):
...     if isinstance(o, (str, bytes)):          # ❶
...         items.append(o)
...     elif isinstance(o, Iterable):
...         for part in o:
...             flatten_safe(part, items)
...     else:
...         items.append(o)
...     return items
...
>>> flatten_safe(('a', ['b', 'c'], {'dee'}), [])
['a', 'b', 'c', 'dee']
>>> flatten_safe(nested, [])
[1, 2, 3, 8, 9, 10, 11, 4, 5, 6, 7, 12, 13, 14, 15, 16, 17, 18]

>>> flatten([b'abc', [100, 101]], [])
[97, 98, 99, 100, 101]                            # ❷
>>> flatten_safe([b'abc', [100, 101]], [])
[b'abc', 100, 101]                                # ❸
```

❶ `bytes` has a slightly different but also annoying issue.

❷ No exception occurred, but probably not what you wanted

❸ Most likely the behavior you were hoping for

It would be nice if Python had a virtual parent class like `collections.abc.NonAtomicIterable`. Unfortunately, it does not, and it *cannot* without substantially changing the semantics of Python strings. Or perhaps, less intrusively, `isinstance()` could conceivably check for something else beyond the presence of an `.__iter__()` when deciding whether an object is an instance of this hypothetical `NonAtomicIterable` interface.

For the current Python version, 3.12 as of this writing, special case checking for string-ness is really the only approach available to handle the dual composite/atomic nature of strings.

7.4   (Often) Use enum **Rather Than** CONSTANT

The enum module was added to Python 3.4, and has grown incremental new capabilities in several versions since then. Prior to that module being added, but also simply because some developers are more accustomed to languages such as bash, C, and Java,[3] it is not uncommon to see capitalized names (usually defined at a module scope) used as constants in Python code.

Informal enumerations using capitalization

```
"This module works with sprites having colors and shapes"

RED = "RED"
GREEN = "GREEN"
BLUE = "BLUE"

CIRCLE, SQUARE, TRIANGLE = range(3)

class Sprite:
    def __init__(self, shape, color):
        self.shape = shape
        self.color = color

    # ... other methods

def process(sprite):
    if sprite.shape == TRIANGLE and sprite.color == RED:
        red_triangle_action(sprite)
    elif something_else:
        # ... other processing
```

---

3. C, Java, Go, Rust, C#, TypeScript, and most programming languages also have enums of varying stripes. But the CONSTANT convention is nonetheless often seen in code in those languages.

In a highly dynamic language like Python, we *can* potentially redefine "constants" since the capitalization is only a convention rather than in the syntax or semantics of the language. If some later line of the program redefines SQUARE = 2, buggy behavior is likely to emerge. More likely is that some other module that gets imported has redefined SQUARE to something other than the expectation of the current module. This risk is minimal if imports are within namespaces, but from othermod import SQUARE, CUBE, TESSERACT is not necessarily unreasonable to have within the current module.

Programs written like the preceding one are not necessarily broken, and not even necessarily mistakes, but it is certainly more elegant to use enums for constants that come in sets.

Using enums for sets of alternatives

```
>>> from enum import Enum
>>> Color = Enum("Color", ["RED", "GREEN", "BLUE"])
>>> class Shape(Enum):
...     CIRCLE = 0
...     SQUARE = 1
...     TRIANGLE = 2
...
>>> my_sprite = Sprite(Shape.TRIANGLE, Color.RED)
>>> def process(sprite):
...     if sprite.shape == Shape.TRIANGLE and sprite.color ==
Color.RED:
...         print("It is a red triangle")
...     elif something_else:
...         pass
...
>>> process(my_sprite)
It is a red triangle
>>> Color.RED = 2
Traceback (most recent call last):
[...]
AttributeError: cannot reassign member 'RED'
```

It's not *impossible* to get around the protection that an Enum provides, but you have to work quite hard to do so rather than break it inadvertently. In effect, the attributes of an enum are *read-only*. Therefore, reassigning to an immutable attribute raises an exception.

There are also "constants" that are not alternatives, but simply values; these likewise cannot actually be enforced as constants in Python. Enums might still be reasonable namespaces with slightly more enforcement against changes than modules have.

Overwriting constants

```
>>> import math
>>> radius = 2
>>> volume = 4/3 * math.pi * radius**3
>>> volume                                  # ❶
33.510321638291124
>>> math.pi = 3.14                          # ❷
>>> 4/3 * math.pi * radius**3
33.49333333333333
>>> from math import pi
>>> 4/3 * pi * radius**3
33.49333333333333
>>> pi = 3.1415                             # ❸
>>> 4/3 * pi * radius**3
33.50933333333333
```

❶ As good as we get with 64-bit floating point numbers

❷ Monkeypatching a bad approximation of pi

❸ A somewhat less bad approximation of pi

Using enums to "enforce" value consistency

```
>>> from enum import Enum
>>> import math
>>> class Math(Enum):
...       pi = math.pi
...       tau = math.tau
...       e = math.e
...
>>> radius = 2
>>> Math.pi.value
3.141592653589793
>>> 4/3 * Math.pi.value * radius**3
33.510321638291124
>>> math.pi = 3
>>> 4/3 * Math.pi.value * radius**3
33.510321638291124
>>> Math.pi.value = 3
Traceback (most recent call last):
[...]
AttributeError: <enum 'Enum'> cannot set attribute 'value'
```

This usage doesn't really use Enum as a way of enumerating distinct values, but it *does* carry with it a modest protection of "read-only" values.

7.5 Learn Less Common Dictionary Methods

Dictionaries are a wonderful data structure that in many ways make up the heart of Python. Internally, most objects, including modules, are defined by their dictionaries.

The sometimes overlooked method `dict.get()` was discussed in Chapter 3, *A Grab Bag of Python Gotchas*, but `dict`s also have a few other methods that are often overlooked, even by experienced Python programmers. As with a number of other mistakes throughout this book, the mistake here is simply one of ignorance or forgetfulness; the result is not usually broken code, but rather just code that is less fast, elegant, and expressive than it might be.

7.5.1 The Dictionaries Defining Objects

This subsection is a digression into Python's internal mechanisms. Feel free to skip it for the actual pitfall; or read it to understand Python a little bit better.

You can use Python for a long time without ever needing to think about the dictionaries at the heart of most non-`dict` objects. There are some exceptions, but many Python objects have a `.__dict__` attribute to store the dictionary providing its capabilities and behaviors.

Let's look at a couple examples.

Module dictionaries

```
>>> import re
>>> type(re.__dict__)
<class 'dict'>
>>> for key in re.__dict__.keys():
...     print(key, end=" ")
...
__name__ __doc__ __package__ __loader__ __spec__ __path__ __file__
__cached__ __builtins__ enum _constants _parser _casefix _compiler
functools __all__ __version__ NOFLAG ASCII A IGNORECASE I LOCALE L
UNICODE U MULTILINE M DOTALL S VERBOSE X TEMPLATE T DEBUG RegexFlag
error match fullmatch search sub subn split findall finditer compile
purge template _special_chars_map escape Pattern Match _cache
_MAXCACHE _compile _compile_repl _expand _subx copyreg _pickle Scanner
```

The various functions and constants in a module are simply its dictionary. Built-in types usually use a slightly different dictionary-like object.

Dictionaries of basic types

```
>>> for typ in (str, int, list, tuple, dict):
...     print(typ, type(typ.__dict__))
...
<class 'str'> <class 'mappingproxy'>
<class 'int'> <class 'mappingproxy'>
<class 'list'> <class 'mappingproxy'>
<class 'tuple'> <class 'mappingproxy'>
<class 'dict'> <class 'mappingproxy'>

>>> int.__dict__["numerator"]
<attribute 'numerator' of 'int' objects>
>>> (7).__class__.__dict__["numerator"]
<attribute 'numerator' of 'int' objects>
>>> (7).numerator
7
```

Custom classes also continue this pattern (their instances have either .__dict__ or .__slots__, depending on how they are defined).

Dictionaries defining classes (and instances)

```
>>> class Point:
...     def __init__(self, x, y):
...         self.x = x
...         self.y = y
...     def from_origin(self):
...         from math import sqrt
...         return sqrt(self.x**2 + self.y**2)
...
>>> point = Point(3, 4)
>>> point.from_origin()
5.0
>>> type(Point.__dict__)
<class 'mappingproxy'>
>>> type(point.__dict__)
<class 'dict'>
>>> Point.__dict__.keys()
dict_keys(['__module__', '__init__', 'from_origin', '__dict__',
'__weakref__', '__doc__'])
>>> point.__dict__
{'x': 3, 'y': 4}
```

7.5.2 Back to Our Regularly Scheduled Mistake

The Method `.setdefault()`

Of all the useful methods of dictionaries, the one I personally forget the most often is `dict.setdefault()`. I have written code like this embarrassingly often:

```
>>> point = {"x": 3, "y": 4}
>>> if 'color' in point:
...     color = point["color"]
... else:
...     color = "lime green"
...     point["color"] = color
...
>>> point
{'x': 3, 'y': 4, 'color': 'lime green'}
```

All the while, I *should* have simply written:

```
>>> point = {"x": 3, "y": 4}
>>> color = point.setdefault("color", "lime green")
>>> color
'lime green'
>>> point
{'x': 3, 'y': 4, 'color': 'lime green'}
>>> point.setdefault("color", "brick red")
'lime green'
```

The first version works, but it uses five lines where one would be slightly faster and distinctly clearer.

The Method `.update()`

The method `dict.update()` is useful to avoid writing:

```
>>> from pprint import pprint
>>> features = {
...     "shape": "rhombus",
...     "flavor": "vanilla",
...     "color": "brick red"}
>>> for key, val in features.items():
...     point[key] = val
...
>>> pprint(point)
```

```
{'color': 'brick red',
 'flavor': 'vanilla',
 'shape': 'rhombus',
 'x': 3,
 'y': 4}
```

Prior to Python 3.9, the friendlier shortcut was:

```
>>> point = {"x": 3, "y": 4, "color": "chartreuse"}
>>> point.update(features)
>>> pprint(point)
{'color': 'brick red',
 'flavor': 'vanilla',
 'shape': 'rhombus',
 'x': 3,
 'y': 4}
```

But with recent Python versions, even more elegant versions are:

```
>>> point = {"x": 3, "y": 4, "color": "chartreuse"}
>>> point | features                              # ❶
{'x': 3, 'y': 4, 'color': 'brick red', 'shape': 'rhombus',
'flavor': 'vanilla'}
>>> point
{'x': 3, 'y': 4, 'color': 'chartreuse'}
>>> point |= features                             # ❷
>>> point
{'x': 3, 'y': 4, 'color': 'brick red', 'shape': 'rhombus',
'flavor': 'vanilla'}
```

❶ Create a new dictionary merging `features` with `point`.

❷ Equivalent to `point.update(features)`

The Methods `.pop()` and `.popitem()`

The methods `dict.pop()` and `dict.popitem()` are also easy to forget, but extremely useful when you need them. The former is useful when you want to find and remove a specific key; the latter is useful when you want to find and remove an unspecified key/value pair:

```
>>> point.pop("color", "gray")
'brick red'
```

```
>>> point.pop("color", "gray")
'gray'
>>> point
{'x': 3, 'y': 4, 'shape': 'rhombus', 'flavor': 'vanilla'}
```

That is much friendlier than:

```
>>> point = {'x': 3, 'y': 4, 'color': 'brick red',
             'shape': 'rhombus', 'flavor': 'vanilla'}
>>> if "color" in point:
...     color = point["color"]
...     del point["color"]
... else:
...     color = "gray"
... color
'brick red'
```

Likewise, to get an arbitrary item in a dictionary, dict.popitem() is very quick and easy. This is often a way to process the items within a dictionary, leaving an empty dictionary when processing is complete. Since Python 3.7, "arbitrary" is always LIFO (last-in, first-out) because dictionaries maintain insertion order. Depending on your program flow, insertion order may or may not be obvious or reproducible; but you are guaranteed *some* order for successive removal:

```
>>> point = {'x': 3, 'y': 4, 'color': 'brick red',
             'shape': 'rhombus', 'flavor': 'vanilla'}
>>> while point and (item := point.popitem()):
...     print(item)
...
('flavor', 'vanilla')
('shape', 'rhombus')
('color', 'brick red')
('y', 4)
('x', 3)
>>> point
{}
```

Making Copies

Another often-overlooked method is dict.copy(). However, I tend to feel that this method is usually properly overlooked. The copy made by this method is a *shallow* copy, so any mutable values might still be changed indirectly, leading to subtle and hard-to-find bugs. Chapter 2, *Confusing Equality with Identity*, is primarily about exactly this kind of mistake.

Most of the time, a much better place to look is `copy.deepcopy()`. For example:

```
>>> d1 = {"foo": [3, 4, 5], "bar": {6, 7, 8}}
>>> d2 = d1.copy()
>>> d2["foo"].extend([10, 11, 12])
>>> del d2["bar"]
>>> d1
{'foo': [3, 4, 5, 10, 11, 12], 'bar': {8, 6, 7}}
>>> d2
{'foo': [3, 4, 5, 10, 11, 12]}
```

This is confusing, and pretty much a bug magnet. Much better is:

```
>>> from copy import deepcopy
>>> d1 = {"foo": [3, 4, 5], "bar": {6, 7, 8}}
>>> d2 = deepcopy(d1)
>>> d2["foo"].extend([10, 11, 12])
>>> del d2["bar"]
>>> d1
{'foo': [3, 4, 5], 'bar': {8, 6, 7}}
>>> d2
{'foo': [3, 4, 5, 10, 11, 12]}
```

Dictionaries are an amazingly rich data structure in Python. As well as the usual efficiency that hash maps or key/value stores have in most programming languages, Python provides a moderate number of well-chosen "enhanced" methods. In principle, if dictionaries only had key/value insertion, key deletion, and a method to list keys, that would suffice to *do everything* the underlying data structure achieves. However, your code can be much cleaner and more intuitive with strategic use of the additional methods discussed.

7.6 JSON Does Not Round-Trip Cleanly to Python

A Python developer can be tempted into mistakenly thinking that arbitrary Python objects can be serialized as JSON, and relatedly that objects that can be serialized are necessarily deserialized as equivalent objects.

7.6.1 Some Background on JSON

In the modern world of microservices and "cloud-native computing," Python often needs to serialize and deserialize JavaScript Object Notation (JSON) data. Moreover, JSON doesn't only occur in the context of message exchange between small cooperating services, but is also used as a storage representation of certain structured data. For example, GeoJSON and the related TopoJSON, or JSON-LD for ontology and knowledge graph data, are formats that utilize JSON to encode domain-specific structures.

In surface appearance, JSON looks very similar to Python numbers, strings, lists, and dictionaries. The similarity is sufficient that for many JSON strings, simply writing eval(json_str) will deserialize a string to a valid Python object; in fact, this will *often* (but certainly not *always*) produce the same result as the correct approach of json.loads(json_str). JSON looks *even more* similar to native expressions in JavaScript (as the name hints), but even there, a few valid JSON strings cannot be deserialized (meaningfully) into JavaScript.

While superficially json.loads() performs a similar task as pickle.loads(), and json.dumps() performs a similar task as pickle.dumps(), the JSON versions do distinctly *less* in numerous situations. The "type system" of JSON is less rich than is that of Python. For a large subset of all Python objects, including (deeply) nested data structures, this invariant holds:

```
obj == pickle.loads(pickle.dumps(obj))
```

There are exceptions here. File handles or open sockets cannot be sensibly serialized and deserialized, for example. But most *data structures*, including custom classes, survive this round-trip perfectly well.

In contrast, this "invariant" is very frequently violated:

```
obj = json.loads(json.dumps(obj))
```

JSON is a very useful format in several ways. It is (relatively) readable pure text; it is highly interoperable with services written in other programming languages with which a Python program would like to cooperate; deserializing JSON does not introduce code execution vulnerabilities.

Pickle (in its several protocol versions) is also useful. It is a binary serialization format that is more compact than text. Or specifically, it is protocol 0, 1, 2, 3, 4, or 5, with each successive version being improved in some respect, but all following that characterization. Almost all Python objects can be serialized in a round-trippable way using the pickle module. However, none of the services you might wish to interact with, written in JavaScript, Go, Rust, Kotlin, C++, Ruby, or other languages, has any idea what to do with Python pickles.

7.6.2   Data That Fails to Round-Trip

In the first place, JSON only defines a few datatypes. These are discussed in RFC 8256 (https://datatracker.ietf.org/doc/html/rfc8259), ECMA-404 (https://www.ecma-international.org/publications-and-standards/standards/ecma-404/), and ISO/IEC 21778:2017 (https://www.iso.org/standard/71616.html). Despite having "the standard" enshrined by several standards bodies in not-quite-identical language, these standards are equivalent.

We should back up for a moment. I've now twice claimed—a bit incorrectly—that JSON has a limited number of datatypes. In reality, JSON has zero datatypes, and instead is, strictly speaking, only a definition of a syntax with no semantics whatsoever. As RFC 8256 defines the highest level of its BNF (Backus–Naur form):

```
value ::= false | null | true | object | array | number | string
```

Here `false`, `null`, and `true` are literals, while object, array, number, and string are textual patterns. To simplify, a JSON object is like a Python dictionary, with curly braces, colons, and commas. An array is like a Python list, with square brackets and commas. A number can take a number of formats, but the rules are *almost* the same as what defines valid Python numbers. Likewise, JSON strings are *almost* the same as the spelling of Python strings, but always with double quotation marks. Unicode numeric codes are mostly the same between JSON and Python (edge cases concern very obscure surrogate pair handling).

Let's take a look at some edge cases. The Python standard library module `json` "succeeds" in two cases by producing output that is *not actually* JSON:

```
>>> import json
>>> import math
>>> print(json.dumps({"nan": math.nan}))              # ❶
{"nan": NaN}
>>> print(json.dumps({"inf": math.inf}))
{"inf": Infinity}
>>> json.loads(json.dumps({'nan': math.nan}))         # ❷
{'nan': nan}
>>> json.loads(json.dumps({'inf': math.inf}))
{'inf': inf}
```

❶ The result of `json.dumps()` is a string; printing it just removes the extra quotes in the echoed representation.

❷ Neither NaN nor Infinity (under any spelling variation) are in the JSON standards.

In some sense, this behavior is convenient for Python programmers, but it breaks compatibility with (many) consumers of these serializations in other programming languages. We can enforce more strictness with `json.dumps(obj, allow_nan=False)`, which would raise `ValueError` in the preceding lines. However, *some* other libraries in *some* other programming languages also allow this almost-JSON convention.

Depending on what you mean by "round-trip," you might say this succeeded. Indeed it does strictly within Python itself; but it fails when the *round-trip* involves talking with a service written in a different programming language, and it talking back. Let's look at some failures within Python itself. The most obvious cases are in Python's more diverse collection types.

Not-quite round-tripping collections with JSON

```
>>> from collections import namedtuple
>>> Person = namedtuple("Person", "first last body_temp")
>>> david = Person("David", "Mertz", "37°C")
>>> vector1 = (4.6, 3.2, 1.5)
>>> vector2 = (9.8, -1.2, 0.4)
>>> obj = {1: david, 2: [vector1, vector2], 3: True, 4: None}
>>> obj
{1: Person(first='David', last='Mertz', body_temp='37°C'),
2: [(4.6, 3.2, 1.5), (9.8, -1.2, 0.4)], 3: True, 4: None}

>>> print(json.dumps(obj))
{"1": ["David", "Mertz", "37\u2103"], "2": [[4.6, 3.2, 1.5],
[9.8, -1.2, 0.4]], "3": true, "4": null}
>>> json.loads(json.dumps(obj))
{'1': ['David', 'Mertz', '37°C'], '2': [[4.6, 3.2, 1.5],
[9.8, -1.2, 0.4]], '3': True, '4': None}
```

In JSON, Python's `True` is spelled `true`, and `None` is spelled `null`, but those are entirely literal spelling changes. Likewise, the Unicode character DEGREE CELSIUS can perfectly well live inside a JSON string (or any Unicode character other than a quotation mark, *reverse solidus*/backslash, and the control characters U+0000 through U+001F). For some reason, Python's `json` module decided to substitute with the numeric code, but such has no effect on the round-trip.

What got lost was that some data was inside a `namedtuple` called `Person`, and other data was inside tuples. JSON only has arrays, that is, things in square brackets. The general "meaning" of the data is still there, but we've lost important type information.

Moreover, in the serialization, only strings are permitted as object keys, and hence our valid-in-Python integer keys were converted to strings. However, this is lossy since a Python dictionary could, in principle (but it's not great code), have both string and numeric keys:

```
>>> json.dumps({1: "foo", "1": "bar"})
'{"1": "foo", "1": "bar"}'
>>> json.loads(json.dumps({1: "foo", "1": "bar"}))
{'1': 'bar'}
```

Two or three things conspired against us here. Firstly, the JSON specification doesn't prevent duplicate keys from occurring. Secondly, the integer `1` is converted to the string `"1"` when it becomes JSON. And thirdly, Python dictionaries always have unique keys, so the second try at setting the `"1"` key overwrote the first try.

Another somewhat obscure edge case is that JSON itself can validly represent numbers that Python does not support:

```
>>> json_str = '[1E400, 3.14159265358979323846264383279]'
>>> json.loads(json_str)
[inf, 3.141592653589793]
```

This is not a case of crashing, nor failing to load numbers at all. But rather, one number overflows to infinity since it is too big for float64, and the other is approximated to fewer digits of precision than are provided.

A corner edge case is that JSON numbers that "look like Python integers" actually get cast to `int` rather than `float`:

```
>>> json_str = f'{"7"*400}'            # ❶
>>> val = json.loads(json_str)
>>> math.log10(val)
399.8908555305749
>>> type(val)
<class 'int'>
```

❶ A string of four hundred `"7"`s in a row

However, since few other programming languages or architectures you might communicate with will support, for example, float128 either, the best policy is usually to stick with numbers float64 can represent.

7.7 Rolling Your Own Data Structures

This section covers a nuanced issue (and a long one). Readers who have come out of a college data structures course, or read a good book on the topic,[4] have learned of many powerful data structures that are neither within Python's standard library nor in the prominent third-party libraries I discuss in various parts of this book. Some of these include treaps, k-d trees, R-trees, B-trees, Fibonacci heaps, tries (prefix tree), singly-, doubly-, and multiply-linked lists, heaps, graphs, bloom filters, cons cells, and dozens of others.

---

4. Perhaps even Donald Knuth's "bible": *The Art of Computer Programming* (various editions among its current five volumes; but especially the 3rd edition of volume 1, Addison-Wesley, 1997).

The choice of which data structures to include as built-ins, or in the standard library, is one that language designers debate, and which often leads to in-depth discussion and analysis. Python's philosophy is to include a relatively minimal, but extremely powerful and versatile, collection of primitives with `dict`, `list`, `tuple`, `set`, `frozenset`, `bytes`, and `bytearray` in `__builtins__` (arguably, `complex` is a simple data structure as well). Modules such as `collections`, `queue`, `dataclasses`, `enum`, `array`, and a few others peripherally, include other data structures, but even there the number is much smaller than for many programming languages.

A clear contrast with Python, in this regard, is Java. Whereas Python strives for simplicity, Java strives to include every data structure users might ever want within its standard library (i.e., the `java.util` namespace). Java has hundreds of distinct data structures included in the language itself. For Pythonic programmers, this richness of choice largely leads only to "analysis paralysis" (https://en.wikipedia.org/wiki/Analysis_paralysis). Choosing among so many only-slightly-different data structures imposes a large cognitive burden, and the final decision made (after greater work) often remains sub-optimal. Giving someone more hammers can sometimes provide little other than more ways for them to hit their thumb.

> **Note   A data structure that hasn't quite made it into Python**
>
> A really lovely example of the design discussions that go into Python is in PEP 603 (https://peps.python.org/pep-0603/), and the python-dev mailing list and Discourse thread among core developers that followed this PEP. The proposal of a new data structure has not been entirely rejected since September 2019, but it also has not been accepted so far.
>
> Internally, CPython utilizes a data structure called a Hash Array Mapped Trie (HAMT). This isn't used widely, but there are specific places in the C code implementing CPython where it is the best choice. A HAMT is a kind of immutable dictionary, in essence. Since this structure *already exists* in the CPython codebase, it would be relatively easy to expose it under a name like `frozenmap` or `frozendict`; this would parallel the existing `frozenset` and `tuple` in being the "immutable version of built-in mutable collections."
>
> HAMT is clearly a useful data structure for some purposes. If it were not, the very talented CPython developers would not have utilized it. However, the current tide of opinion among these developers is that HAMT is not general purpose enough to add to the cognitive load of tens of millions of Python developers who *probably won't need it.*

7.7.1   When Rolling Your Own Is a Bad Idea

Writing any of the data structures mentioned thus far is comparatively easy in Python. Doing so is often the subject of college exams and software engineering interviews, for example. Doing so is also *usually* a bad idea for most software tasks you will face. When you reach quickly for an opportunity to use one of these data structures you have learned—each of which genuinely *does* have concrete advantages in specific contexts—it often reflects an excess of cleverness and eagerness more than it does good design instincts.

A reality is that Python itself is a relatively slow bytecode interpreter. Unlike compiled programming languages, including just-in-time (JIT) compiled languages, which produce machine-native instructions, CPython is a giant bytecode dispatch loop. Every time an instruction is executed, many levels of indirection are needed, and basic values are all relatively complex wrappers around their underlying data (remember all those methods of datatypes that you love so much?).

Note   Python implementations

Several alternative implementations of Python exist besides CPython. In particular, a few of these include JIT compilation. The most widely used such implementation is PyPy (https://www.pypy.org/), which JITs everything, and does so remarkably well. Its main drawbacks are that it has fallen behind version compatibility with CPython, and that using compiled extensions created for CPython can encounter overheads that reduce the speed advantages greatly.

Less widely used attempts at JIT Python interpreters include Pyston (https://github.com/pyston/pyston), Cinder (https://github.com /facebookincubator/cinder), and Pyjion (https://github.com/tonybaloney /Pyjion). While all of these have good ideas within them—and all are derived from CPython source code (unlike PyPy)—these open source projects still largely have a focus within the private companies that developed them. Those are Dropbox, Meta, and Microsoft, respectively (Alphabet—i.e., Google—subsidiary DeepMind abandoned its similar S6 project).

Reservations mentioned, it is well possible that a custom data structure developed as pure Python but used in a JIT interpreter will achieve the speed and flexibility advantages that those developed in compiled languages have.

Accompanying the fact that Python is relatively slow, most of the built-in and standard library data structures you might reach for are written in highly optimized C. Much the same is true for the widely used library NumPy, which has a chapter of its own.

On the one hand, custom data structures such as those mentioned can have significant big-O complexity advantages over those that come with Python.[5] On the other hand, these advantages need to be balanced against what is usually a (roughly) constant

---

5. See note 1 on page 156.

multiplicative disadvantage to pure-Python code. That is to say, implementing the identical data structure purely in Python is likely to be 100x, or even 1000x, slower than doing so in a well-optimized compiled language like C, C++, Rust, or Fortran. At some point as a dataset grows, big-O dominates any multiplicative factor, but often that point is well past the dataset sizes you actually care about.

Plus, writing a new data structure requires actually writing it. This is prone to bugs, takes developer time, needs documentation, and accumulates technical debt. In other words, doing so might very well be a mistake.

7.7.2 When Rolling Your Own Is a Good Idea

Taking all the warnings and caveats of the first subsection of this discussion into account, there remain many times when *not* writing a custom data structure is its own mistake. Damned if you do, damned if you don't, one might think. But the real issue is more subtle; it's a mistake to make a poor judgment about which side of this decision to choose.

I present in the following subsections a "pretty good" specialized data structure that illustrates both sides. This example is inspired by the section "Deleting or Adding Elements to the Middle of a List" earlier in this chapter. To quickly summarize that section: Inserting into the middle of a Python list is inefficient, but doing so is very often a matter of *solving the wrong problem*.

For now, however, let's suppose that you genuinely *do need* to have a data structure that is concrete, strictly ordered, indexable, iterable, and into which you need to insert new items in varying middle positions. There simply is not any standard library or widely used Python library that gives you exactly this. Perhaps it's worth developing your own.

Always Benchmark When You Create a Data Structure

Before I show you the code *I* created to solve this specific requirement, I want to reveal the "punch line" by showing you performance. A testing function shows the general behavior we want to be performant.

The insert_many() function that exercises our use case

```
from random import randint, seed
from get_word import get_word                       # ❶
def insert_many(Collection, n, test_seed="roll-your-own"):
    seed(test_seed)                                 # ❷
    collection = Collection()
    for _ in range(n):
        collection.insert(randint(0, len(collection)), get_word())
    return collection
```

❶ The get_word() function available at this book's website is used in many examples. It simply returns a different word each time it is called.

❷ Using the same random seed assures that we do *exactly* the same insertions for each collection type.

The testing function performs however many insertions we ask it to, and we can time that:

```
>>> from binary_tree import CountingTree

>>> %timeit insert_many(list, 100)
92.9 µs ± 742 ns per loop (mean ± std. dev. of 7 runs, 10,000 loops
each)
>>> %timeit insert_many(CountingTree, 100)
219 µs ± 8.17 µs per loop (mean ± std. dev. of 7 runs, 1,000 loops
each)

>>> %timeit insert_many(list, 10_000)
13.9 ms ± 193 µs per loop (mean ± std. dev. of 7 runs, 100 loops each)
>>> %timeit insert_many(CountingTree, 10_000)
38 ms ± 755 µs per loop (mean ± std. dev. of 7 runs, 10 loops each)

>>> %timeit insert_many(list, 100_000)
690 ms ± 5.84 ms per loop (mean ± std. dev. of 7 runs, 1 loop each)
>>> %timeit insert_many(CountingTree, 100_000)
674 ms ± 20.1 ms per loop (mean ± std. dev. of 7 runs, 1 loop each)

>>> %timeit insert_many(list, 1_000_000)
1min 5s ± 688 ms per loop (mean ± std. dev. of 7 runs, 1 loop each)
>>> %timeit insert_many(CountingTree, 1_000_000)
9.72 s ± 321 ms per loop (mean ± std. dev. of 7 runs, 1 loop each)
```

Without having yet said just what a `CountingTree` is, I can say that I spent more time ironing out the bugs in my code than I entirely want to admit. It's not a large amount of code, as you'll see, but the details are futzy.

Notable points are that even though I've created a data structure optimized for *exactly* this task, it does worse than `list` for 100 items. `CountingTree` does worse than `list` for 10,000 items also, even by a slightly larger margin than for 100. However, my custom data structure pulls ahead *slightly* for 100,000 items; and then *hugely* so for a million items.

It would be painful to use `list` for the million-item sequence, and increasingly worse if I needed to do even more `collection.insert()` operations.

Performing Magic in Pure Python

The source code for `binary_tree.py` is available at the book's website (https://gnosis.cx /better). But we will go through most of it here. The basic idea behind my *Counting Binary Tree* data structure is that I want to keep a binary tree, but I also want each node to keep a count of the total number of items within it and all of its descendants. Unlike some other tree data structures, we specifically *do not* want to order the node values by their inequality comparison, but rather to maintain each node exactly where it is inserted.

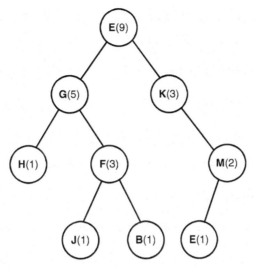

Figure 7.1   A graph of a Counting Binary Tree.

In Figure 7.1, each node contains a value that is a single letter; in parentheses we show the *length* of each node with its subtree. Identical values can occur in multiple places (unlike, e.g., for a set or a dictionary key). Finding the len() of this data structure is a matter of reading a single attribute. But having this length available is what guides insertions.

It is very easy to construct a *sequence* from a tree. It is simply a matter of choosing a deterministic rule for how to order the nodes. For my code, I chose to use *depth-first, left-to-right*; that's not the only possible choice, but it is an obvious and common one. In other words, every node value occurs at exactly one position in the sequence, and every sequence position (up to the length) is occupied by exactly one value. Since our use case is approximately random insertion points for new items, no extra work is needed for rebalancing or enforcing any other invariants.

The code shown *only* implements insertions, our stated use case. A natural extension to the data structure would be to implement deletions as well. Or changing values at a given position. Or other capabilities that lists and other data structures have. Most of those capabilities would remain inexpensive, but details would vary by the specific operation, of course.

The basic implementation of Counting Binary Tree

```
class CountingTree:
    def __init__(self, value=EMPTY):
        self.left = EMPTY
        self.right = EMPTY
        self.value = value
        self.length = 0 if value is EMPTY else 1
```

```
def insert(self, index: int, value):
    if index != 0 and not 0 < index <= self.length:
        raise IndexError(
            f"CountingTree index {index} out of range")

    if self.value is EMPTY:
        self.value = value
    elif index == self.length:
        if self.right is EMPTY:
            self.right = CountingTree(value)
        else:
            self.right.insert(
                index - (self.left.length + 1), value)
    elif index == 0 and self.left is EMPTY:
        self.left = CountingTree(value)
    else:
        if index > self.left.length:
            self.right.insert(
                index - (self.left.length + 1), value)
        else:
            self.left.insert(index, value)

    self.length += 1
```

This much is all we actually need to run the benchmarks performed here. Calling
CountingTree.insert() repeatedly creates trees much like that in the figure. The .left
and .right attributes at each level might be occupied by the sentinel EMPTY, which the
logic can utilize for nodes without a given child.

It's useful also to define a few other behaviors we'd like a collection to have.

Additional methods within Counting Binary Tree

```
def append(self, value):
    self.insert(len(self), value)

def __iter__(self):
    if self.left is not EMPTY:
        yield from self.left
    if self.value is not EMPTY:
        yield self.value
    if self.right is not EMPTY:
        yield from self.right

def __repr__(self):
    return f"CountingTree({list(self)})"
```

```
    def __len__(self):
        return self.length

    def tree(self, indent=0):
        print(f"{'· '*indent}{self.value}")
        if self.left is not EMPTY or self.right is not EMPTY:
            self.left.tree(indent+1)
            self.right.tree(indent+1)
```

These other methods largely just build off of .insert(). A CountingBinaryTree is iterable, but along with .__iter__() it would be natural to define .__getitem__() or .__contains__() to allow use of square bracket indexing and the in operator. These would be straightforward.

For the .tree() method we need our sentinel to have a couple specific behaviors. This method is just for visual appeal in viewing the data structure, but it's nice to have.

The EMPTY sentinel

```
# Sentinel for an unused node
class Empty:
    length = 0

    def __repr__(self):
        return "EMPTY"

    def tree(self, indent=0):
        print(f"{'· '*indent}EMPTY")


EMPTY = Empty()
```

Observing the Behavior of Our Data Structure

By no means am I advocating the general use of this specific skeletal data structure implementation. It's shown merely to illustrate the general way you might go about creating something analogous for well-understood use cases and with a knowledge of the theoretical advantages of particular data structures. Let's look at a few behaviors, though:

```
>>> insert_many(CountingTree, 10)
CountingTree(['secedes', 'poss', 'killcows', 'unpucker',
'gaufferings', 'funninesses', 'trilingual', 'nihil', 'bewigging',
'reproachably'])
>>> insert_many(list, 10)                          # ❶
['secedes', 'poss', 'killcows', 'unpucker', 'gaufferings',
```

```
       'funninesses', 'trilingual', 'nihil', 'bewigging', 'reproachably']

>>> ct = insert_many(CountingTree, 1000, "david")
>>> lst = insert_many(list, 1000, "david")
>>> list(ct) == lst                                     # ❷
True

>>> insert_many(CountingTree, 9, "foobar").tree()       # ❸
loaf
· acknown
· · spongily
· · · saeculums
· · · EMPTY
· · EMPTY
· fecundities
· · EMPTY
· · input
· · · boddle
· · · · sots
· · · · shrifts
· · · EMPTY
```

❶ Insertions into `list` or `CountingTree` preserve the same order.

❷ Equivalence for some operations between `list` and `CountingTree`

❸ Display the underlying tree implementing the sequence.

The tree is fairly balanced, and sometimes a given subtree fills only one or the other of its left and right children. This balance would be lost if, for example, we always used `.append()` (it would degenerate to a singly-linked list).

7.7.3 Takeaways

This section has had a long discussion. The takeaway you should leave with isn't a simple one. The lesson is "be subtle and accurate in your judgments" about when to create and when to avoid creating custom data structures. It's not a recipe, but more vaguely an advocacy of a nuanced attitude.

As a general approach to making the right choice, I'd suggest following a few steps in your thinking:

1. Try implementing the code using a widely used, standard Python data structure.

2. Run benchmarks to find out if any theoretical sub-optimality *genuinely* matters for the use case your code is put to.

3. Research the wide range of data structures that exist in the world to see which, if any, are theoretically optimal for your use case.

4. Research whether someone else has already written a well-tested Python implementation of the less common data structure you are considering. Such a library might not be widely used simply because the niche it fulfills is relatively narrow. On the other hand, it is also easy to put partially developed, poorly tested, and buggy libraries on PyPI, conda-forge, GitHub, GitLab, Bitbucket, or other public locations.

5. Assuming you are writing your own after considering the preceding steps, create both tests and benchmarks either in conjunction with—or even before—the implementation of the data structure.

6. If your well-tested implementation of a new data structure makes your code better, ask your boss for a raise or a bonus... and then share the code with the Python community under an open source license.

7.8 Wrapping Up

Sometimes a powerful object method or general technique can also lead you in the wrong direction, even in seemingly ordinary uses. This wrong direction might cause bad complexity behavior; at times it might work for initial cases but then fail in cases you had not yet considered.

In this chapter we probed at some operations on lists—generally one of the best optimized and flexible data structures Python has—where a different data structure is simply better. We also looked at how recursive algorithms need to remember that strings are both scalar and iterable, which means they often need to be special-cased in program flow.

Two more mistakes in this chapter looked at "sins of omission" where a facility that may be less familiar provides a more convenient and more readable approach to common tasks. Specifically, two mistakes served as reminders of the `enum` module and of some of the less widely used methods of dictionaries.

In the penultimate mistake of this chapter, the capabilities and limitations of the widely used JSON format were explored. In particular, we saw how Python developers might forget the (relatively minor) lossiness of JSON representations of data.

The final mistake discussed is one of nuance and complex decision-making. Often, creating custom data structures is premature optimization; but at other times they can significantly improve your code. The (long) discussion provides some guidance about making this choice wisely.

8

Security

This book is not the one you should read to understand either cryptography or computer security built on top of cryptographic primitives. Of course, in a very general way, it's a mistake to wire money to fraudulent entities phishing under various get-rich-quick or tug-on-heartstrings pretenses. However, that's life advice that might touch on using computers, not Python advice.

What the mistakes in this chapter discuss are simply approaches to security concerns that I have frequently seen Python developers do badly. Often this reflects a misunderstanding of some very general security concepts. At other times an unawareness of the appropriate modules and functions to use (standard library or third-party) is evidenced.

For an actual background on cryptography, Bruce Schneier's *Applied Cryptography: Protocols, Algorithms, and Source Code in C* is a quite old, but still classic, text (2nd edition, John Wiley & Sons, 1996; it even has a few errata corrected from the first edition by your current author). Schneier's somewhat more recent 2010 text, with coauthors Niels Ferguson and Tadayoshi Kohno, *Cryptography Engineering: Design Principles and Practical Applications*, is also excellent (John Wiley & Sons).

There is a distinction to be made between cryptography and security, with the latter being more broad. Cryptography is an important element of secure software designs, but it is not the only concern, nor even the only building block. Cryptography concerns itself with mathematical mechanisms of enforcing confidentiality, integrity, non-repudiation, and authentication. Security more broadly concerns itself also with risk management, access control, classification of information, business continuity, disaster recovery, and laws and regulations. Addressing the broad security concerns often utilizes cryptographic protocols, but puts them in the context of a general "threat model" against which protection is sought.[1]

Threat modeling and security procedures involve many concerns beyond what Python programmers can or cannot do. For example, it considers corporate training about when

---

1. The term *threat model* is a rather elegant one, to my eyes; but it's also likely unfamiliar to many readers. It basically amounts to posing a collection of "what if?" questions about potential (malicious) actions that might cause a failure in computer systems. What are the ways the system *can possibly* go wrong? This is only occasionally a matter of "someone breaks the encryption protocol." Far more often concerns like social engineering (convincing people to act unwisely through misrepresentation) or denial of service (causing systems to break without an intruder per se getting access to information) are threats modeled.

and with whom employees should share secrets. It includes physical locks on buildings. It includes procedures used for in-person or telephone verification of an identity. It includes background checks before giving humans particular access rights. It includes physical securing of transmission wires or server rooms.

You don't need to read any of the recommended external texts to understand this chapter, but they provide some general background to the mathematical and algorithmic design of particular functions and modules this chapter discusses. The broader concerns around "social engineering" (i.e., convincing people to do things that compromise security) are even further outside the direct scope of this chapter.

8.1   Kinds of Randomness

The module `random` in the standard library—with the exception of the `random.SystemRandom()` class—uses the Mersenne Twister (MT) pseudo-random number generator (PRNG).[2] This algorithm is used by numerous other programming languages and libraries; older languages and libraries might use linear congruential generators (LCGs),[3] and some newer systems use permuted congruential generators (PCGs).[4] Several other pseudo-random generators are occasionally used.

A great deal of mathematical theory goes into each of these, but PRNGs all operate in a similar manner at a high level. They begin with a state, derived from a seed. Then they deterministically move between a very large cycle of other states (for example, among $2^{19937}-1$ states for MT). The distribution of states *resembles* a stochastic process according to numerous statistical tests, but it is actually a completely deterministic progression from the current state. If you know the current state, you know with certainty exactly what the next state will be.

The module `secrets` in the standard library builds on `random.SystemRandom()`, but it is nearly always a better practice to use the wrappers within `secrets`. The purpose of `secrets` is to generate non-repeatable, cryptographically strong, random numbers. The functions in `secrets` utilize system entropy (what is called `/dev/random` on Unix-like systems) and will actually block (if needed, which is uncommon) until sufficient entropy becomes available to provide "random" data. Entropy comes from interrupt timing for various kinds of devices (e.g., disk, keyboard, network), CPU execution time jitter, and hardware RNGs if they are available.

8.1.1   Use `secrets` for Cryptographic Randomness

Many developers who want a random value such as a generated password or token will reach towards the `random` module. The `random` module is widely used, familiar to most users of Python, and usually feels "good enough" at being unpredictable.

---

2. See a description of Mersenne Twister at https://en.wikipedia.org/wiki/Mersenne_Twister.
3. See a description of linear congruential generators at https://en.wikipedia.org/wiki/Linear_congruential
_generator.
4. See a description of permuted congruential generators at https://en.wikipedia.org/wiki/Permuted
_congruential_generator.

However, for actual cryptographic needs, `random` falls short. When a seed is not specified to `random.seed()`, a small number of truly random entropy bytes are used as a seed. In many circumstances that makes a "random" token sufficiently unpredictable.

Many circumstances are not *all circumstances*, and for applications that care about cryptographic security, it is better simply to start by using `secrets` in case your code becomes used in a situation where vulnerabilities are exposed. The `secrets` module has been available since Python 3.6, so it is not anything very new.

An excellent, fairly informal, analysis of vulnerabilities in the Mersenne Twister was done by James Roper.[5] The short summary is that if you can observe 624 consecutive integers produced by the Mersenne Twister, you can reconstruct its complete state, and thereby every output it will produce in the future. Even if fewer consecutive values can be observed by a malicious intruder, indirect vulnerabilities can likely be exploited.

Besides the vulnerability Roper points out, we also commonly spin up virtual images with little initial entropy and/or reproducing an exact known state of the MT generator. Running on your local machine, which has been in operation for hours or weeks, provides sufficient strength in a generated seed. Running on a Docker image that Kubernetes spins up frequently, on an AWS Lambda, or Google Cloud Function very well may not.

The code you run today in a circumstance where "`random` is fine" will probably be ported to an environment where it is not tomorrow.

There are only a few functions in the `secrets` module. The most commonly used one generates tokens of arbitrary length in a few different formats:

```
>>> secrets.token_bytes(12)
b'\xe7Wt\x96;\x829a\xc9\xbd\xe1\x94'
>>> secrets.token_hex(20)
'b397afc44c9cac5dba7900ef615ad48dd351d7e3'
>>> secrets.token_urlsafe(24)
'QYNBxUDVGO4feQUyetyih8V5vKKyy8nQ'
```

For security against brute-force attacks by state-level actors, a length of at least 32 is recommended. A few additional functions are available as well, specifically `secrets.choice()`, `secrets.randbelow()`, and `secrets.randbits()`, but not the full range of distributions and other types of pseudo-randomness that `random` provides.

The very interesting `secrets.compare_digest()` is also present and will compare two string or byte values in constant time to avoid timing attacks. This situation is a very specific threat model, which only occasionally exists. That said, if you are comparing tokens rather than simply generic strings, there is no harm in using this function rather than a simple == just in case you've overlooked such an attack.

---

5. See Roper's "Cracking Random Number Generators - Part 3" at https://jazzy.id.au/2010/09/22/cracking_random_number_generators_part_3.html, and "Cracking Random Number Generators - Part 4" at https://jazzy.id.au/2010/09/25/cracking_random_number_generators_part_4.html.

8.1.2 Reproducible Random Distributions

The preceding section could possibly have left readers with a mistaken impression, if read hastily. True randomness is a valuable feature for cryptographic and security concerns. However, for equally many *other* purposes, cryptographic randomness is specifically *not* what we want (and it is a mistake to use it).

As well as offering a reasonably large number of random distributions, random has an essential feature that secrets in its nature never can: reproducibility. Distributions provided include random.random() (uniform over interval [0.0, 1.0)); random.uniform(a, b) (uniform over interval [a, b]); random.triangular(), random.betavariate(), random.expovariate(), random.gammavariate(), random.gauss(), random.lognormvariate(), random.vonmisesvariate(), random.paretovariate(), and random.weibullvariate(). As well, random provides other useful selectors such as random.randint(), random.randrange(), random.randbytes(), random.choice(), random.choices(), and random.sample() (the last two varying by whether they are taken with or without replacement).

The preceding paragraph listed a large number of distributions. Don't worry if you don't know what most of them do; those people who work in domains that need them understand why they need them. For a variety of scientific and numeric purposes, each of these is useful, and few are present in secrets. However, with algebraic manipulation, you could, in principle, obtain each of those numeric distributions from calls to, for example, secrets.randbelow(a), which picks an integer uniformly from the interval [0, a).

More fundamentally, random contains random.seed(), random.setstate(), and random.getstate(). This enables *reproducibility* of a sequence of random values. Here is an example.

Reproducible random choice from SOWPODS wordlist

```
>>> import random, secrets
>>> words = [w.strip() for w in open('data/sowpods')]
>>> random.seed('reproducible-abc123')
>>> for _ in range(9_999_999):
...     random.choice(words)
...
>>> random.choice(words)
'spekboom'
>>> for _ in range(secrets.randbelow(1_000_000)):    # ❶
...     random.choice(words)
...
>>> random.choice(words)                             # ❷
'remotivations'
>>> random.seed('reproducible-abc123')
>>> for _ in range(9_999_999):
```

```
...        random.choice(words)
...
>>> random.choice(words)
'spekboom'
```

❶ This loop performs a genuinely unknowable number of steps through the Mersenne Twister generator.

❷ This choice of "remotivations" will not occur if I run the code again, or if you run it. However, "spekboom" will remain stable if you use my wordlist.

Not only was "spekboom" (a South African succulent commonly kept as a houseplant) the 10 millionth word chosen following initialization of the MT generator with the seed I used, but also the prior nine million, nine hundred ninety-nine thousand, nine hundred ninety-nine words were the same (although were not displayed in the output).

If we wish to save the state of the generator after these 10 million choices, that is easy to do.

Saving the state of a Mersenne Twister generator

```
>>> mt_state = random.getstate()
>>> print(f"{len(mt_state[1])} numbers: {mt_state[1][:4] + ('...',)}")
625 numbers: (3974703532, 1779565825, 1928569991, 1391398096, '...')
>>> random.choice(words)
'labdacisms'
>>> for _ in range(secrets.randbelow(1_000_000)):   # ❶
...        random.choice(words)
...
>>> random.choice(words)                            # ❷
'carnotite'
>>> random.setstate(mt_state)
>>> random.choice(words)
'labdacisms'
```

❶ Again, an unknowable number of steps through the Mersenne Twister generator

❷ The choice of "carnotite" is also a one-off occurrence. Or at least a 1/267,752 chance of happening.

Every time the state is reset to mt_state, the very next word chosen will be "labdacisms" (a phonological shift in which /l/ is substituted with /r/).

Why Do We Want Repeatability?

We've seen a bit of the API for using seeds and state in random, but the reason we want that repeatability may remain unclear. There are a couple of clear reasons to want this.

Just as a quick reminder, even though the preceding example worked with `random.choice` from a wordlist, simply to create memorable outputs, the same reproducibility and APIs work the same way when drawing from any of the numeric distributions.

Perhaps the most obvious need for "repeatable randomness" is in creating unit tests or functional tests of our software. We would like to ensure that our software—for example, a long-running web server—given a particular sequence of inputs continues to behave the same way.

For 10 million inputs, we could probably save those in a data file without outrageous waste on modern computers. But if it were 10 billion inputs, saving a sequence of inputs is enormously wasteful when one seed of a few-character string, or one state of 625 numbers, would suffice.

Another common related need is when you have a complex process that you believe you can optimize, but want to ensure that identical behavior is retained. As a contrived example, we have a function `blackbox()` that takes a string and an iterable of integers as arguments, and returns a permutation of that string. Again, for short iterables, simply saving them as static data is fine, but for long ones repeatability is relevant.

Let's run the existing implementation.

An inefficient but important `blackbox()` function

```
from typing import Iterable
def blackbox(s: str, nums: Iterable[int]) -> str:
    # some non-optimized computation
    return new_s
```

Observing the behavior of `blackbox()` we find:

```
>>> def test_sequence(seed="abc", count=10, floor=0, ceil=100):
...     random.seed(seed)
...     for _ in range(count):
...         yield random.randint(floor, ceil)
...
>>> s = "Mary had a little lamb!"
>>> blackbox(s, [5, 9999, 34, -65, 4, 2])
'Mryaa hd a itltle lamb!'
>>> blackbox(s, test_sequence(count=10_000_000))
'aMt!r ahbma i  letllyda'
>>> %timeit blackbox(s, test_sequence(count=10_000_000))
28 s ± 195 ms per loop (mean ± std. dev. of 7 runs, 1 loop each)
```

We could create other test sequences of varying lengths, with varying seeds, and with varying floor and ceiling of the integers produced. But across a reasonable collection of such configurations, we would like our new `blackbox_fast()` function to produce the same outputs as a previous slow implementation.

Examining implementation of `blackbox_fast()`

```
>>> blackbox_fast(s, [5, 9999, 34, -65, 4, 2])
'Mryaa hd a itltle lamb!'
>>> (blackbox(s, test_sequence(count=10_000_000)) ==
...  blackbox_fast(s, test_sequence(count=10_000_000)))
True
>>> (blackbox(s, test_sequence(seed="xyz", count=1_000_000)) ==
...  blackbox_fast(s, test_sequence(seed="xyz", count=1_000_000)))
True
>>> (blackbox(s, test_sequence(count=1000, ceil=500)) ==
...  blackbox_fast(s, test_sequence(count=1000, ceil=500)))
True
>>> %timeit blackbox_fast(s, test_sequence(count=10_000_000))
3.6 s ± 36 ms per loop (mean ± std. dev. of 7 runs, 1 loop each)
```

We can see that the new implementation is considerably faster, while also remaining consistent in behavior across our range of test cases. Constructing a collection of such tests over large iterables would be impractical without "deterministic randomness."

8.2 Putting Passwords or Other Secrets in "Secure" Source Code

Far too often, I have seen password information included within the source code of project files. Usually when this is done, developers have carelessly thought that in their particular scenario, these source code files will not be directly exposed to users, so this style does not matter.

Often the systems in question are web servers or other kinds of data servers, where in normal operation access is only via URLs or other encapsulated mechanisms. The passwords in source code are used to access additional resources, such as other websites or databases protected by credentials. Such developers often try to reassure themselves by asserting that the resource is itself inside a firewall zone or otherwise whitelist the particular applications or servers making such requests.

Approaching secrets this way is *always* a bad idea, and is usually motivated by mere laziness (although ignorance can certainly be at play as well). The assumptions you make about underlying source code not being exposed to malicious actors almost inevitably are proved wrong, through one mechanism or another. Sometimes that happens by so-called "hackers" deliberately looking for exploits; probably even more often it occurs simply because access to the source code is not well regulated within version control systems, shared drives, backup storage, and so on.

A typical example of this mistake can resemble the following code. This example uses an HTTPS request, but a very similar pattern would apply to a request using Python's DB-API to talk to a database that uses credentials.

Insecure and badly designed credential storage

```
import requests
from requests.auth import HTTPBasicAuth

def get_other_data():
    _username = "DavidMertz"
    _password = "jNeyQIyE6@pR"
    _localservice1 = "192.168.227.1
    _localservice2 = "192.168.227.2
    _localservice3 = "192.168.227.3

    for service in [_localservice1, _localservice2, _localservice3]:
        resp = requests.get(f"https://{service}/latest-data",
                            auth = HTTPBasicAuth(_username,
                            _password))
        if resp.status_code == 200:
            data = process(resp.text)
            break

    return data
```

The same general principles apply for passwords, tokens, session keys, or any other information that should generally be kept secure.

A first, and sometimes adequate, approach is to store secrets in environment variables.

User environment variables to store secrets semi-securely

```
import os

def get_other_data():
    _username = os.environ.get("LOCAL_SERVICE_USER")
    _password = os.environ.get("LOCAL_SERVICE_PASSWORD")
    _localservice1 = os.environ.get("LOCAL_SERVICE_ADDR_1")
    _localservice2 = os.environ.get("LOCAL_SERVICE_ADDR_2")
    _localservice3 = os.environ.get("LOCAL_SERVICE_ADDR_3")

    # ... rest of code ...
```

This becomes a vulnerability only if an attacker can gain shell access, or equivalent, to a system where the code is running. However, these secrets are visible in unencrypted form within an OS shell. Developers (myself included) often lose track of which environment variables were previously set, and thereby forget explicitly to unset them after an application using them has terminated.

A step better is to use the "dotenv" approach. This style *does* keep secret information within a file on the filesystem, usually with the special name .env. Specifically, this file must always be excluded from being kept under version control (e.g., in `.gitignore`), and should be distributed by a separate secure channel, as needed. As well, permissions to a `.env` file should be restricted to the specific user or group that has legitimate access rights.

Using dotenv for storing secrets semi-securely in filesystem

```
# pip install python-dotenv
import os
from os.path import join, dirname
from dotenv import load_dotenv

dotenv_path = join(dirname(__file__), ".env")
load_dotenv(dotenv_path)

def get_other_data():
    _username = os.environ.get("LOCAL_SERVICE_USER")
    _password = os.environ.get("LOCAL_SERVICE_PASSWORD")
    _localservice1 = os.environ.get("LOCAL_SERVICE_ADDR_1")
    _localservice2 = os.environ.get("LOCAL_SERVICE_ADDR_2")
    _localservice3 = os.environ.get("LOCAL_SERVICE_ADDR_3")

    # ... rest of code ...
```

This looks very similar to directly loading environment variables; it is, since the code is identical. However, these environment variables are only loaded at the time this code runs, and are not in the environment of the parent process.

The `.env` file used in this example would look like:

```
# Local service settings
LOCAL_SERVICE_USER=DavidMertz
LOCAL_SERVICE_PASSWORD="jNeyQIyE6@pR"
LOCAL_SERVICE_PREFIX=192.168.227
LOCAL_SERVICE_ADDR_1=${LOCAL_SERVICE_PREFIX}.1
LOCAL_SERVICE_ADDR_2=${LOCAL_SERVICE_PREFIX}.2
LOCAL_SERVICE_ADDR_3=${LOCAL_SERVICE_PREFIX}.3
```

A better approach still is to use your operating system's keyring service. This is handled somewhat differently by macOS, Windows, Linux, and even Android, but all have secure systems that do not store plaintext passwords. The module `keyring` wraps those OS-specific details and provides a common interface in Python.

Using `keyring` for storing secrets securely

```
# pip install keyring
import keyring as kr
```

```
def get_other_data():
    _username = kr.get_password("data-service", "user")    # ❶
    _password = kr.get_password("data-service", "pw")
    _localservice1 = kr.get_password("data-service", "1")
    _localservice2 = kr.get_password("data-service", "2")
    _localservice1 = kr.get_password("data-service", "3")

    # ... rest of code ...
```

❶ Must have previously run `kr.set_password("data-service", "user",` `"DavidMertz")` on the system running code

Using the `keyring` module is straightforward, and will not keep unencrypted versions of any secrets anywhere on your filesystem. If at all possible, use this final approach. However, the first two solutions are still *vastly* better than putting secrets directly into source code.

8.3 "Rolling Your Own" Security Mechanisms

It is a mistake to construct cryptographic protocols if you are not a professional cryptographer. Something that *seems obviously strong* probably is not.

The Python standard library does not include most accepted cryptographic primitives. There are reasons for this exclusion that are not mere laziness or oversight by the core developers of CPython. Libraries dealing with cryptography evolve and fix discovered vulnerabilities at a different pace than the Python release cycle. The developers of Python are not themselves necessarily cryptologists or cryptanalysts.

Debate sometimes arises among the CPython developers about whether this exclusion is the best policy, but it is *not* a lack of thought and discussion that led to the decision. Even environments like those installed by Miniconda, which include a *little bit* beyond the standard library, do not add general cryptographic primitives.

A temptation arises—one which your author has himself been guilty of far too often—to just create something "good enough" based on those primitives that *are* in the standard library. For example, the standard library has `secrets`, `hmac`, and `hashlib`, which include *some* well-accepted cryptographic primitives. If it feels like the threat model for your code is limited and you are only aiming for "quick and dirty," you might quickly write something like the following.

Hastily designed symmetric encryption developed by the author

```
>>> def amateur_encrypt(plaintext: str, key: str) -> bytes:
...     encoded_text = plaintext.encode()                # ❶
...     m = hashlib.sha256()                             # ❷
...     m.update(key.encode())                           # ❸
...     # Expand length of key to match the full plaintext
```

```
...         hashed_key = m.digest() * (1 + len(encoded_text)//32)
...         ciphertext0 = b"".join(                          # ❹
...             (a ^ b).to_bytes()
...             for a, b in zip(encoded_text, hashed_key))
...         ciphertext = b"".join(                           # ❺
...             (a ^ b).to_bytes()
...             for a, b in zip(reversed(ciphertext0), hashed_key))
...         return ciphertext
...
>>> hidden = amateur_encrypt("Mary had a little lamb",
...                           "MyStrongKey!!17")
>>> hidden
b'\x8f}\xe5SDz\xb4f\xc5\x8f\x8d\xc1\x87\x91v\xb9wDF\xf6q\xa0'
```

❶ Bytes rather than Unicode codepoints

❷ A cryptographically strong hash

❸ A hash of the key as bytes

❹ XOR between each key byte and encoded plaintext byte

❺ I *think* I'm so "clever" as to obscure a frequency attack on a Vigenère-like cipher by XORing with a reversed cipher.

This encryption algorithm is good enough that *I do not know* any better way to attack it than a brute-force search on the key. Decrypting is pretty much symmetrical with the encryption, and works.

Hastily designed matching decryption

```
>>> def amateur_decrypt(ciphertext: bytes, key: str) -> str:
...         m = hashlib.sha256()
...         m.update(key.encode())
...         hashed_key = m.digest() * (1 + len(ciphertext)//32)
...         plainbytes0 = b"".join(
...             (a ^ b).to_bytes()                           # ❶
...             for a, b in zip(ciphertext, hashed_key))
...         plainbytes = b"".join(
...             (a ^ b).to_bytes()
...             for a, b in zip(reversed(plainbytes0), hashed_key))
...         return plainbytes.decode()
...
>>> amateur_decrypt(hidden, "MyStrongKey!!17")
'Mary had a little lamb'
```

❶ Under Python 3.11+ .to_bytes() has a default length of 1. For older Python versions, you need to specify .to_bytes(length=1).

Here's the thing. I'm not nearly smart enough to know how to attack this encryption algorithm, even if I were given many plaintexts and many ciphertexts. However, my sliver of intelligence tells me that there are actual cryptanalysts who are *vastly* better at such attacks than I am. It is extremely likely that you readers are not better cryptographers than I am.[6] Just because you can't think of how to compromise an algorithm, that doesn't mean that someone else can't.

Rather than rely on amateur cryptography, the correct approach is to obtain the third-party pyca/cryptography library (https://cryptography.io/en/latest/). This is implemented correctly by people who genuinely understand security, and is updated quickly if weaknesses are discovered.

The protocol setup is probably slightly cumbersome, but is well documented in the module documentation. What I show can easily be wrapped in functions with simple signatures similar to the amateur ones I created earlier.

Symmetrical encryption done right

```
>>> from pprint import pprint
>>> import secrets
>>> from cryptography.hazmat.primitives.kdf.scrypt import Scrypt
>>> from cryptography.hazmat.primitives.ciphers import (
...     Cipher, algorithms, modes)

>>> salt = secrets.token_bytes(16)                       # ❷
>>> kdf = Scrypt(salt=salt, length=32, n=2**14, r=8, p=1)  # ❶
>>> key = kdf.derive(b"MyStrongKey!!17")

>>> iv = secrets.token_bytes(16)                         # ❷
>>> cipher = Cipher(algorithms.AES(key), modes.CBC(iv))
>>> encryptor = cipher.encryptor()

>>> plaintext = b"Mary had a little lamb"
>>> padded = plaintext.ljust(32, b"\x00")                # ❸
>>> encrypted = encryptor.update(padded) + encryptor.finalize()
>>> pprint(encrypted, width=68)                          # ❹
(b'\xfd\xaf}s\x9e8#\xe4\x94Fh\x83\x18\x17j\xa1\xe7\x8a\x98 '
 b'\xc3\xd9\x07\xee\x1e\xe9\x9c\xf2\xec\x90\xf74')
```

---

6. As an idle diversion, I have created a challenge at https://gnosis.cx/better. For this challenge, I have created 1000 ciphertexts, all of which are encrypted with the same key, using *exactly* the encryption code published here. Moreover, all 1000 plaintexts these are encryptions of are sentences from a draft of this book (they may not occur verbatim after later editing, though). If any reader can identify the key used, or even two of the plaintext sentences, I will deliver to them a signed copy of the print version of this book.

```
>>> decryptor = cipher.decryptor()
>>> restored = decryptor.update(encrypted) + decryptor.finalize()
>>> restored.rstrip(b"\x00")
b'Mary had a little lamb'
```

❶ Key derivation function for 32-byte key based on password

❷ To reconstruct the `cipher` object, the value of `salt` and `iv` will need to be retained somewhere. It is important that these are unique per message, but their secrecy is not important. In other words, they are often aggregated with the message itself, as plaintext.

❸ Must pad the plaintext to a multiple of 32 bytes for the Advanced Encryption Standard

❹ The encrypted text is also 32 bytes, identical to padded plaintext.

There are a great many cryptographic protocols in the `cryptography` module beyond only Advanced Encryption Standard (AES; https://en.wikipedia.org/wiki/Advanced_Encryption_Standard). In fact, there is a great deal beyond symmetric encryption algorithms. Everything you will find therein is well audited and coded correctly.

Even though the templates for using high-quality encryption are not entirely friendly or obvious, it is worth using proper cryptography as soon as you begin a project that uses it.

8.4 Use SSL/TLS for Microservices

Using Transport Layer Security is very important for communication over HTTP(S), but is often omitted during local development and/or with a false confidence that firewalls around locally connected server nodes suffice for security.

Transport Layer Security (TLS) is a cryptographic protocol that provides communications security over a computer network. The protocol allows client/server applications to communicate in a way that is designed to prevent eavesdropping, tampering, or message forgery. TLS supersedes the now-deprecated SSL (Secure Sockets Layer).

A great deal of Python software is now written as "microservices," also often called "web service." The choice of name often, but not consistently, reflects how limited the functionality of a particular server is intended to be.

In a typical arrangement, a small number of endpoints are created using a RESTful web server (https://en.wikipedia.org/wiki/Representational_state_transfer). Many such servers can run, and provide services to each other, with general independence from the particular hosting approach. Very often cloud hosting providers (e.g., AWS, GCP, or Azure) and/or container orchestration systems (e.g., Docker Swarm or Kubernetes) are used in production, often with arrangements for demand scaling, load balancing, and other related capabilities.

Typically, Python web services are written in Flask (https://flask.palletsprojects.com/) or FastAPI (https://fastapi.tiangolo.com/), which are both very lightweight, and more or less designed around microservices. The heavyweight web framework, Django, has a side project, Django REST framework (https://www.django-rest-framework.org/), as well.

As a toy example of a web service, I wrote this Flask application.

Source code of `HelloServer.py`

```
# pip install flask[async]
from flask import Flask

app = Flask(__name__)

@app.route("/")
async def hello_world():                          # ❶
    return "<p>Hello, World!</p>"
```

❶ To enable async routes, I installed with `pip install flask[async]`.

When launched locally, in development mode, we see:

```
[code]$ flask --app HelloServer run
 * Serving Flask app 'HelloServer'
 * Debug mode: off
WARNING: This is a development server. Do not use it in a production
  deployment. Use a production WSGI server instead.
 * Running on http://127.0.0.1:5000
Press CTRL+C to quit
```

Read the Flask documentation for details on how to launch using a robust WSGI server. You can also modify IP addresses and ports exposed. The key point for this mistake is that we only published an `http://` route by launching this way.

We can access the data this server provides from within the same *localhost*, for example:

```
>>> import requests
>>> resp = requests.get("http://127.0.0.1:5000")
>>> resp.text
'<p>Hello, World!</p>'
```

However, I am not entirely secure in the belief that this server might not be accessed externally via exposed ports on my system (or on the hosting Docker image, for example). It would be better only to provide the data from this server over an encrypted TLS channel.

Obtaining and installing SSL certificates is a somewhat cumbersome task. The availability of the community project Let's Encrypt (https://letsencrypt.org/) or commercial company Cloudflare's free SSL/TLS, even on free accounts (https://www .cloudflare.com/ssl/), makes this somewhat easier. However, your employer or project is

> **IMPORTANT   Transport Layer Security is not authentication**
>
> The discussion in this mistake describes the value and procedures for utilizing
> TLS/SSL. Using this means that *channels* are protected against
> eavesdroppers.
>
> However, in this example, no mechanism was created or described around
> using *authentication* for access. Anyone with access to the IP address and
> port used in the example can access the demonstration server. If we also
> wanted to require credentials for access, that would be a separate discussion.
> All the web servers we mention can certainly do that, but the specifics are not
> documented herein.

likely to have its own certificate creation and distribution system, which you should,
obviously, follow for production.

Fortunately, for local development and testing purposes, using ad hoc certificates is very
simple (but not ideal; we will improve that shortly):

```
[code]$ pip install pyopenssl
# messages about installation progress
[code]$ flask --app HelloServer run --cert=adhoc
 * Serving Flask app 'HelloServer'
 [...]
 * Running on https://127.0.0.1:5000
Press CTRL+C to quit
```

At this point, no `http://` route has been created. We can try connecting again, to both
the TLS and the unencrypted channel.

Connecting to ad hoc SSL certified route

```
>>> import requests
>>> resp = requests.get('https://127.0.0.1:5000', verify=False)
InsecureRequestWarning: Unverified HTTPS request is being made
to host '127.0.0.1'. Adding certificate verification is strongly
advised.
>>> resp.text
'<p>Hello, World!</p>'

>>> try:
...     resp = requests.get("http://127.0.0.1:5000", verify=False)
... except Exception as err:
```

```
...        print(err)
...
('Connection aborted.',
 ConnectionResetError(104, 'Connection reset by peer'))
```

The connection to the unencrypted route is simply refused. The unverified certificate settles for a warning, but still provides its data. However, it would be best to heed this warning. Doing so is not difficult. You will need openssl installed (https://www .openssl.org/).

Generating a self-signed cert and using it in microservice

```
[code]$ openssl req -x509 -newkey rsa:4096 -nodes \
            -out cert.pem -keyout key.pem -days 365
# ...shows key generation process...
You are about to be asked to enter information that will be
incorporated into your certificate request.
What you are about to enter is what is called a Distinguished
Name or a DN.
There are quite a few fields but you can leave some blank
For some fields there will be a default value,
If you enter '.', the field will be left blank.
-----
Country Name (2 letter code) [AU]:US
State or Province Name (full name) [Some-State]:Maine
Locality Name (eg, city) []:
Organization Name (eg, company) [Internet Widgits]:KDM Training
Organizational Unit Name (eg, section) []:
Common Name (e.g. server FQDN or YOUR name) []:localhost
Email Address []:

[code]$ % flask --app HelloServer run --cert=cert.pem --key=key.pem
 * Serving Flask app 'HelloServer'
 [...]
 * Running on https://127.0.0.1:5000
Press CTRL+C to quit
```

We are now able to connect to the local microservice, but only using the specific domain name "localhost" and by pointing to the correct cert.pem. We could have configured the FQDN as "127.0.0.1" instead if we wished, but using the symbolic name is generally the recommended practice.

Connecting to generated self-signed certificate

```
>>> resp = requests.get('https://localhost:5000',
...                      verify="code/cert.pem")
```

```
>>> resp.text
'<p>Hello, World!</p>'
>>> try:
...     resp = requests.get("http://localhost:5000",
...                         verify="code/other-cert.pem")
... except Exception as err:
...     print(err)
...
('Connection aborted.',
 ConnectionResetError(104, 'Connection reset by peer'))
>>> try:
...     resp = requests.get("http://127.0.0.1:5000",
...                         verify="code/cert.pem")
... except Exception as err:
...     print(err)
...
('Connection aborted.',
 ConnectionResetError(104, 'Connection reset by peer'))
```

In the example, `code/other-cert.pem` is an actual valid (signed) certificate for an unrelated domain that I copied into that directory (and renamed). The error message shown, unfortunately, would be the same if I had pointed to a file that did not exist (but some details in the full error object would differ).

8.5 Using the Third-Party requests Library

The Python standard library provides several mid-level capabilities within the `urllib` module, and specifically within its `urllib.request`, `urllib.error`, `urllib.parse`, and `urllib.robotparser` submodules. For low-level SSL/TLS, it is possible to work with the standard library `ssl` module.

The `urllib.request` Python documentation (https://docs.python.org/3/library /urllib.request.html#module-urllib.request) states:

> The urllib.request module defines functions and classes which help in opening URLs (mostly HTTP) in a complex world — basic and digest authentication, redirections, cookies and more.

This very same page immediately states, however, that the third-party `requests` package (https://requests.readthedocs.io/en/latest/) is "recommended for a higher-level HTTP client interface." There is a good reason for this recommendation: Working with the low-level modules Python's standard library provides is cumbersome and error prone. You very rarely need to deal with the low-level details of SSL/TLS contexts, DNS resolution, proxies, and many other issues that are needed to make HTTP(S) requests on the modern web.

There is a very crucial part of the quoted documentation to pay attention to: "mostly HTTP." Using `urllib.request` with modern HTTPS websites (or microservices) is exceedingly difficult. It is *possible*, but only just barely and after great frustration.

For example, a footnote in this chapter mentions challenges accompanying this book. It happens that my website is proxied by Cloudflare (https://www.cloudflare.com/) to provide it with SSL/TLS and content caching (under their free plan, for my limited needs); the underlying content is contained on GitHub Pages (https://pages.github.com/). On my local computer I use a VPN. None of this is an uncommon kind of configuration for static pages, but it is indeed not a 2003-style page on a single server with a fixed DNS entry.

Let's try to retrieve that page.

Retrieving an HTTPS page using `requests`

```
>>> import requests
>>> domain = "www.gnosis.cx"
>>> resource = "better"
>>> resp = requests.get(f"https://{domain}/{resource}/")
>>> resp.status_code
200
>>> for header in ["Content-Type", "Date", "Server"]:
...     print(f"{header}: {resp.headers[header]}")
...
Content-Type: text/html; charset=utf-8
Date: Mon, 20 Feb 2023 03:37:25 GMT
Server: cloudflare
>>> len(resp.text)
24974
```

There is nothing difficult here, and I feel confident that the maintainers of `requests` are following all relevant security and transport protocols. What about if we try to do the same thing with the Python standard library?

Failing to retrieve an HTTPS page using `urllib`

```
>>> import urllib.request
>>> try:
...     url = f"https://{domain}/{resource}/"
...     resp = urllib.request.urlopen(url)
... except Exception as err:
...     print(f"{err.__class__.__name__}: {err}")
...
HTTPError: HTTP Error 403: Forbidden                  # ❶

>>> import ssl                                         # ❷
>>> try:
```

```
...     ctx = ssl.create_default_context(ssl.Purpose.CLIENT_AUTH)
...     url = f"https://{domain}/{resource}/"
...     resp = urllib.request.urlopen(url, context=ctx)
... except Exception as err:
...     print(f"{err.__class__.__name__}: {err}")
...
URLError: <urlopen error Cannot create a client socket with a
PROTOCOL_TLS_SERVER context (_ssl.c:795)>

>>> cert = ssl.get_server_certificate((domain, 443))
>>> print(f"{cert[:157]}\n...\n{cert[-145:]}")       # ❸
-----BEGIN CERTIFICATE-----
MIIFMTCCBNigAwIBAgIQDJeUxb0DI0d5ZhI2SbcvOzAKBggqhkjOPQQDAjBKMQsw
CQYDVQQGEwJVUzEZMBcGA1UEChMQQ2xvdWRmbGFyZSwgSW5jLjEgMB4GA1UEAxMX
...

MAoGCCqGSM49BAMCA0cAMEQCIFv5r9ARdjfr5ctvjV57d2i18tOwGWRAsT9HwDr/
zyy8AiA4V5gjyLS5wRF24bqfyly64AnKQqOJyAMMCXy5HAK95A==
-----END CERTIFICATE-----

>>> import socket                                    # ❹
>>> answers = socket.getaddrinfo("www.gnosis.cx", 443)
>>> (family, type_, proto, canonname, (address, port)) = answers[0]
>>> address
'172.67.139.241'

>>> try:
...     ctx = ssl.create_default_context(cadata=cert)
...     url = f"https://{address}:{port}/{resource}/"
...     resp = urllib.request.urlopen(url, context=ctx)
... except Exception as err:
...     print(f"{err.__class__.__name__}: {err}")
...
URLError: <urlopen error [SSL: WRONG_VERSION_NUMBER] wrong
version number (_ssl.c:992)>
```

❶ Trigger a frantic search for error explanations at this point.

❷ The Python docs and some user bugs suggest we need an SSL/TLS context.

❸ Some vague hints suggest we are not finding the needed certificate.

❹ Or maybe we need the actual IP address DNS resolves to?

I am confident that there genuinely is *some magic incantation* that would convince
Python's standard library to fetch the content of this rather ordinary, static web page. With
a great deal more effort, I would probably eventually find it.

In the meanwhile, I will be happy and productive (and secure) using the third-party `requests` library, as the CPython developers themselves recommend.

8.6   SQL Injection Attacks When Not Using DB-API

SQL injection attacks are a general security vulnerability across almost all languages that are able to utilize SQL databases. It's not a *mistake* that is specific to Python, but the solution is specifically to use the full capabilities of Python's DB-API. Other programming languages and other libraries or drivers have their own solutions, but in Python, it falls under the DB-API, which almost all database drivers follow.

Part of what the DB-API provides is a way of passing parameters to an SQL call in a way that is guaranteed to be safe against injection attacks. For most modern RDBMSs (relational database management systems), the query parameters are, in fact, passed as a separate stream from the query template. However, other than feeling happy that efficiency is improved thereby, you do not need to worry about that internal detail. You simply can be assured that the DB-API and driver module are keeping you safe.

Let's see a simple example of using the DB-API.

A simple (and safe) example of using the DB-API

```
>>> password = keyring.get_password("postgres", "pw")     # ❶
>>> import psycopg                                          # ❷
>>> with psycopg.connect(
...         dbname='mistakes',
...         host='localhost',
...         user='developer',
...         password=password) as conn:
...     with conn.cursor() as cur:
...         cur.execute("SELECT * FROM wordlist")
...         for record in cur:
...             print(record)
...     conn.commit()
...
('biochips',)
('fluoroacetate',)
('potentialities',)
('steelwares',)
('edacity',)
('platter',)
('pulverizations',)
('entertains',)
('photoionising',)
```

❶ Per the mistake of putting secrets in source code, a good approach is used here.

❷ The Psycopg 3 driver to connect to PostgreSQL

However, there may be quite a few words in this wordlist, so we'd like to limit it. Specifically, we'd like to limit it based on a criterion provided by a user; in our case, users may request to only see words having a certain prefix.

A seemingly simple function with exposed injection attack

```
>>> def some_words():
...     prefix = input("[Prefix]? ")
...     print("-"*40)
...     with psycopg.connect(
...             dbname='mistakes',
...             host='localhost',
...             user='developer',
...             password=password) as conn:
...         with conn.cursor() as cur:
...             cur.execute(f"SELECT word FROM wordlist "
...                         f"WHERE word LIKE '{prefix}%'")
...             for record in cur:
...                 print(record[0])
...         conn.commit()
...
>>> some_words()
[Prefix]? p
----------------------------------------
potentialities
platter
pulverizations
photoionising
```

So far, it is all still straightforward and simple. But let's try calling the function another time.

An injection attack in action

```
>>> some_words()
[Prefix]? ';DELETE FROM wordlist;--
----------------------------------------
```

The problem is not, of course, simply that nothing matches the strange user input. It's that we actually did the following:

- Select words matching ' '
- Delete *everything* in the table
- Include a final comment of --'

An unsanitized user-provided input just deleted the entire content of our table! Requesting the "e" prefix words ("edacity" and "entertains") shows the empty table, as does trying the "p" prefix again:

```
>>> some_words()
[Prefix]? e
-----------------------------------------
>>> some_words()
[Prefix]? p
-----------------------------------------
```

Note Exploits of a mom

Randall Munroe's brilliant comic strip XKCD, as often, captures the concern of this mistake very pithily.[7]

Python itself also has a wonderful reference to XKCD. Try typing `import antigravity` in a Python shell sometime.

Let's repopulate the table with some new words, and try a safer version of the function. Showing a special fondness for the letter "b", I ran this query in the `psql` shell:

```
mistakes=> INSERT INTO wordlist (word) VALUES
    ('blondness'),
    ('disinures'),
    ('starchily'),
    ('behoveful'),
    ('berming');
INSERT 0 5
```

---

7. Comic strip used with permission from Randall Munroe (xkcd), granted by The Gernert Company.

Before we do that, however, it is worth mentioning that the DB–API actually allows for several different styles of parameter specification, which drivers are free to choose among. These are specified in PEP 249 (https://peps.python.org/pep-0249/).

paramstyle	**Meaning**
qmark	Question mark style, e.g., …WHERE name=?
numeric	Numeric, positional style, e.g., …WHERE name=:1
named	Named style, e.g., …WHERE name=:name
format	ANSI C printf format codes, e.g., …WHERE name=%s
pyformat	Python extended format codes, e.g., …WHERE name=%(name)s

Inquiring into the current `psycopg` driver:

```
>>> psycopg.paramstyle
'pyformat'
```

Armed with that knowledge, let's secure our function.

A function with query parameters sanitized and protected against injection

```
>>> def some_words():
...     prefix = input("[Prefix]? ")
...     print("-"*40)
...     with psycopg.connect(
...             dbname='mistakes',
...             host='localhost',
...             user='developer',
...             password=password) as conn:
...         with conn.cursor() as cur:
...             cur.execute(
...                 "SELECT word FROM wordlist WHERE word LIKE %s;",
...                 (f"{prefix}%",))                        # ❶
...             for record in cur:
...                 print(record[0])
...         conn.commit()
...
>>> some_words()
[Prefix]? b
----------------------------------------
behoveful
berming
blondness
```

❶ The interaction between % as an SQL wildcard and in a Python string requires a bit of special care for this example.

If we try a similar injection with this corrected code, nothing bad happens. We just get zero results because `'';DELETE FROM wordlist;--` isn't a word in the `wordlist` table. Or if it *is* an unusual word, we get the harmless result:

```
>>> some_words()
[Prefix]? '';DELETE FROM wordlist;--
----------------------------------------
'';DELETE FROM wordlist;--more stuff after prefix
```

8.7   Don't Use `assert` to Check Safety Assumptions

Assertions are a wonderful means of communicating your intent to other developers who read the code you write. It can be tempting to extend this utility to guarding against dangers in code, but doing so is a mistake for a simple reason. Code run in production sometimes uses the `-O` or `-OO` switch to (very slightly) optimize code performance.

When Python code is "optimized" one of the basic such optimizations is removal of assertions. During development they are a good way to enforce assumptions in the code; however, to eke out a few percent faster production systems, optimization switches are commonly used. The difference these flags make is small, and I myself rarely use them; but be aware that they might be used, and my own habits are far from universal in this respect.

Here is a short example of a reasonable use of assertions. This is an echo of the example in "Directly Accessing a Protected Attribute" in Chapter 4, *Advanced Python Usage*. We presented there a class-based version of a pseudo-random linear congruential generator. The details of this algorithm are discussed somewhat more in that chapter, as well as in the "Kinds of Randomness" section earlier in this chapter.

The algorithm presented here is a perfectly reasonable pseudo-random number generator, but for production use, you should use the `random` module from the standard library, and thereby implicitly the Mersenne Twister algorithm (at least as of Python 3.12). The focus of this section is simply to show *some* algorithm with invariants, not to discuss pseudo-random number generation in general.

We can implement this algorithm as a generator function.

Generator function implementing an LCG

```
def lcg(
    seed: int = 123,
    multiplier: int = 1_103_515_245,
    modulus: int = 2**32,
    increment: int = 1
):
```

```
    # Simple constraints we should follow
    assert 0 < modulus
    assert 0 < multiplier < modulus
    assert 0 <= increment < modulus
    assert 0 <= seed < modulus

    # One initial application of recurrence relation
    state = (multiplier * seed + increment) % modulus

    while True:
        state = (multiplier * state + increment) % modulus
        yield state / modulus
```

We can utilize the generator to obtain pseudo-random numbers in the interval $[0,1)$:

```
>>> from lcg import lcg
>>> for x, _ in zip(lcg(), range(5)):
...     print(x)
...
0.7730483340565115
0.7532131555490196
0.8828994461800903
0.6617866707965732
0.1618147783447057
```

The assertions made were concretely useful when I was first debugging this code. Moreover, they communicate to other developers some of my expectations about the reasonable preconditions for the algorithm to work (some are much more nuanced; what makes a "good" modulus and multiplier would take full papers in number theory, not single lines).

However, suppose that a naive developer wanted to enhance this code by having a fallback to Python's standard library random module when disallowed parameters were passed in.

Source code of code/bad_lcg.py

```
def bad_lcg(
    seed: int = 123,
    multiplier: int = 1_103_515_245,
    modulus: int = 2**32,
    increment: int = 1
):
```

```
        # Skip LCG algorithm if parameters are not usable
        try:
            assert 0 < modulus
            assert 0 < multiplier < modulus
            assert 0 <= increment < modulus
            assert 0 <= seed < modulus

            # One initial application of recurrence relation
            state = (multiplier * seed + increment) % modulus

            while True:
                state = (multiplier * state + increment) % modulus
                yield state / modulus

        except AssertionError:
            import random
            while True:
                yield random.random()

if __name__ == '__main__':
    for x, _ in zip(bad_lcg(multiplier=-1), range(5)):
        print(x)
```

At first brush, this seems to work. At least in the sense of getting *some* pseudo-random numbers (albeit not ones that are easily reproducible as in the non-fallback case):

```
[BetterPython]$ python code/bad_lcg.py
0.9091770816298352
0.5190613689590089
0.911898811723727
0.8066722366593495
0.5563737722223733
[BetterPython]$ python code/bad_lcg.py
0.19828280342458238
0.3661064573367322
0.02637664736327605
0.04362950928898546
0.32456135199248937
```

This breaks down rather badly once we run the code with the optimization flag, however:

```
[BetterPython]$ python -O code/bad_lcg.py
2.8638169169425964e-08
0.9999999715946615
```

```
2.8638169169425964e-08
0.9999999715946615
2.8638169169425964e-08
```

These pseudo-random numbers are very bad at their job. Specifically, the same two numbers (close to the extremes of the unit interval) will alternate forever, which is not an expected distribution. Moreover, if you are using this numeric stream for anything vaguely security related, many attack vectors are opened up by failing to fall back to the alternate code path. Depending on the context, of course, many other problems might occur as well; for example, performance problems, errors in modeling, excessive collisions of, for instance, hash keys, and so on.

The wisdom of this specific fallback is a separate matter; there are absolutely many other contexts where a fallback is reasonable. The solution to this error is extremely simple, happily. Simply use explicit checks for the conditions that are permitted or prohibited within `if/elif` or `match/case` blocks, and use those to fall back to alternate behavior. Using an explicit `raise` of an exception other than `AssertionError` within those blocks is perfectly reasonable as well.

8.8 Wrapping Up

In Python, as in every modern programming language, a background concern in the creation of any software system is the vulnerabilities it might create. Software can do things wrong in the sense of not producing the output or interactions that we had in mind when writing it; but it can also do things wrong in the sense of allowing bad actors to cause harm through the use of that software.

Genuine security analysis of software is a broad topic, and one requiring a great deal of knowledge ranging over many things not in this book. However, there are a number of often repeated mistakes that Python developers make, each of which can be relatively straightforwardly rectified by following the advice in this chapter. These few things will not address all possible concerns, but they will fix surprisingly much of what we Python developers often get wrong.

For a more in-depth look at a number of security issues, the Open Worldwide Application Security Project (OWASP; https://owasp.org/) is a good resource. They discuss and provide resources for some of the vulnerabilities I discuss, and for a great many others as well.

There are many security mistakes not specifically addressed in this chapter, of necessity. Security is a broad concern, with many books wholly about it, and many professionals employed to understand a range of concerns. However, a few mistakes that are already well described in the Python documentation are still worth quickly mentioning.

- Unpickling pickles with uncontrolled sources can cause execution of arbitrary code.

- Loading YAML has the same concern as with pickles, but an easy solution is `yaml.safe_load()`.

- Loading XML can enable denial-of-service attacks; these are discussed in detail at https://docs.python.org/3/library/xml.html.

- Temporary files created with `tempfile.mktemp()` are unsafe, but Python documents this and provides `tempfile.mkstemp()` as a drop-in replacement.

Use the right libraries. Choose a few of the right APIs. Avoid some missteps that will be obvious once you internalize the mistake in this chapter. After those few small actions, the so-called *attack surface* of the software you create will be vastly reduced.

9

Numeric Computation in Python

Working with numbers is, of course, one of the most common things we do in programming languages. And yet, there are a great many ways that our numeric code can go subtly wrong. For larger scale and more intensive work with numbers, the third-party libraries NumPy and Pandas make a great many tasks easier and faster. Other important numeric libraries also exist, but those two are so widespread in the Python ecosystem as to merit independent discussion. Several such libraries are discussed briefly in the appendix, *Topics for Other Books*.

While reaching out to "vectorized" or "unboxed" numeric libraries can often be useful,[1] we should and do perform much numeric computation in Python itself.

Many of the mistakes we can make in working with numbers derive from subtle edge cases of the behavior of floating point numbers. In a general way, this class of issues applies just as much to the third-party libraries as it does to pure Python. In fact, three of the four mistakes discussed in the IEEE-754 section of this chapter apply almost identically to most programming languages other than Python, but remain concerns for Python developers, so are discussed here.

Some mistakes Python developers can make relate to other kinds of *numeric domains*, perhaps with choosing the wrong one for a given task. The last two mistakes in this chapter touch on `decimal.Decimal` and `fractions.Fraction` and when those are good choices for numeric types.

9.1 Understanding IEEE-754 Floating Point Numbers

Had he lived 75 years later, J. B. S. Haldane likely would have remarked:

---

1. Wikipedia's articles on vectorization (https://en.wikipedia.org/wiki/Array_programming) and numeric boxing (https://en.wikipedia.org/wiki/Boxing_(computer_science)) are good starting points for understanding these computer programming topics.

> Now, my own suspicion is that [IEEE-754] is not only queerer than we
> suppose, but also queerer than we can suppose … I suspect that there are more
> things in numeric approximation than are dreamed of, or can be dreamed of,
> in any philosophy.[2]

This section looks at several common mistakes Python programmers make when
working with floating point numbers, which often occur in places that are unlikely to raise
immediate suspicion among developers who have not yet been bitten by them.

9.1.1 Comparing NaNs (and Other Floating Point Numbers)

The IEEE-754-1985 standard for floating point numbers includes a special kind of value
called "Not a Number" (NaN).[3] Nearly all programming languages and computer
architectures implement IEEE-754 and NaN values. As well as being perfectly good
floating point values in plain Python, NaNs serve special roles when they are individual
values within NumPy arrays or Pandas DataFrames (and Xarray DataArrays, and
Vaex/Polars DataFrames, and in other numeric special collections).

Note   Getting pedantic about NaNs

To be precise about things, a NaN is not *a value*, but rather a family of values
marked by a particular bit pattern. There are 16,777,214 32-bit NaNs, and
9,007,199,254,740,990 64-bit NaNs. Moreover, within this vast space of
possible NaNs, the bit patterns are split evenly between *signaling* and *quiet*
NaNs.

This is a lot of complication that the original designers of IEEE-754,
including main architect William Kahan, hoped would be utilized to carry
payloads describing the circumstances within a computation where a
non-representable floating point value arose. As things panned out, no widely
used computing system makes any use of the many NaN values, and all
basically treat every NaN as the same value.

Let's dig a bit deeper into the weeds. These details apply to many concerns. A floating
point number is represented as a sign bit, followed by an exponent, followed by a
mantissa.[4] A NaN is simply a number that has all of its exponent bits set to 1s.

---

2. J. B. S. Haldane, *Possible Worlds*. New Brunswick, NJ: Transaction Publishers, 2000.
3. See discussion at https://en.wikipedia.org/wiki/IEEE_754-1985 for more information. Unfortunately, these
standards themselves are not available free of charge, but their technical requirements are widely published in
other forms. Technically, this standard was superseded by IEEE-754-2008, and then by IEEE-754-2019, but
nothing relevant herein was modified.
4. To get even more technical, an alternate representation exists for *subnormal numbers* (https://en.wikipedia.org
/wiki/Subnormal_number) where we want to represent floating point numbers close to zero with greater precision.

Whatever happens to occur in the mantissa, it remains a NaN and is treated in the same special manner. Let's see this in action.

Looking at bit patterns of floating point numbers

```
>>> import struct, math
>>> def show32(num):                                    # ❶
...     pack32 = struct.pack("!f", num)
...     bits = ''.join(f"{c:0>8b}" for c in pack32)
...     sign = bits[0]
...     exp = bits[1:9]
...     mantissa = bits[9:]
...     print("- exponent mantissa")
...     print(f"{sign} {exp} {mantissa}")
...
>>> show32(3.1415)
- exponent mantissa
0 10000000 10010010000111001010110
>>> show32(-math.pi)
- exponent mantissa
1 10000000 10010010000111111011011
```

❶ We "cast" a floating point to 32-bit, even if its native format is wider.

We can see that a very rough approximation of π has the same exponent and most of the same mantissa bits as the best approximation we can make of negative pi within IEEE-754. The sign bit is flipped between the two numbers spelled out as bits. But what about operations that result in NaNs?

Looking at NaN bit patterns generated by Python

```
>>> show32(math.nan)
- exponent mantissa
0 11111111 10000000000000000000000
>>> show32(math.inf/math.inf)
- exponent mantissa
1 11111111 10000000000000000000000
>>> show32(-math.nan)
- exponent mantissa
1 11111111 10000000000000000000000
>>> show32(1e500-1e500)
- exponent mantissa
1 11111111 10000000000000000000000
>>> show32(0 * math.inf)
- exponent mantissa
1 11111111 10000000000000000000000
```

Python, like almost all other programming languages, simply uses one of the millions (or quadrillions) of possible NaNs, regardless of how we arrived at it. The leading 1 in the mantissa technically makes it a signaling NaN, but no Python library I know of pays any attention to this fact. It's technically possible in Python to construct a NaN with a different bit pattern, but it requires arcana from the `struct` or `ctypes` modules; no "normal Python" operation will do this, nor pay any attention to the special value.

Let's try a comparison that at first, certainly, *seems like* it should succeed.

Comparing floating point numbers, including NaNs

```
>>> a = [math.pi, math.e, float('nan'), math.tau]
>>> b = [math.pi, math.e, math.nan, math.tau]
>>> a == b
False
```

The bit patterns stored for the NaNs in a and b are, in fact, identical. Likewise for the other mentioned mathematical constants. The problem is that according to IEEE-754, no NaN will ever compare as equal to another, even if their payloads are identical:

```
>>> math.nan == math.nan, math.nan is math.nan
(False, True)
>>> math.isnan(math.nan)                                # ❶
True
```

❶ The cleanest way to check whether a value is a NaN

A NaN is a peculiar Python object that can be self-identical, yet unequal to itself. Moreover, the example shown allows us to fix another common problem with floating point numbers that other sections will also address. While the examples for a and b *do* produce bit-wise identical values for the non-NaN constants, in general, "mathematically" equal numbers that we arrive at by different sequences of floating point operations will more often than not be unequal because of rounding issues. A robust way to compare two iterables of floating point numbers is shown.

Robustly comparing floating point numbers with NaN equivalence

```
>>> def approxEqualNums(seq1, seq2):
...     for x, y in zip(seq1, seq2, strict=True):
...         if math.isnan(x) and math.isnan(y):
...             continue
...         elif math.isclose(x, y):                     # ❶
...             continue
...         else:
...             return False
```

```
...       return True
...
>>> approxEqualNums(a, b)
True
```

❶ The function `math.isclose()` has `rel_tol` and `abs_tol` optional arguments to
   fine-tune what "closeness" means. See the Python documentation for details.

The function `approxEqualNums()` will raise a `ValueError` if the iterables passed to
it are of different lengths, but will raise a `TypeError` if some of the elements are
non-numeric. The function is not restricted to lists, but will work on anything where
`isinstance(o, collections.abc.Iterable)` holds. In practice, you usually want
something that is specifically a `collections.abc.Sequence` since unordered collections
may accidentally produce either `True` or `False` answers. For example:

```
>>> approxEqualNums((1, 2, 3), {1:None, 2:None, 3:None})
True
>>> approxEqualNums((1, 2, 3), {1, 2, 3})          # ❶
True
>>> approxEqualNums((3, 2, 1), {3, 2, 1})          # ❷
False
>>> approxEqualNums([0, 1, 2, 3], range(4))
True
```

❶ Do not rely on the ordering of sets, even though this example is coincidentally order
   preserving. Dicts preserve insertion order

❷ An example where sets do not preserve their "order" during iteration

9.1.2 NaNs and `statistics.median()`

In the preceding section, we discussed the sometimes surprising behavior of NaNs in
extensive detail. Please refer back to the footnotes, notes, and discussion there if you need
to familiarize yourself.

One of the main modules in the Python standard library for working with collections
of floating point numbers is `statistics`. As we saw in the earlier discussion, when you
think about collections of floating point numbers you should keep in mind that some
floating point numbers are NaNs.

Most of the functions within `statistics` *propagate* NaNs. That is, if some of the
numbers in a collection are NaNs, the result simply becomes NaN as well. Two such
functions are `statistics.mean()` and `statistics.fmean()`; these functions differ from
each other in that the former tries to preserve the specific numeric datatype of elements
while the latter automatically converts everything to floating point numbers (and is thereby
generally faster).

Comparing `statistics.mean()` with `statistics.fmean()`

```
>>> import statistics
>>> from fractions import Fraction as F
>>> a = [F(3, 7), F(1, 21), F(5, 3), F(1, 3)]
>>> statistics.mean(a)
Fraction(13, 21)
>>> statistics.fmean(a)
0.6190476190476191
>>> from decimal import Decimal as D
>>> b = [D("0.5"), D("0.75"), D("0.625"), D("0.375")]
>>> statistics.mean(b)
Decimal('0.5625')
>>> statistics.fmean(b)
0.5625
```

When we introduce NaNs, it becomes impossible to say what the "mean value" is, regardless of which approach we are using.

Taking a mean in the presence of NaN values

```
>>> import math
>>> statistics.fmean([math.nan] + b)
nan
>>> statistics.mean(a + [math.nan])
nan
```

Similar behavior is encountered with functions like `statistics.stdev()`, `statistics.variance()`, `statistics.correlation()`, and others, for essentially the same reason. Interestingly, `statistics.mode()` and `statistics.multimode()` are "NaN aware" rather than "NaN propagating":

```
>>> from math import nan
>>> statistics.mode([nan, nan, nan, 4, 3, 3, 3.0])
nan
>>> statistics.multimode([nan, nan, nan, 4, 3, 3, 3.0])
[nan, 3]
```

I would likely argue that this behavior of `statistics.mode` is nonobvious, or perhaps even wrong. Those several NaN values should never be equal to one another (although they are identical), and it's not clear the sense in which "the same" value occurs multiple times. However, this behavior remains clear and easy to understand, even if purity concerns are possibly pushed aside.

Where we find a genuinely odd corner of module behavior is with `statistics.median()` (and its close relatives `statistics.median_low()`, `statistics.median_high()`, and `statistics.median_grouped()`). In all of these, the presence of NaN values makes the results completely nonsensical.

Median becomes silly in the presence of NaNs

```
>>> statistics.median([nan, nan, nan, 4, 3, 3, 7])
3
>>> statistics.median_grouped([nan, nan, nan, 4, 3, 3, 7])
3.2
>>> statistics.median_high([7, 4, 3, 3, nan, nan, nan])
7
>>> statistics.median_grouped([7, 4, 3, 3, nan, nan, nan])
6.625
```

Depending on where elements occur within a list of numbers, the median might be the lowest number, the highest number, a NaN (with some orderings not shown), or in the case of `statistics.median_grouped()`, some number that incorporates a fairly meaningless mean into the overall result (for strictly non-NaN values, this "value between the elements" is sometimes quite useful).

There are basically two ways we might go about *fixing* this. I have argued on the python-ideas mailing list that these functions should grow an optional argument to clarify behavior; I've never completely convinced the module's main author. One approach is to introduce NaN propagation, the other is to introduce NaN stripping. Notably, these two approaches are the default behaviors of NumPy and Pandas, respectively (but varying from each other).

Fortunately, choosing either of these behaviors is easy to achieve in Python; you just have to remember to do it.

Median with NaN propagation

```
>>> c = [nan, nan, nan, 4, 3, 3, 7]
>>> d = [4, 3, 3, 7, 0, 10, 4]
>>> math.nan if math.nan in c else statistics.median(c)
nan
>>> math.nan if math.nan in d else statistics.median(d)
4
```

Notice that this ternary clause works because in will do an identity check before it tries an equality test. As we've seen, nan != nan, so the fact it checks this way is necessary for the suggestion to work. Here is the code for the latter option.

Median with NaN stripping

```
>>> statistics.median([x for x in c if not math.isnan(x)])
3.5
>>> statistics.median([x for x in d if not math.isnan(x)])
4
```

9.1.3   Naive Use of Floating Point Numbers: Associativity and Distributivity

It is famously easy to forget that basic algebraic operations on floating point numbers are neither associative nor distributive in general. Even when we rule out special values like `math.inf` and `math.nan`, basic "ordinary numbers" only approximate Rational or Real numbers. We can exclude infinities and NaNs with the function `math.isfinite()`.

To put it very simply, we cannot assume in IEEE-754—whether in Python or in any of the other majority of programming languages that use floating point numbers as built-ins or standard library types—that these properties hold.

Absence of associativity and distributivity

```
>>> from math import isfinite
>>> a, b, c, d = 0.1, 0.2, 0.3, 0.4
>>> isfinite(a) and isfinite(b) and isfinite(c) and isfinite(d)
True
>>> (a + b) + c == a + (b + c)
False
>>> (a + b) + d == a + (b + d)
True
>>> a * (b + c) == (a * b) + (a * c)
True
>>> c * (a + b) == (c * a) + (c * b)
False
```

Associativity and distributivity do not *always* fail, of course. We see examples in the preceding code block of these properties both holding and failing, all with very ordinary numbers. However, predicting exactly which series of operations will preserve exact equality and which will not is exceedingly subtle.

The solution to this Gordian Knot, of course, is not to understand all the rounding errors in a computation that might consist of thousands or millions of floating point operations, but rather to settle for "plausible equality." For what it's worth, the problem gets even more tangled in the face of concurrency, wherein you may not even be able to predict the order in which operations are performed.

Both Python's `math.isclose()` and NumPy's `numpy.isclose()` provide such plausible answers.

Approximate associativity and distributivity

```
>>> import numpy as np
>>> import math
>>> math.isclose((a + b) + c, a + (b + c))
True
>>> np.isclose((a + b) + c, a + (b + c))
True
```

```
>>> math.isclose(c * (a + b), (c * a) + (c * b))
True
>>> np.isclose(c * (a + b), (c * a) + (c * b))
True
```

Note *Remembrance of Things Past*

I had already previously commented in a 2003 book that "If you think you *understand* just how complex IEEE 754 math is, you are not yet aware of all of its subtleties." In that ancient text, I noted that my friend, colleague, and erstwhile professor of numeric computing, Alex Martelli, had written:

> Anybody who thinks he knows what he's doing when floating point is involved is either naive, or Tim Peters (well, it *could be* W. Kahan I guess).

Tim Peters (after whom "Timsort," the sorting algorithm used in Python and in many other modern programming languages), replied:

> I find it's possible to be both (wink). But *nothing* about fp comes easily to anyone, and even Kahan works his butt off to come up with the amazing things that he does.

Peters illustrated further by way of Donald Knuth (*The Art of Computer Programming*, 3rd edition, Addison-Wesley, 1997: 229):

> Many serious mathematicians have attempted to analyze a sequence of floating point operations rigorously, but found the task so formidable that they have tried to be content with plausibility arguments instead.

Both `math.isclose()` and `numpy.isclose()` come with optional arguments to fine-tune their meanings of "closeness." However, note that these corresponding functions are *not* algorithmically identical. In fact, quoting the NumPy documentation:

> Unlike the built-in `math.isclose`, the above equation is not symmetric in a and b — it assumes b is the reference value — so that `isclose(a, b)` might be different from `isclose(b, a)`.

In other words, `numpy.isclose()` is also not itself commutative (the property of an operator in mathematics in which $A \oplus B$ is always equal to $B \oplus A$).

9.1.4   Naive Use of Floating Point Numbers: Granularity

The dark corners of floating point arithmetic include not only associativity and distributivity, as we have seen, but also granularity. The IEEE-754 standard allows for expression of numbers across a very large numeric range in comparatively few bits; this section looks at an implication of that choice in places where errors become tempting.

Let's examine a problem, then one solution and one failed try at a solution.

Trying to find the mean of three floating point numbers

```
>>> import statistics
>>> import numpy as np
>>> nums = [1e20, 1.0, -1e20]
>>> sum(nums)/len(nums)
0.0
>>> statistics.mean(nums)
0.3333333333333333
>>> np.mean(nums)
0.0
```

We are able to say at this point that the module `statistics` does a good job of averaging, and both the arithmetically obvious hand-rolled approach and NumPy do a much worse job (that is, they are flatly wrong).

I suppose we might stop at commenting "solve your problem by using `statistics`." This is not terrible advice for those operations that `statistics` includes, and where the operation assumes samples without an inherent order. We've seen in another puzzle that this list does not include `statistics.median()` in the presence of NaNs. But for mean, geometric mean, harmonic mean, mode, multimode, quantiles, standard deviation, variance, linear regression, population variance, covariance, and a few other operations, the advice is sound.

Let's look deeper into this quandary. The underlying problem is that the structure of floating point numbers, with a sign, an exponent, and a mantissa, causes the distribution of representable numbers to be uneven. In particular, the gap between one floating point number and the next representable floating point number can be more than another number in a sample collection.

Granularity of floating point numbers

```
>>> math.nextafter(1e20, math.inf)          # ❶
1.0000000000000002e+20
>>> math.nextafter(1e20, -math.inf)         # ❶
9.999999999999998e+19
>>> 1e20 + 1.0 == 1e20
True
```

❶ The second argument indicates which *direction* to go for this "next" float. Pedantically, any floating point number will work there, but in most cases positive or negative infinity is used.

Since the gap between the closest floating point numbers is more than 1.0 in the region of `1e20`, adding or subtracting 1.0 can have no effect. The best representation remains the number we started with. In fact, this example is based around the 64-bit floating point numbers native to the system I am writing on; the problem is much worse for 32-bit floating point numbers, and absurdly terrible for 16-bit numbers.

Granularity of floating point by bit width

```
>>> from numpy import inf, nextafter
>>> nextafter(np.array(1e20, np.float32), inf)      # ❶
1.0000000200408775e+20
>>> nextafter(np.array(1e15, np.float32), inf)      # ❷
999999986991104.1
>>> nextafter(np.array(1e6, np.float16), inf)       # ❸
inf
>>> nextafter(np.array(50_000, np.float16), inf)    # ❹
49984.00000000001
```

❶ The next 32-bit float after 1e20 is 2,004,087,750,656 larger!

❷ The "next" 32-bit float after 1e15 is 13,008,896 *smaller*! 1e15 is represented as a still smaller number than the "next" one!

❸ Even the next 16-bit float after a million is infinity.

❹ The "next" 16-bit float after 50,000 is actually smaller than 50k.

Despite the doom and gloom of some of these examples, there is *often* (but not always) a pretty straightforward way to address these granularity issues. If your operation involves adding together numbers of widely different sizes, sorting them in reverse order by absolute value first will generally achieve the best stability you can find with floating point numbers.

Note   Being absolutely precise about numeric error

Although the heuristic I provide is worth keeping in mind, it is *not* what the `statistics` module does. Instead (simplifying a bit), that module first converts all numbers to numerically exact (but much slower) Fractions, then down-converts back to floats as needed.

A "usually correct" heuristic for adding collections of numbers

```
>>> nums = [1e20, 1.0, -1e20]
>>> sum(sorted(nums, key=abs, reverse=True))/len(nums)
0.3333333333333333
```

There is, unfortunately, currently no direct way of doing the equivalent stabilization in NumPy. You can, of course, convert a 1-D NumPy array to a Python list, and back again, but at the cost of orders-of-magnitude slowdowns.

Floating point numbers are both ubiquitous and enormously useful as approximations of Real numbers from mathematics. However, since finite computers cannot truly represent the Real number line completely, many compromises and errors are introduced by this approximation. Python developers, as nearly all software developers, should keep attuned to the places where the inevitable errors (in a mathematical sense) become *mistakes* in a programming sense.

9.2   Numeric Datatypes

Choosing the right datatype might not simply mean using the system-default floating point. For users of NumPy, one mistake often encountered is choosing an inappropriate bit width for floating point numbers; this concern applies equally for Pandas users. Within Pandas, an additional quasi-datatype mistake arises around using categorical data where appropriate. However, as the appendix discusses, those libraries are outside the scope of this particular book.

This section looks at places where developers might choose nonideal—or indeed, dangerously flawed—datatypes.

9.2.1   Avoid Floating Point Numbers for Financial Calculations

Python developers, as with those in most other popular programming languages, generally reach for floating point numbers when performing numeric calculations. However, sometimes those calculations concern financial quantities—most commonly units of currency, but also sometimes specified shares of assets or other units.

Very often when financial calculations are involved, the exact manner of the calculation is specified by laws or regulations. Unlike with, for example, extrapolations from scientific data where more precision is generically better—or at least precision might be a trade-off against speed of calculation—financial regulations indicate an exact procedure that must be used. Moreover, such procedures are almost universally given in terms of rounding and precision of base-10 numbers. For example, exact whole dollars and cents must be determined within each stage of a series of calculations.

Suppose that you make a deposit at a bank, and they tell you that the bank will pay you 3.95% interest on your deposit, with interest compounded daily. By the rules of daily compounding, this will be an effective interest rate of approximately 4.03% if you leave your money in the bank for a whole year. Moreover, to simplify things for this discussion, we will simply assume that the current year is not a leap year.[5] In Python:

---

5. There are diverse methods of accounting for leap years in actual use by different lenders, and permitted by different regulatory jurisdictions. An example of how complex this can be is discussed at the JS Coats Capital LLC page "Interest Calculation Methods" (https://jscoats.com/interest-calculation-methods/).

```
>>> f"{100 * ((1 + 0.0395/365)**365 - 1):.3f}%"
'4.029%'
```

However, the regulatory jurisdiction the bank falls under specifies the following rules.

- The daily balance must be stored internally in tenths-of-a-cents. These daily internal balances must round fractional balance half-a-hundredth amounts to an even number of tenths.

- The customer-available daily balance is based on the internal balance, but when rounding half-a-tenth, the cents are rounded down.

- Exact daily records are audited by the regulatory agency on a recurring basis, and errors face stiff fines.

We know that 64-bit floating point numbers have a great deal more precision than these required amounts. A 64-bit float carries approximately 17 decimal digits of precision with it, which is certainly quite a lot more than the two or three digits (cents or tenths) that we apparently need. Perhaps we can get by with a program that simply stores approximations as needed.

Source code of code/daily_interest_float

```
#!/usr/bin/env python
import sys

def print_daily_balance(deposit, interest_rate):
    balance = deposit
    daily_interest = interest_rate/365
    print(" Day | Customer | Internal")
    print("-----+----------+----------")
    for day in range(1, 366):
        print(f" {day:>3d} | {balance:8.2f} | {balance:8.3f}")
        balance = balance * (1 + daily_interest)

if __name__ == '__main__':
    deposit = float(sys.argv[1])
    interest_rate = float(sys.argv[2]) / 100
    print_daily_balance(deposit, interest_rate)
```

Let's take a look, in part, at what this program outputs.

Incorrect abridged daily balance sheet for interest-bearing account

```
[BetterPython]$ code/daily_interest_float 500 3.95
 Day | Customer | Internal
-----+----------+----------
   1 |   500.00 |  500.000
   2 |   500.05 |  500.054
```

```
  3 |    500.11 |   500.108
  4 |    500.16 |   500.162
  5 |    500.22 |   500.216
  6 |    500.27 |   500.271            # ❶
... |       ... |      ...
360 |    519.81 |   519.807            # ❶
361 |    519.86 |   519.863            # ❶
362 |    519.92 |   519.919            # ❷
363 |    519.98 |   519.975            # ❷
364 |    520.03 |   520.032            # ❶
365 |    520.09 |   520.088            # ❷
```

❶ Customer-available balance rounds to correct, but internal balance is in error.

❷ Both customer-available and internal balance are in error.

This program just rounds where needed using f-string formatting. We *could* also use a round(balance, 3) within the loop to periodically approximate in an attempt to meet the regulatory rules. Neither this naive approach nor such period approximation will produce *exactly* the right balances, though.

On its face, the customer has earned *approximately* the correct amount of interest at the end of the year, and even pretty close to the right amount at each intervening day. However, the *true* balance sheet should read like this.

Correct abridged daily balance sheet for interest-bearing account

```
[BetterPython]$ code/daily_interest_decimal 500 3.95
 Day | Customer | Internal
-----+----------+----------
   1 |   500.00 |  500.000
   2 |   500.05 |  500.054
   3 |   500.11 |  500.108
   4 |   500.16 |  500.162
   5 |   500.22 |  500.216
   6 |   500.27 |  500.270
 ... |      ... |     ...
 360 |   519.80 |  519.802
 361 |   519.86 |  519.858
 362 |   519.91 |  519.914
 363 |   519.97 |  519.970
 364 |   520.03 |  520.026
 365 |   520.08 |  520.082
```

The divergence between the actually correct calculation and the purely floating point one occurs slowly, and numeric error is hardly overwhelming. If these were scientific calculations—or even if they were predictive models within finance—these numeric divergences would be trivial. Under laws, treaties, and regulatory rules they are not, however.

The `decimal` module treats decimal arithmetic correctly, including precision and rounding rules. There are separate available rounding modes for ROUND_CEILING, ROUND_DOWN, ROUND_FLOOR, ROUND_HALF_DOWN, ROUND_HALF_EVEN, ROUND_HALF_UP, ROUND_UP, and ROUND_05UP. The code that solves this specific problem utilizes two of these, and would produce slightly different (wrong) results if it had not chosen exactly the two it does.

Source code of `code/daily_interest_decimal`

```python
#!/usr/bin/env python

import sys
from decimal import Decimal, ROUND_HALF_EVEN, ROUND_HALF_DOWN

def print_daily_balance(deposit, interest_rate):
    balance = deposit
    daily_interest = interest_rate/365
    print(" Day | Customer | Internal")
    print("-----+----------+----------")
    cents = Decimal('1.00')
    tenths = Decimal('1.000')
    for day in range(1, 366):
        balance = balance.quantize(tenths, rounding=ROUND_HALF_EVEN)
        customer = balance.quantize(cents, rounding=ROUND_HALF_DOWN)
        print(f" {day:>3d} | {customer:8.2f} | {balance:8.3f}")
        balance = balance * (1 + daily_interest)

if __name__ == '__main__':
    deposit = Decimal(sys.argv[1])
    interest_rate = Decimal(sys.argv[2]) / 100
    print_daily_balance(deposit, interest_rate)
```

We can notice that the method ROUND_HALF_EVEN is entirely statistically balanced. In the long run, on data that does not contain inherent distortions, trends and tendencies will balance exactly. But that does not ensure that *every* result will be the same as if a greater (false) precision were used.

Using ROUND_HALF_DOWN is systematically biased; however, in this particular code it never propagates, but is simply a repeatedly derived quantization. Had we used that within the internal balance running total, we would systematically trend down versus the "true" floating point approximations (albeit very slowly so in this example).

Half the solution to mistakes that result from using (binary) floating point numbers for financial math is simply "use the `decimal` module." While these numbers are not *as fast* as IEEE-754 floating point numbers, Python provides a pretty efficient machine-native implementation. The second half of the solution is more subtle; it requires accurately understanding the rounding and precision rules that are imposed by regulatory or administrative concerns. The exact details of solutions will vary based on those concerns, but the `decimal` module provides options for all such widely used rules.

9.2.2 Nonobvious Behaviors of Numeric Datatypes

The so-called "numeric tower" in Python is more of a "garden of forking paths."[6] As with many edge cases in Python, there are widely discussed and well-reasoned motivations for things being as they are. These reasons are not necessarily obvious to ordinary developers. Getting these details wrong can lead to you mistakenly winding up with an unexpected numeric datatype.

In parallel with the concrete numeric types provided within Python's built-ins, or in modules in its standard library, are a hierarchy of *abstract base classes* within the module `numbers`. These abstract base classes *can* be inherited from if you implement the relatively large collection of methods they require; however, more often they are used for purposes of "virtual inheritance." Before we get there, let's look at the actual inheritance diagram of numeric types, including the abstract ones (marked in italic and with rounded edges in Figure 9.1).

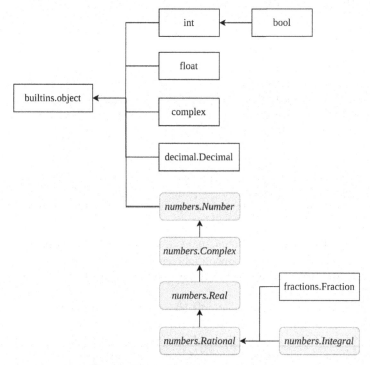

Figure 9.1   Python's numeric garden.

---

6. The phrase "garden of forking paths" is borrowed from the translated title of Jorge Luis Borges' wonderful 1941 short story "El Jardín de Senderos que se Bifurcan".

> **Note   A digression on virtual parents**
>
> Let's take a look at an abstract base class. For this purpose, we wish to create a class called `BigNumber` whose instances "contain" all big numbers (of all comparable numeric types, in fact). The class doesn't do much else, nor much useful, but *virtually* contains all the big numbers (here defined as more than one thousand):
>
> ```
> >>> class BigNumber:
> ...     def __contains__(self, value):
> ...         return value > 1000
> ...
> >>> big_numbers = BigNumber()
> >>> 5.7 in big_numbers
> False
> >>> 1_000_000 in big_numbers
> True
>
> >>> from collections.abc import Container
> >>> isinstance(big_numbers, Container)
> True
> >>> BigNumber.__mro__
> (<class '__main__.BigNumber'>, <class 'object'>)
> ```
>
> Even though `Container` is nowhere in the inheritance tree of `BigNumber`, the mere fact it implements the required protocol of having a `.__contains__()` method makes it act *as if* it did have that ancestor class.

The abstract classes within the module `numbers` are "virtual parents" of various concrete numeric classes. However, the particular parent–child relationships that exist virtually are not necessarily the ones that make obvious sense.

Estranged children

```
>>> from fractions import Fraction
>>> from decimal import Decimal
>>> frac = Fraction(1, 1)
>>> dec = Decimal("1.0")
>>> 1 == 1.0 == Fraction(1, 1) == Decimal("1.0")     # ❶
True

>>> (1.0).as_integer_ratio()                         # ❷
(1, 1)
>>> (0.3).as_integer_ratio()                         # ❷
(5404319552844595, 18014398509481984)
```

```
>>> isinstance(1, numbers.Integral)          # ❸
True
>>> isinstance(1, numbers.Rational)          # ❹
True
>>> isinstance(frac, numbers.Integral)       # ❺
False
>>> isinstance(frac, numbers.Rational)       # ❻
True
>>> isinstance(dec, numbers.Integral)        # ❺
False
>>> isinstance(dec, numbers.Rational)        # ❼
False
>>> isinstance(dec, numbers.Real)            # ❼
False
>>> isinstance(dec, numbers.Number)          # ❽
True
>>> isinstance(0.3, numbers.Rational)        # ❾
False
>>> isinstance(0.3, numbers.Real)            # ❾
True
```

❶ Various kinds of "one" are equal to each other.

❷ Every float is a ratio of integers, even if approximated in base-2.

❸ Sensibly, integers are Integral.

❹ And Integral numbers inherit from Rational.

❺ Fractions and Decimals are not generally Integral, even when equal to `int`.

❻ A Fraction is indeed a synonym for Rational.

❼ A Decimal is finitely many digits, why not Rational, nor even Real?!

❽ And yet, Decimal *is* a Number!

❾ Why is a float with numerator and denominator Real but not Rational?!

Cycles within Cycles of Confusion

It is very hard to reconcile the virtual parentage of Python concrete numeric datatypes with what I learned in middle school algebra. Some of the fault can be assigned to IEEE-754 floating point numbers, the subject of numerous mistakes addressed in this book. However, even other numeric types without rounding errors suffer oddities as well.

Moreover, we can wonder what happens when we perform an operation that combines different kinds of numbers.

Comingling with `decimal.Decimal` numbers

```
>>> dec + 1
Decimal('2.0')
>>> 1 + dec
Decimal('2.0')
>>> dec + 1.0
[...]
TypeError: unsupported operand type(s) for +:
    'decimal.Decimal' and 'float'

>>> dec + frac
[...]
TypeError: unsupported operand type(s) for +:
    'decimal.Decimal' and 'Fraction'
>>> dec + 1+0j
[...]
TypeError: unsupported operand type(s) for +:
    'decimal.Decimal' and 'complex'
```

Decimal numbers mostly refuse to engage in operations with other kinds of numbers, but make an exception for integers. One might question this decision by Python since `decimal.Decimal` already carries a specific precision, and could simply round even if a result would be inexact, but the decision isn't obviously wrong.

What seems worse is the tendency of `float` to take over almost anything else it interacts with.

One datatype to rule them all (almost)

```
>>> frac + frac
Fraction(2, 1)
>>> frac + 1, 1 + frac                          # ❶
(Fraction(2, 1), Fraction(2, 1))

>>> frac + 1.0, 1.0 + frac                      # ❷
(2.0, 2.0)
>>> 1 + 1.0, 1.0 + 1                             # ❷
(2.0, 2.0)

>>> f"{frac + 0.3:.17f}"                         # ❸
'1.30000000000000004'
>>> frac + Fraction(0.3)                         # ❸
Fraction(23418718062326579, 18014398509481984)
```

```
>>> frac + Fraction("0.3")                        # ❹
Fraction(13, 10)
```

❶ Integers are quite deferential to other datatypes.

❷ Floating point tends to take over, which might not be terrible.

❸ The floating point initializer loses precision before creating a `Fraction`.

❹ A string initializer produces the simplest exact fraction.

Trying to Maintain Precision

We have seen that floating point numbers—under the hood—are always just imprecise fractions for the rational number we want. There *is* a good reason that floating point numbers are used so widely: Working precisely with rational numbers often grows resulting numerators and denominators unboundedly.

As we combine various fractions with large least common denominators, the size of numerators and denominators grows, operations become slower, and more memory is consumed. Small examples we could show here using a handful of numbers will never become that bad; but real-world code that performs millions or billions of numeric operations can quickly become burdensomely sluggish. IEEE-754 is a reasonable compromise.[7]

Although floating point approximations of rational numbers can easily have seemingly insanely large numerators and denominators, the `fractions.Fraction` class provides a rough and heuristic way to limit this at the cost of introducing its own kind of numeric error:

```
>>> f"{0.3:.17f}"                                  # ❶
'0.29999999999999999'
>>> Fraction(*(0.3).as_integer_ratio())            # ❷
Fraction(5404319552844595, 18014398509481984)
>>> Fraction(*(0.3).as_integer_ratio()).limit_denominator(1000)
Fraction(3, 10)
>>> Fraction(*(0.3).as_integer_ratio()).limit_denominator(9)
Fraction(2, 7)
```

❶ No precise representation of 0.3 is possible in base-2.

❷ It would be nice to obtain a much simpler `Fraction(3, 10)`.

Limiting the denominator manually can often produce the *result we want*. Unfortunately, there is no obvious or computable rule about exactly how much of a limitation we actually

---

7. Posits and unums (https://en.wikipedia.org/wiki/Unum_(number_format)) are a proposed alternative machine representation for approximations of real numbers that in many ways use a finite number of bits more efficiently, and that can be hardware friendly. They have not yet been widely adopted, but it is possible they will be in the future.

want in the abstract. In simple examples like that shown, the choice seems obvious; but there is no mechanism to provide that in a completely general way.

Casting Down

Rather than allow floats to annex all the results from operations that combine `Fraction` with `float`, we could create a custom class to do the reverse. Yes, we might need to consider periodic approximation with `Fraction.limit_denominator()`, but the rounding would be our explicit choice. For example, let's start with this:

```
>>> class Ratio(Fraction):
...     def __add__(self, other):
...         if isinstance(other, float):
...             numerator, denominator = other.as_integer_ratio()
...             other = Fraction(numerator, denominator)
...             self = Fraction(self.numerator, self.denominator)
...         return Ratio(self + other)
...
>>> Ratio(3, 10) + 0.3
Ratio(54043195528445951, 90071992547409920)
>>> 0.3 + Ratio(3, 10)                               # ❶
0.6
>>> f"{0.3 + Ratio(3, 10):.17f}"
'0.59999999999999998'
```

❶ The Python shell performs some "friendly" rounding in its display, so we might mistakenly think it is producing an exact result.

We've moved in the right direction. The `Ratio` class can cause addition with a float to maintain a `Ratio`. However, we lost commutivity in the process. That was an easily rectified oversight:

```
>>> class Ratio(Fraction):
...     def __add__(self, other):
...         if isinstance(other, float):
...             numerator, denominator = other.as_integer_ratio()
...             other = Fraction(numerator, denominator)
...             self = Fraction(self.numerator, self.denominator)
...         return Ratio(self + other)
...
...     __radd__ = __add__
...
>>> 0.3 + Ratio(3, 10)
```

```
Ratio(54043195528445951, 90071992547409920)
>>> Ratio(3, 10) + 0.3
Ratio(54043195528445951, 90071992547409920)
```

The problem is that we've only handled addition this way. Other operators obviously exist as well:

```
>>> Ratio(3, 10) * 1.0
0.3
```

Adding a full suite of dunder methods for all the operators would be straightforward, merely slightly tedious. Start with `.__mul__()` and `.__rmul__()` and work your way through the rest in similar fashion.

What to Do with All of These Numbers?

If we enforce a rule within our own projects that all the numbers we are operating on are `decimal.Decimal`, or that they are all `fractions.Fraction`, operations will remain sensible. It creates doubts about the meaningfulness of the hierarchy of numeric virtual types, but we would remain within just one numeric domain.

As mentioned earlier, the problem with the domain of `Fraction` is that as the numerator and denominator often grow unboundedly larger as a result of performing many operations, the speed and memory usage get dramatically worse. Doing many calculations on many numbers can become a major bottleneck in this numeric domain.

The domain of `Decimal` remains a fixed length, which can be set by a context (defaulting to 28 digits), and is reasonably fast in performing operations. Floating point remains about 2× to 5× faster than `Decimal` at a similar precision, but the latter is not terrible. The problem is that for scientific or other observation-based measurements, base-2 minimizes the accumulation of numeric bias *far better* than does base-10. Base-10 is easier for most humans to understand, but its rounding errors are *not* numerically superior.

Using a bit of cleverness—arguably too much of it—we could also create custom classes that forced results of operations into their own numeric domain, as shown, in partially fleshed-out form, with the `Ratio` class.

Choosing the right numeric datatype is often a relevant concern for Python programmers, and happily Python provides several options beyond floating point. Creating custom classes with more specialized numeric datatypes is also relatively easy in Python, although only occasionally needed.

9.3 Wrapping Up

In this chapter, we looked at a variety of "obvious" numeric operations that can go wrong, both within the *numeric domain* of floating point numbers and in other domains. There are numerous assumptions that developers tend to make about numbers—perhaps because we learned about how they should work in elementary school or middle school—that become less obvious when we write actual computer programs.

A

Appendix: Topics for Other Books

There are, of course, many domains of Python programming in which you might make mistakes, or face trade-offs. Not all such topics can fit within this book, but those not touched on are not necessarily less important. For the most part, those topics not addressed are simply big enough to warrant their own full books.

A.1 Test-Driven Development

Good software development practice should *always* include extensive tests. There is a great amount of detail, and sometimes subtlety, to how to do tests right. But the biggest mistake, and the far most common one I've seen in real-life codebases, is simply not to have tests at all. Only barely less bad than tests not existing is to have test suites that have not been maintained. It is always difficult and painful to encounter production code in which tests are only run occasionally and erratically, and developers just live with an assumption that most tests will fail. Usually when you see this, it is far from obvious which of the failing tests might once have succeeded, and which were never completed or functional in the first place.

A good test suite should be a barrier placed before every code merge. Either upon every push, or upon every merge (at least to production branches), CI/CD (continuous integration/continuous development) tests should be run by automated means. For more time-consuming tests, scheduling them to be run nightly or weekly can also be appropriate; by all means, though, such tests should be required to run and pass before code can enter production use.

Whether or not development is strictly TDD (test-driven development) is a subject of reasonable debate. However one comes down in that debate, developers should *always* simply assume that untested code is broken code. Of course, the advice of these few paragraphs applies equally to every programming language, and is not specific to Python.

Within Python itself, my advice is to always use pytest (https://docs.pytest.org) rather than the standard library `unittest`. Pytest supports `unittest` suites in a backward-compatible way, provides an enormously better syntax and, more capabilities, and is simply more Pythonic overall. The third-party nose2 (https://docs.nose2.io/en /latest/) is also not a terrible choice, but generally I recommend pytest over nose2. The standard library `doctest` module is also very useful for the kinds of tests that are easily expressed as docstrings (which is surprisingly many, and providing them is enormously helpful to future maintainers).

A.2   Concurrency

At some point during development of this book, I wanted to discuss a number of concurrency pitfalls and trade-offs. It's a big topic, though; too big for a chapter or two of this moderately sized book to treat adequately. The fact that this is not the book for discussion of concurrency does not diminish the importance of the topic, nor suggest that the choices you make are not subject to pitfalls and trade-offs.

Within Python itself, there are three main approaches to concurrency. Python's standard library has a `threading` module to work with threads. Threads are famously subject to gotchas like deadlocks, race conditions, priority inversion, data structure corruption, and other glitches. Moreover, within pure Python, threading does not enable CPU parallelism because of the infamous GIL (global interpreter lock). That said, many third-party modules "release the GIL" and allow true parallelism.

Python's standard library also contains the `multiprocessing` module, which is largely similar in API to `threading`, but works with processes rather than threads. This module provides a means of running parallel tasks on multiple CPU cores, but is also constrained by not being able to share data directly among processes and in being "heavier weight." In general, in order to communicate, processes require message passing, usually by means of pipes and queues (which are available in the `multiprocessing` module).

A useful and higher-level abstraction for both threading and multiprocessing is the `concurrent.futures` module of the standard library. Many problems can be more easily and more safely expressed using the "futures" abstraction, and where possible, concurrency is easier using this mechanism.

A third abstraction in Python for concurrency is asynchronous programming with coroutines. This is supported via the `async` and `await` keywords, and is managed by the `asyncio` standard library module, or by third-party async event loops such as uvloop (https://uvloop.readthedocs.io/), Trio (https://trio.readthedocs.io/en/stable/), Curio (https://curio.readthedocs.io/en/latest/), and Twisted (https://twisted.org/). The general idea behind coroutines is that async functions can *yield* control in the middle of their operations, allowing an event loop to give attention to other coroutines within the same thread and process. This is typically useful when operations are I/O bound (since I/O is generally several orders of magnitude slower than CPU-bound computation).

The official Python documentation contains a good discussion of many of the trade-offs among different approaches to concurrency (see https://docs.python.org/3/library /concurrency.html to get started).

A.3 Packaging

A large part of the Python ecosystem is about packaging software for distribution. Actually, pretty much the same is true of *every* programming language. When you write software, whether executables, libraries, or other systems, you usually wish to share your work with other users and developers.

For some languages newer than Python, the design of the language itself was simultaneous with the design of its packaging system. So, for example, users of the Go programming language will use `go get` ... to install packages. Users of Rust will use `cargo` and `rustup`. In Julia, it is a combination of `using Pkg; Pkg.add(...)`. In R, it's generally always `install.packages(...)`. For these languages, there is one and only one way to install a package, and pretty much exactly one way to publish the packages or tools you have created. Other languages like Ruby have mostly congealed around `gem`, and JavaScript is split between `npm` and `yarn`, but the two are *mostly* compatible.

Python is not as old as C, or Fortran, or even Perl, Bash, Haskell, or Forth. All of those have, arguably, a greater disarray around packaging than Python does. But Python is *pretty old*, having started in 1991, and going through numerous not-quite-compatible packaging and installation systems over that time, while starting relatively late on putting serious effort into this aspect. Over the past five to 10 years, Python packaging has become solid and relatively stable, but a number of competing tools remain, as do a number of package formats.

Wheels are supported and endorsed by the Python Packaging Authority (https://www.pypa.io/en/latest/), but so are *sdist* archives for source-only packages. Numerous tools for creating wheels are largely, but not entirely, compatible with one another. Conda packages use a different format and a different build system, but allow completely non-Python packages to be created, distributed, and installed. A large number of tools allow creation of platform-specific executables for Python, including often the native packaging system of operating system distributions. Moreover, especially with so much software being deployed in "cloud native" or at least "cloud-centric" ways now, containerization, such as with Docker and Kubernetes, has become a popular alternative approach as well.

This book simply does not attempt to address software packaging, but rather recommends that you read some of the excellent online material on the topic, starting with https://packaging.python.org/en/latest/overview.

A.4 Type Checking

On top of the mostly orthogonal nature of type-checking mistakes and the conceptual mistakes addressed in this book, the use of type checking and its associated tools is somewhat divisive among Python developers. I do not hesitate to be opinionated in this book about many things, but I have chosen not to weigh in on the virtues and drawbacks of using or adding extensive type annotations in Python codebases. There are many excellent books and other resources that delve into this topic, and these debates, in great detail.

The Python documentation on type hints is a good place to start if this topic interests you: https://docs.python.org/3/library/typing.html. The mypy project (https://mypy.readthedocs.io/) is the tool closest to an "official" type-checking tool for Python. The Pyre project (https://pyre-check.org/) is a popular type-checking tool, and is especially useful for large codebases. Pyright (https://microsoft.github.io/pyright) and Pytype (https://google.github.io/pytype/) likewise serve similar purposes. The PyCharm IDE (https://www.jetbrains.com/pycharm/) has excellent support for type checking and type inference, and is worth considering if you are looking for a Python IDE.

A.5   Numeric and Dataframe Libraries

At the heart of much of the numeric computation performed in Python is the library NumPy (https://numpy.org/). NumPy provides a powerful and efficient multidimensional array type, and a large number of functions for operating on these arrays. NumPy is developed in C, and a bit for Fortran, but is explicitly a Python library that cannot be used outside of Python. The idioms used for vectorized computation in NumPy are often quite different from those used in "native Python," and a number of books and articles have been and will be written on its idioms.

For the purpose of leaving NumPy best practices out of this book, it's sufficient to note that those best practices are generally different from those used in "native Python." In many ways, learning NumPy is like learning a domain-specific language (DSL) for numeric computation that resides *within* Python.

Tensor libraries such as TensorFlow (https://www.tensorflow.org/), PyTorch (https://pytorch.org/), CuPy (https://cupy.dev/), and JAX (https://jax.readthedocs.io) borrow many concepts from NumPy, but are reimplemented in C++ and CUDA, and are often used for machine learning applications. Probably even more than with NumPy, using these Python libraries is effectively using DSLs inside Python code (not strictly syntactically so, but in feel, yes).

A powerful abstraction for working with tabular data is *dataframes*. This concept was popularized by the R programming language, and is mostly widely used in Python via the Pandas library (https://pandas.pydata.org/). Pandas is itself built on top of NumPy. Other libraries, such as Polars (https://www.pola.rs/) and RAPIDS (https://rapids.ai/) via its GPU-accelerated cuDF library, provide similar functionality, and some advantages over Pandas.

As with NumPy, using Pandas and other dataframe libraries requires quite different idioms than those used in "native Python." In particular, these libraries very commonly use "method chaining" or "fluent interfaces" to express intentions. This style is quite powerful and expressive, and is the topic of a great many books (e.g., *Pandas for Everyone: Python Data Analysis*, 2nd edition, by Daniel Y. Chen [Addison-Wesley, 2022]), ISBN-13: 9780137891054), but is omitted from this one.

Index

Note: Italic letters following page numbers refer to special formats—*f* for figures, *n* for footnotes, and *t* for tables.

Photo by Marvent/Shutterstock

VIDEO TRAINING FOR THE **IT PROFESSIONAL**

LEARN QUICKLY
Learn a new technology in just hours. Video training can teach more in less time, and material is generally easier to absorb and remember.

WATCH AND LEARN
Instructors demonstrate concepts so you see technology in action.

TEST YOURSELF
Our Complete Video Courses offer self-assessment quizzes throughout.

CONVENIENT
Most videos are streaming with an option to download lessons for offline viewing.

Learn more, browse our store, and watch free, sample lessons at
informit.com/video

Save 50%* off the list price of video courses with discount code **VIDBOB**

Register Your Product at informit.com/register

Access additional benefits and save up to 65%* on your next purchase

- Automatically receive a coupon for 35% off books, eBooks, and web editions and 65% off video courses, valid for 30 days. Look for your code in your InformIT cart or the Manage Codes section of your account page.
- Download available product updates.
- Access bonus material if available.**
- Check the box to hear from us and receive exclusive offers on new editions and related products.

InformIT—The Trusted Technology Learning Source

InformIT is the online home of information technology brands at Pearson, the world's leading learning company. At informit.com, you can

- Shop our books, eBooks, and video training. Most eBooks are DRM-Free and include PDF and EPUB files.
- Take advantage of our special offers and promotions (informit.com/promotions).
- Sign up for special offers and content newsletter (informit.com/newsletters).
- Access thousands of free chapters and video lessons.
- Enjoy free ground shipping on U.S. orders.*

* Offers subject to change.
** Registration benefits vary by product. Benefits will be listed on your account page under Registered Products.

Connect with InformIT—Visit informit.com/community

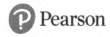

Addison-Wesley • Adobe Press • Cisco Press • Microsoft Press • Oracle Press • Peachpit Press • Pearson IT Certification • Que